W0230050

Industry Innovation in the Era of Artificial Intelligence

This book explores the multifaceted nature of AI implementation in modern business strategy, focusing on its present and future impact on various sectors. The book will spark fresh thinking and provide a driving force for global industrial innovation. Author Xiaomei Wang, Founder and CEO of PathoAI, former Global Leader of Big Data and Analytics at IBM, as well as General Manager of IBM Growth Markets Unit Big Data Centers, draws on over 20 years of experience in data analytics and AI to offer unique insights and a rich collection of compelling industry case studies.

Designed for business leaders, tech enthusiasts, and policymakers alike, this book is not just a manual for understanding AI, but a roadmap for harnessing its potential. By offering a blend of theoretical insight and practical guidance, this book empowers readers to embrace AI as a catalyst for innovation and sustainable growth in their respective fields.

Xiaomei Wang is Chairman of Global AI Inclusive Networks, where she champions the empowerment of future AI professionals. Her steadfast commitment to inclusivity and diversity embodies her vision for an equitable AI landscape. Leading this nonprofit organization, she merges extensive experience with a passion for cultivating a skilled AI community. As Founder and CEO of PathoAI, Xiaomei spearheads innovation in AI-driven diagnostics and pharmaceutical R&D, recently pioneering multimodal models that analyse complex medical data with remarkable accuracy, transforming healthcare outcomes.

With a distinguished 19-year career at IBM and credentials as a Certified Independent Director, Xiaomei stands as a prominent voice in the global AI dialogue. An accomplished author, her works include *AI 3.0* and *Understanding DB2*.

CRC Press Women in AI Series

There is no denying the gender gap in AI. In this dynamic industry where innovations focus on enabling computers to perform tasks that have traditionally required human intelligence, representation needs to go well beyond diversity of thought. This CRC Press series aims to increase equality in AI globally by highlighting women's accomplishments in this critical field. Books in the series are dedicated to showcasing, supporting, and championing contemporary women's work in AI.

Industry Innovation in the Era of Artificial Intelligence: The AI Compass
Xiaomei Wang

Industry Innovation in the Era of Artificial Intelligence

The AI Compass

Xiaomei Wang

CRC Press
Taylor & Francis Group
Boca Raton London New York

CRC Press is an imprint of the
Taylor & Francis Group, an **informa** business

A CHAPMAN & HALL BOOK

Designed cover image: @ShetuNetwork

First edition published 2025
by CRC Press
2385 NW Executive Center Drive, Suite 320, Boca Raton FL 33431

and by CRC Press
4 Park Square, Milton Park, Abingdon, Oxon, OX14 4RN

CRC Press is an imprint of Taylor & Francis Group, LLC

© 2025 Xiaomei Wang

British Library Cataloguing-in-Publication Data
A catalogue record for this book is available from the British Library

ISBN: 978-1-032-83239-5 (hbk)
ISBN: 978-1-032-83225-8 (pbk)
ISBN: 978-1-003-51060-4 (ebk)

DOI: 10.1201/9781003510604

Typeset in Minion
by SPi Technologies India Pvt Ltd (Straive)

Contents

Foreword 1: Mastery Determines Success

I OFTEN LIKEN THE FIELDS OF BIG DATA AND ARTIFICIAL INTELLIGENCE to a fertile ground, one that I've passionately nurtured and from which I've reaped abundant rewards—technological breakthroughs, vibrant industries, and like-minded partners.

Xiaomei is one such partner. I've had the privilege of working closely with her, and from the very beginning, her enthusiasm, creativity, wisdom, and collaborative spirit have deeply impressed me. Over the past decade, she has led numerous technology projects around the globe, successfully guiding many companies to triumph in their digital transformations, with several becoming shining examples of innovation in the industry.

Yet, her dedication goes far beyond this. For years, Xiaomei has been recognized as a thought leader, evangelist, and practitioner in the realm of big data and AI, actively engaging with audiences worldwide. Understanding the needs and challenges of industries on the front lines, she has poured her energy into the practical applications of AI technology. Early on, she astutely recognized the immense potential AI would unleash in the next wave of digital transformation, fervently advocating for industries to prepare for the arrival of this new era.

For the past few years, I've been closely following Xiaomei's remarkable journey in the AI field. As an entrepreneur focused on cutting-edge technology, she has led her company to successfully bring AI innovations to the healthcare and pathology field. Her work has helped achieve industry-wide breakthroughs, providing doctors in numerous countries with highly efficient and accurate diagnostic support, as well as AI-driven tools for drug development.

In the era of large models, Xiaomei's team has made groundbreaking strides by integrating multimodal AI models, creating a revolutionary diagnostic product in pathology. This new technology transcends the conventional "single-disease, single-model" approach, achieving the leap to a "single model, multi disease" system.

Additionally, she has drawn upon her diverse experience working across North America, Asia-Pacific, Europe, and South America, merging global insights and innovative services into her endeavors. She plays an integral role in the construction of Global AI Inclusive Networks (GAINetworks), a global non-profit aimed at advancing AI technology. Together with her ecosystem partners, she helps foster pioneering innovations while advocating for digital inclusivity driven by these technological advancements.

This expansive vision is also reflected in her unwavering dedication as an advocate and practitioner of women in AI, consistently championing gender equality and inclusivity for professionals in the field. Both Xiaomei's and my own experiences actively demonstrate how women can bring fresh perspectives and innovative thinking to technological advancement.

As a longtime collaborator and dear friend, I eagerly anticipate her upcoming book. I am confident that her insights and viewpoints will inspire global business leaders in profound ways.

Josephine Cheng
Member of the United States National
Academy of Engineering
IBM Fellow
San Jose, California, USA

Foreword 2: The Era of AI Value Creation Has Arrived

AS THE MAGNET PASSED THROUGH THE COIL-WRAPPED CYLINDER, THE needle on the ammeter flickered.

That was electricity! Yes, it had to be electricity!

I still vividly recall that high school physics class where we witnessed Faraday's electromagnetic induction in action for the first time. It was in that moment that I grasped how electricity—an invisible, untouchable force with incredible power—was actually created.

Later, I delved into the history of the electrical revolution. In 1831, Michael Faraday discovered electromagnetic induction and invented the first disk generator. Forty-eight years later, Thomas Edison invented the mass-producible incandescent light bulb, then went on to establish the first commercial central power station in New York, ushering in the era of electric lighting. Along the way, numerous scientists continually improved generators, leading to the rise of great companies like General Electric, Siemens, and Westinghouse.

Years later, as I built my own career in investment and industry, I gained a deeper understanding: behind every great technological revolution lies an insightful grasp of "demand." It's this relentless pursuit of needs that drives the journey from scientific discovery to commercial application, and finally to large-scale development.

In the electrical age, Edison keenly recognized that electricity itself wasn't the direct demand—lighting was what truly created value for customers. That's why he simultaneously developed the generator and the light bulb, bringing illumination to countless homes. Over a century later,

Jeff Bezos led Amazon to the pinnacle of the internet era, and his secret was the same: a customer-centric business model. You can see this clearly in his 24 letters to shareholders starting in 1997, where "customer" is the most frequently used word.

As the era of AI surges forward, I, as an investor, have been pondering: Was this true in the electrical age? Was it true in the internet age? Will it hold true for the AI age? The answer, without a doubt, is yes! In any era, the fundamental business question remains: Who is your customer, and how can you create real value for them?

Take the healthcare and media industries as examples. For AI to succeed, it must deeply understand the needs and relationships between various stakeholders—patients, hospitals, insurers—and identify who the true decision-makers and payers are. In media content creation, AI needs to grasp the dynamics between PGC (professionally generated content), UGC (user-generated content), and AIGC (AI-generated content) in relation to users, to determine the most effective channels for delivering content.

So, how is value creation reflected in the new generation of AI, represented by LLM (large language model) technology? It requires actively exploring the fit between LLM technology and the product-market fit, achieving a T-P-M-2-W-F (Technology – Product – Market Two-Way Fit). This demands robust infrastructure such as powerful chips, computing power, and development tools. In vertical industries, it also requires dedicated systems for proprietary data, security assessments, and industry-specific policies. The more challenges there are to solve, the more opportunities there are for value creation—and thus the more space for entrepreneurship and investment.

This wave of AI, led by LLM technology, has seen massive investments from the "Magnificent 7" (Apple, Microsoft, Google, Amazon, Nvidia, Tesla, Meta). Behind star startups like OpenAI and Anthropic, you can see the clear influence of these tech giants.

In the future, more industries like healthcare, biopharma, insurance, finance, manufacturing, and media will see their Corporate Venture Capital (CVC) arms actively investing in AI startups. Through capital as a bridge, these industries will integrate AI with proprietary data and real-world business scenarios, enabling AI to truly drive intelligent transformation across sectors.

My recent travels around the world have deepened my belief that AI belongs to all of humanity and will benefit us all. Today, every country and region has both the right and its own unique approach to developing AI.

The U.S. leads with cutting-edge innovation and market-driven venture capital, China brings national ambition and the advantage of a massive market, Europe excels with its wealth of Public-Private Partnership experience, Southeast Asia offers an open market attracting global capital, the Middle East is backed by powerful sovereign wealth funds, and even across the vast continents of Australia, Africa, and the Americas, AI is being pursued and invested in unique ways.

Whether or not you believe LLMs are the path to AGI (Artificial General Intelligence), AI represents the most certain and transformative opportunity in human society today, as far as the eye can see.

Embracing it is the best choice!

Jason Dong
TMT and Deep Tech Investor
Singapore

Preface: Boundless Imagination, Relentless Growth

M Y ENTRY INTO THE WORLD OF COMPUTER SCIENCE STEMMED FROM a beautiful misunderstanding. From a young age, I had a passion for art, which led me to choose a computer science major focused on graphics and imaging in university. I was eager to elevate my artistic journey through technology. However, I was met with a screen full of code and algorithms, far removed from the imagery I had envisioned. Yet it was the focus and creativity honed through my art studies that propelled me forward on this new path, launching an entirely new chapter in my life.

If this serendipitous choice was rooted in my youthful love for art, the passion I've maintained over the decades amidst the tide of digital transformation reflects my unwavering love for innovation and adaptability in the face of change.

After my studies in North America, I was fortunate to join IBM Toronto lab, renowned for its cutting-edge information management technologies. For over 20 years, I have immersed myself in the fields of big data and artificial intelligence, participating firsthand in the journey of turning cutting-edge concepts into industry realities. Between 2012 and 2017, my team and I implemented over a thousand projects globally, helping many Fortune 500 companies leverage big data and AI to achieve breakthroughs and completely rejuvenate their business models.

Of course, there have been regrets along the way. I witnessed numerous companies, including leading traditional industries, miss crucial opportunities by neglecting or outright ignoring the need for digital transformation. Many of these organizations are now grappling with the painful consequences of lacking digital capabilities, while their competitors pull ahead in business strategy, operational efficiency, and data innovation. Each time I reflect on this, I feel a sense of loss; had these companies recognized the significance of big data and AI from a strategic standpoint and had concrete guidance, the outcomes could have been vastly different.

The motivation behind writing this book is to share my passion, insights, and reflections from over two decades in the field. I aim to sketch a roadmap for the "AI industry landscape" using my usual analytical lens. This is a strategic framework and tactical approach developed through iterative methodologies and practical validation, designed to assist those navigating this domain. How can we integrate data and related technologies as key production elements into strategic planning? How can robust AI capabilities reshape business operations, allowing companies to rise again and gain competitive advantages? I hope this book serves as a catalyst, offering new perspectives and inspiration for business leaders and practitioners alike.

Unlike other works focusing solely on AI technology, this book expands on two key themes that resonate with my views on artificial intelligence:

1. **From "Intrinsic" to "Extrinsic"**: AI is not just about the technologies used to create intelligence; it also encompasses data and business contexts. The essence of competition in AI has become clear: it is a contest of data. The key to winning in this industrial race lies in rooting our strategies in business contexts, formulating data strategies, and diligently applying technology to realize and cultivate our ideas. Notably, with the recent rapid development of large models and the swift evolution of generative AI, the landscape of AI is advancing at breakneck speed. Thus, we must adopt a higher-level understanding and view the entire "AI industry chain," encompassing technology, infrastructure, ecosystems, people, and ethics.

2. **From "Technological Application" to "Strategic Co-Winning"**: AI transformation is neither mysterious nor unattainable; it brings opportunities that can create richer ecosystems. We have seen innovative companies thrive amid the AI surge while traditional businesses leverage unique data resources in critical scenarios. By consciously utilizing these advantages and collaborating effectively, companies can build new competitive edges and ecosystems that benefit all parties involved. This places higher demands on decision-makers: to see

the bigger picture, identify key opportunities, embrace challenges, and dare to innovate, thereby guiding their organizations towards a future of growth.

I have always considered myself incredibly fortunate to embark on this imaginative journey. The river of history flows ever forward, and no one can escape its current. The only way to avoid being left behind is to embrace change and become a brave explorer and innovator. This mindset fuels my relentless pursuit of "vastness of spirit, vibrancy of imagination, and diligence of mind."

I am wholeheartedly committed to the wave of AI development, working closely with industry partners to welcome an equitable and accessible AI future.

All that has come before is merely prologue. May we all continue to dream without limits and grow in our pursuits!

Xiaomei Wang
Chairman, Global AI Inclusive Networks
New Tech Entrepreneur
Toronto, Canada

CHAPTER 1

When Machines Gain Intelligence

On a June evening in 2023, my phone suddenly lit up with a message from the lead screener Ms. Ika: "working on it," followed by "still excited." Accompanying the text was a photo she had snapped of her computer screen, giving me a glimpse into her fervent work in progress.

This vibrant creation, made up of blue, pink, and purple blocks, dark spots, and square frames, is none other than *PathoInsight-T*—the AI-powered cervical cancer diagnostic system developed by our company, PathoAI. At this very moment, it's hard at work in the Premier Integrated Labs (PIL) at Pantai Hospital in Kuala Lumpur, alongside Dr. Patsy and her team, providing crucial support for the initial screening of cervical cancer.

I can still vividly recall the scene from early May when we deployed *PathoInsight-T* at Pantai Hospital. This was the very first hospital where PathoAI's AI-driven pathology diagnostic solution was put into action, following our partnership with IHH Healthcare Berhad, Asia's largest private healthcare group. On-site, Dr. Patsy made her expectations crystal clear to me and my team: the system needed to be user-friendly, highly accurate, fast, and capable of easing the workload of the initial screening staff.

At this moment, Ms. Ika's excitement over her "AI assistant" practically leaps off the screen—a glowing testament to her satisfaction with the project's outcomes. Her enthusiasm is the best feedback we could hope for and also reinforces my confidence in PathoAI and the exciting strides we're about to make in the field of pathology AI.

PIL, one of the top diagnostic service providers for cervical cancer screening in Malaysia, handles a staggering volume of around 140,000

DOI: 10.1201/9781003510604-1

cases per year. 70% of the workload falls on a team of three patholo-gists and several cytotechnologists based in their Kuala Lumpur laboratory at Pantai Hospital. These initial screeners work in shifts, each examining nearly a hundred slides daily, with about 60% of these slides requiring confirmation by two separate screeners.

In the past, each slide required around 5 minutes under the micro-scope—up to 6 or 7 minutes for positive slides. However, with the intro-duction of *PathoInsight-T*, AI analysis of each scanned slide is completed in just 30 seconds. Thanks to the AI's highlighted regions of interest (ROIs) and diagnostic results, screeners can swiftly pinpoint high-risk cells and microorganisms, rapidly reaching conclusions. This advancement dramati-cally boosts screening efficiency, reduces missed diagnoses, and enhances overall accuracy.

Now, over a year since the launch of *PathoInsight-T*, I'm seeing an ever-increasing number of such cases come to light. Thanks to its highly sensi-tive and specific AI models, the PathoAI pathology AI-assisted diagnostic system has supported pathologists in various global markets in reviewing over 3 million cases. It boasts an impressive sensitivity of 99.20% and a specificity of 87.50%. Capable of handling 80% of initial screening tasks, this system significantly reduces missed diagnoses and provides doctors with reliable support and assistance.

Our next frontier involves advancing to large AI models, which will further unleash the potential of artificial intelligence in diagnosing and monitoring malignant tumors. We're gearing up to make the leap from "single-disease models" to "multi-disease models," aiming to provide broader coverage for clinical tasks and expand the reach of AI in healthcare.

I find myself reminiscing about my journey with artificial intelligence. Over the past two decades of study and professional work, I've passion-ately engaged with the surge of AI commercialization. Despite my daily engagement with this field, I'm still exhilarated by every progress made and excited by each milestone humanity achieves in the progression of artificial intelligence.

SECTION 1: AI THROUGH MY EYES

Over the past 70 years, artificial intelligence has experienced a roller-coaster of highs and lows. Today, amid the waves of data and technological advancements, AI has once again become a hot topic, with interpretations and discussions ranging widely. With over 20 years of experience in this field, I have had the privilege of working with numerous Fortune 500 com-panies on data analytics and AI projects. In the early days, I led the estab-lishment of IBM's big data centers in growth markets and participated in pioneering projects across China, the Asia-Pacific region, and South America. Therefore, my insights are grounded in real-world experiences and hands-on observations.

Unveiling the Core of AI

At the heart of artificial intelligence lies the machine's ability to understand, reason, and learn.

I clearly recall November 2015, when I attended Shelly Palmer's Innovation Series Breakfast event in New York. As one of the keynote speakers, I discussed the arrival of the AI era and its industrial evolution. I shared insights and recent advancements from my team's global AI deployments with the influential figures of the American media industry present. At that time, many in the industry were still unfamiliar with the definition of AI, its industrial significance, and the driving forces behind it.

Although this topic has been around for many years, it remains as relevant today as ever and is definitely worth sharing with everyone.

There are many interpretations of artificial intelligence in the market. However, one clear and widely accepted perspective is that the core pillars of AI development are **Understanding, Reasoning, and Learning**. These three capabilities not only distinguish AI from traditional programmed systems but also drive profound changes in commercial applications. It is through these abilities that AI is evolving from a mere tool into an intelligent system capable of independently tackling complex problems.

▪ U—Understanding: AI's "Conversational Ability" with the World

Most AI applications revolve around facilitating interactions between humans and machines. Today's common commercial scenarios involve using natural language processing and text analysis to enable machines to understand users' historical behavior, make contextual inferences, and communicate in natural language. Models like GPT, for example, can generate coherent text based on user prompts, mimicking the way humans think and respond.

Imagine a retail company using natural language processing to automate customer service. AI not only swiftly addresses common queries but also comprehends customer emotions and intentions, enhancing the overall user experience. This "understanding" capability has become a pivotal force driving the automation of customer interactions.

■ **R—Reasoning: The Ultimate Evolution from AI to Intelligent Decision-Making**

If "Understanding" serves as the bridge between AI and the external world, then "Reasoning" is widely regarded as one of the most essential capabilities of artificial intelligence. It enables AI to extract insights from known information, draw new conclusions, and solve complex problems through logical thinking, akin to human cognition. In many business decisions, reasoning is crucial—it helps companies predict future trends based on past data or derive optimal solutions from intricate information, unlocking new insights previously unimaginable.

A dramatic showcase of reasoning in the real world occurred in 2016 when Google's AlphaGo used its reasoning abilities to defeat human champions in the highly complex game of Go. In the financial sector, AI employs reasoning to assist institutions with risk assessment. For instance, AI systems can analyze vast amounts of historical transaction data to forecast market trends, helping investors craft precise investment strategies and mitigate risks.

During the writing of this book, the industry has once again been rocked by a "reasoning bombshell." On September 13, 2024, OpenAI unveiled its next-generation reasoning model, GPT-o1—the long-awaited model previously known by the codename "Strawberry." Compared to its predecessors like GPT-4o, GPT-o1 marks a significant leap in handling complex reasoning tasks. For instance, it achieved an 83% problem-solving rate in the International Mathematical Olympiad qualification exam, while GPT-4o managed only 13%. This means GPT-o1 delivers notably more accurate results in solving mathematical puzzles, coding, and tackling multi-step logical problems.

GPT-o1 employs a reasoning technique called Chain of Thought (CoT), which simulates the process humans use to solve intricate problems. This advancement not only enhances the model's performance in fields such as science, mathematics, and programming but also allows it to explain the logical steps behind its reasoning. Thus, AI is no longer merely providing answers; it is offering comprehensive support for future intelligent decision-making and problem-solving, marking a pivotal moment in AI's evolution from thought to action.

■ L—Learning: The Eternal Drive for Self-Optimization

This is, in fact, the most crucial driving force behind AI's impact across various industries. Artificial intelligence continuously evolves and provides more accurate answers based on new information, results, and actions, while also tracking decision history. This process can be summarized as autonomous learning. The ability to self-learn is the primary engine propelling the commercialization of AI. Currently, AI is capable of offering valuable recommendations for human decisions. The future trend will see AI engaging in even more autonomous learning to provide decision-making advice, including recommendations, analyses, and necessary actions.

Machine learning forms the foundation of this capability. By analyzing vast amounts of data, models can uncover patterns and optimize themselves. Technologies like deep learning and reinforcement learning have made significant strides in the field of machine learning, particularly excelling in areas such as computer vision and natural language processing. Deep neural networks enable AI to learn complex patterns and features from large datasets. For instance, image recognition systems like Google's DeepMind can continuously learn and train to identify specific objects within massive data collections, evolving from "data learning" to "accurate recognition."

Therefore, true artificial intelligence is defined and assessed by these three dimensions: whether a machine possesses the abilities of Understanding, Reasoning, and Learning.

Defining Moments: The Pivotal Early Steps in Shaping AI

Artificial intelligence began its journey at the Dartmouth Conference in 1956. It experienced a golden decade of progress in its early years but faced setbacks in the 1970s and 1990s due to limitations in hardware and data. However, with breakthroughs in neural network technology and advances in computational power, AI saw the dawn of modernity after the year 2000. This period set the stage for the flourishing of deep learning and machine learning that we witness today.

In the late 1990s, after earning my master's degree in computer science, I ventured to Toronto, Canada, for further academic exploration. In 1999,

I was invited to join the prestigious IBM Toronto Lab, where I initially worked on database technologies. This opportunity marked the beginning of my journey witnessing the full cycle of artificial intelligence—from its dormant phase to its remarkable resurgence.

Toronto became a pivotal chapter in my educational and professional journey, where I lived for over 20 years. Remarkably, it was in this very city that the revival of artificial intelligence took root, making it a fortuitous epicenter for AI's renaissance.

■ The Dawn of the AI Era

To trace the history of "artificial intelligence," we must journey back to 1956. That August, Dartmouth College in the northern U.S. hosted the "Dartmouth Summer Research Project on Artificial Intelligence." Initiated by John McCarthy, Marvin Minsky, Claude Shannon, and other luminaries of the computer science field, this seminal conference gathered the foremost minds of the era. Their ambitious goal was to explore how to imbue machines with human-like intelligence, focusing particularly on using symbolic logic to solve problems and simulate the complex processes of human thought. It was at this conference that McCarthy first coined the term "artificial intelligence."

The brainstorming session lasted for two months, delving into how machines could tackle issues such as natural language processing and neural networks, with the hope of creating machines that could mimic human intelligence. While these ideas seemed far-fetched at the time, they laid the theoretical groundwork for the advancements in AI that would unfold over the following decades.

■ The Golden Decade of Artificial Intelligence

In the decade following the Dartmouth Conference, the field of artificial intelligence saw a surge of groundbreaking innovations. For instance, Marvin Minsky and Seymour Papert established the AI Laboratory at MIT, where they delved into neural networks and symbolic logic reasoning. Meanwhile, Alan Newell and Herbert Simon developed the "Logic Theorist" program, which successfully proved mathematical theorems and marked a significant milestone in early AI.

During the 1960s, AI researchers primarily understood intelligence through the lens of symbolic logic processing. They created systems capable of handling specific tasks, such as chess-playing programs and problem solvers. While these early AI systems demonstrated impressive computational power, they fell short when it came to handling ambiguous and unstructured data.

▪ **The Bottlenecks of Computing Power and Data: The AI Winters of the 1970s and 1990s**

Despite early breakthroughs in AI, the 1970s were marred by significant bottlenecks in computing power and limited data resources, which impeded further progress. Symbolic logic models held great theoretical promise but required substantial computational resources that the hardware of that era could not support. Additionally, many AI programs relied on small, structured datasets, struggling to handle the complexities and uncertainties of the real world.

A critical report by British scientist James Lighthill cast a harsh light on the slow progress of AI, arguing that the investment did not yield proportional returns. This led to a reduction in government and corporate funding for AI research, ushering in the first "AI Winter." During this period, enthusiasm for AI waned, but it inadvertently set the stage for future technological advancements.

The 1990s ushered in another AI Winter, despite ongoing progress in algorithms and theories. The limitations of hardware and data resources became even more pronounced, exacerbating the difficulties faced by AI in practical applications. Most AI systems struggled with real-world problems, particularly in fields like speech and image recognition that demanded extensive computational power.

▪ **The Dawn of Modern AI: From Revival to Revolution (1980–2000)**

In the 1980s, the resurgence of neural networks heralded a new era of optimism for AI. Researchers like Geoffrey Hinton introduced the backpropagation algorithm, overcoming the technical barriers that had stymied neural networks in the 1960s. This breakthrough revealed fresh potential for AI in tasks such as speech recognition and image classification. By the late 1980s, Yann LeCun and others introduced Convolutional Neural Networks (CNNs), which became the hallmark algorithms of deep learning.

Despite these advances in neural network theory, the 1990s were still marred by limitations in computing power and data scarcity, constraining broader practical applications of AI.

By 2000, the landscape began to shift dramatically. The rise of the internet led to a surge in available data, while advancements in computing power—particularly the advent of GPU technology—significantly lowered the costs and complexities of AI research. GPUs provided the parallel processing capabilities essential for accelerating model training, and the internet became a vast reservoir of data for AI systems. This marked the beginning of AI's transition into the modern era of deep learning.

The Third Wave of AI: The Revolution Fueled by Deep Learning

After experiencing two major waves and two harsh winters in the history of artificial intelligence, the academic community gradually recognized that only by meeting the three foundational pillars—data, computational power, and algorithms—could AI achieve groundbreaking advancements. Everything was in place, except for the final catalyst. We must remember the year 2012, a pivotal moment that marked a historic breakthrough for AI, and the names of a remarkable mentor-mentee duo who played a crucial role throughout this transformative period.

One weekend in 2003, an 18-year-old student from Russia knocked on Professor Geoffrey Hinton's office door at the University of Toronto.

"He told me he was more eager to work in my lab than to spend his summer frying French fries," Hinton recalls. This student, named Ilya Sutskever, was soon recruited to join Hinton's research team.

It was this dynamic mentor-mentee duo, Hinton and Sutskever, along with numerous other distinguished figures from academia and industry, who collectively propelled the third wave of artificial intelligence to new heights.

The Deep Learning Renaissance: From Shadows to Spotlight
In the early 2000s, artificial intelligence was considered a niche field, with progress in fundamental tasks like image and speech recognition advancing at a sluggish pace. However, around 2006, the wave of deep learning began to surge, marking a pivotal shift in the AI landscape.

Traditional data processing methods involved using various units or models to cover possible input spaces, which worked well for low-dimensional scenarios. But as data dimensions increased, traditional statistical methods quickly faltered, leading to what is known as the "curse of dimensionality." This made it challenging to handle the burgeoning data volumes driven by the IT revolution. Both academia and industry were in search of new solutions, and their paths converged dramatically.

In 2009, Geoffrey Hinton's research team used NVIDIA's CUDA platform to train neural networks for recognizing human language. Pleased with the results, Hinton publicly endorsed NVIDIA's GPUs at that year's NIPS (Conference and Workshop on Neural Information Processing Systems), recommending them to the research community.

Three years later, Hinton's students—Alex Krizhevsky and Ilya Sutskever—heeding their mentor's advice, purchased two GeForce GPUs from Amazon. Using NVIDIA's parallel computing platform, they trained a neural network called AlexNet (named after Krizhevsky) for visual recognition, feeding it millions of images over a week. The results were exceptional.

Earlier that year, Google researcher Andrew Ng had trained a neural network to recognize cat videos, using approximately 16,000 CPUs across 1,000 computers, costing a million dollars to achieve his goal. This student experiment would later serve as a foundation for NVIDIA's rise.

In 2012, AlexNet, representing Hinton's team, competed in the ImageNet annual visual recognition competition. The results were astonishing—AlexNet's performance far surpassed other algorithms, leading organizers to question if cheating had occurred. Hinton described it as a "big bang moment" and a paradigm shift.

Tech giants quickly recognized that deep learning was breaking through previous AI technological barriers and held immense commercial potential. That same year, IBM, Microsoft, and Google released reports showing that deep learning could significantly enhance speech recognition accuracy.

Following AlexNet's success, Google acquired Hinton and his students' startup, DDNresearch, for $45 million, with Microsoft also bidding. The trio joined Google, where their technology swiftly improved Google's photo classification capabilities.

The following year, Yann LeCun was invited to lead Facebook's AI research center, joining the ranks of the "three giants" of AI research, with only Bengio remaining in academia.

From that point, competitors in the ImageNet competition rapidly turned to neural networks, propelling their status in academia. This academic revolution would soon capture public attention through a high-profile competition four years later.

In 2016, Google's DeepMind unleashed its groundbreaking AI program, AlphaGo, upon the world. In a stunning display of prowess, AlphaGo defeated the reigning Go champion, Lee Sedol, with a decisive 4–1 victory. This wasn't just any triumph; it was a profound showcase of AI's capabilities. AlphaGo demonstrated not only exceptional memory and computational skills but also an unprecedented level of learning. During the match, it played moves that no human had ever considered—most notably, its move 37 in the second game, which exhibited a form of "human-like intuition," left experts astounded.

The public was jolted awake to the reality that the era of AI applications had truly arrived. Soon, a wave of innovations powered by deep learning emerged, from facial recognition and reading recommendations to intelligent customer service. This technological leap extended into new realms, including autonomous driving and drug discovery.

Little did anyone anticipate that, just a decade later, Geoffrey Hinton and his protégé would propel artificial intelligence into yet another transformative era.

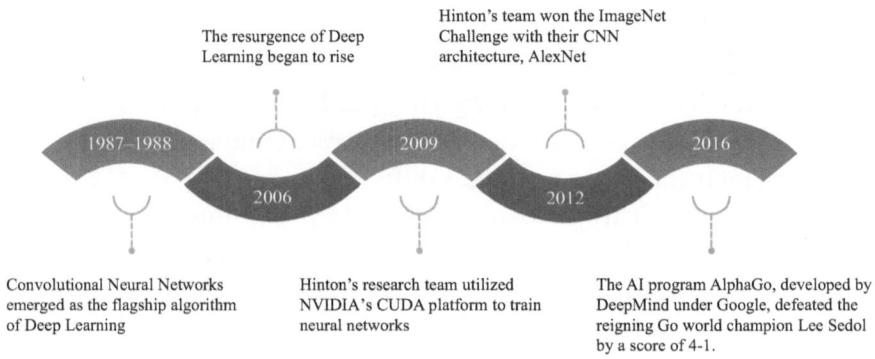

FIGURE 1.1   Pivotal moments in the rise of deep learning.

The Emergence of Giants: The Era of Large Models

After gaining fame from the ImageNet competition, Ilya Sutskever, following Geoffrey Hinton, joined Google Brain to apply deep learning's recognition capabilities to sequences of data, such as words, sentences, and images.

In July 2015, the 30-year-old scientist was invited to a private dinner at the luxurious Rosewood Sand Hill Hotel in Silicon Valley. Hosted by Sam Altman, head of the startup incubator Y Combinator, the guest list was a who's who of tech elites, including Tesla CEO Elon Musk, his former

PayPal colleague Peter Thiel, and Greg Brockman, CTO of payment processing company Stripe.

At the time, Google had just spent $400 million acquiring DeepMind, a London-based neural network startup that had attracted a group of industry leaders. It was rumored that out of the 50 real experts in deep learning, 12 were at DeepMind.

During the dinner, the participants discussed founding a lab to prevent Google from monopolizing the field and committed to making the lab non-profit. They promised to make all research public and open-source all technologies, underscoring their commitment to transparency. The founding donors decided to invest $1 billion in the new venture (though this pledge was ultimately unfulfilled), naming the lab OpenAI.

Sam Altman took on the role of CEO to spearhead OpenAI's formation, while Sutskever joined as Chief Scientist, publicly stating that OpenAI aimed to achieve Artificial General Intelligence (AGI).

In 2017, Google introduced a novel training architecture known as Transformer. Sutskever quickly adopted this architecture to create the first "Generative Pre-trained Transformer" or GPT. He believed that by increasing computational resources, data scale, and model parameters, these systems could become significantly more intelligent. His intuition proved correct, as model performance continued to improve in line with Moore's Law.

Subsequently, OpenAI distilled the secret of this model training into what is known as Scaling Law. Scaling Law outlined a potential path to AGI, suggesting that by absorbing vast amounts of text, machines could understand natural language similarly to humans, eventually achieving human-like cognition.

Meanwhile, Microsoft CEO Satya Nadella eagerly wanted Microsoft to play a leading role in AI. OpenAI was keen to partner with a competitor to Google. In July 2019, the two companies joined forces, with Microsoft becoming OpenAI's "preferred commercial partner," making an initial investment of $1 billion.

The rewards of big models exceeded expectations. As the parameter counts increased, researchers observed surprising and hard-to-explain bursts in capability, known as emergent phenomena.

At the end of 2022, OpenAI's release of the ChatGPT chatbot to the public sparked global attention and debate, marking the official dawn of the era of large models. Its impact continues to grow every moment.

The rise of large models has brought a stronger influence from industry power and capital investment. While AlexNet's success was primarily a hot topic within academic circles, the release of ChatGPT immediately made ordinary people users, creating a massive industry explosion.

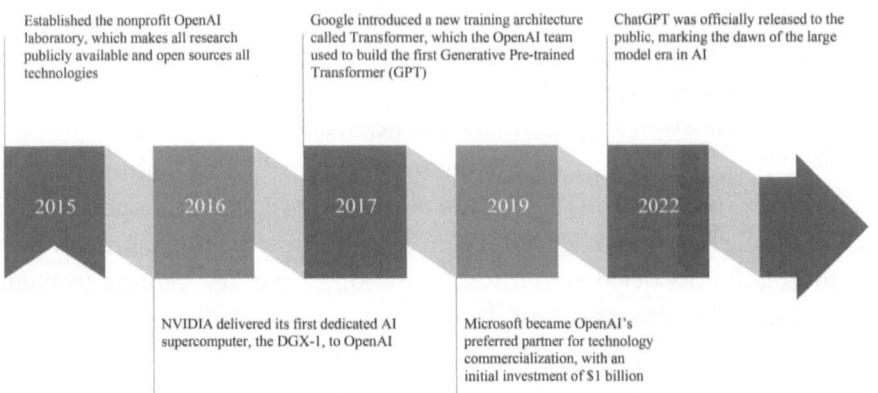

FIGURE 1.2   Defining epochs in the evolution of large models.

SECTION 2: PIONEERS OF THE AI RENAISSANCE

The rise of large models has spearheaded the contemporary "AI Renaissance"—if earlier discussions focused on the three waves of AI development, then this undeniably represents a "tectonic-shift tsunami." Models like the GPT series and BERT, through massive data training and deep learning, have showcased unprecedented capabilities in language processing and knowledge reasoning, profoundly transforming societal paradigms.

These models have not only propelled automation into more complex domains such as medical diagnostics, financial forecasting, and content generation but also nudged humanity closer to Irving Good's prophecy of an "intelligence explosion": an era where machine intelligence continuously self-optimizes and surpasses human cognition. As these large models evolve, they will reshape how society functions, redefine business models, and alter human roles, ushering in a new chapter of human-machine coexistence.

The Technological Foundation of Large Models

Large models are neural networks characterized by their exceptionally vast parameter scales, marking an advancement in deep learning technology. At their core, these models are sophisticated algorithms developed using deep learning methods, designed to harness vast amounts of data and computational power to tackle complex tasks with unprecedented accuracy and efficiency.

Mainstream Power Engine: Transformer

In the world of large language models, such as OpenAI's GPT-4o and Google's Gemini, one might liken them to different car brands; however, they all essentially rely on the same underlying engine—the Transformer.

The Transformer is a neural network architecture introduced in a groundbreaking 2017 paper, "Attention Is All You Need," by an eight-member team at Google. At the time, neural networks had achieved remarkable successes in image recognition, and Google sought to apply these advancements to create more human-like responses, such as auto-completing email sentences or developing relatively simple customer service chatbots.

Yet, researchers encountered a significant challenge: Recursive Neural Networks struggled with parsing longer text blocks. For example, to comprehend the terms "9-dan," "playing black," and "midgame" in the context of Lee Sedol's first game against AlphaGo, a language model is needed to retain context about "Go." While humans easily recognize and remember the term "Go," computers traditionally process sequences strictly in order, missing out on potentially vital contextual clues.

Around 2014, Google's research team began conceptualizing a novel approach called self-attention. This mechanism allows a network to reference other parts of a document to clarify the intent of words, thus aiding in more accurate translations. From a neuroscience perspective, attention mechanisms mimic the brain's selective focus, where humans concentrate on specific information while disregarding irrelevant details. For instance, when viewing the Mona Lisa, our initial focus might be on her enigmatic smile, possibly overlooking her hand's position.

In computational terms, attention mechanisms offer a dynamic weighting approach. Unlike traditional neural networks, which assign fixed weights to each input feature, attention mechanisms adjust weights dynamically based on different parts of the input data, enabling more flexible information processing.

In simpler terms, the self-attention used by Transformers learns probabilistic relationships between words within a sequence. For example, in the sentence "The boy was late for work because he didn't catch the early bus," the model establishes connections between the word "he" and other words. The core function of the Transformer model is to map these connections, helping the model understand which words, like "he" and "boy," are most closely related, thereby improving its comprehension of text sequences.

When interacting with ChatGPT, the model's understanding of each word is guided by this self-attention mechanism, allowing it to interpret our meanings effectively.

The Transformer's approach is distinct from linear methods (processing each word in sequence) by using parallel methods (analyzing words collectively). The popularity of NVIDIA GPUs can be attributed to their prowess in handling such parallel processing tasks.

Despite the transformative impact of the Transformer, Google's leadership hesitated to fully embrace its potential for training large networks, missing out on early opportunities. This led to the development of Transformer-based products like the chatbot Bard, but the initial advantage was lost.

In contrast, OpenAI acted swiftly. Ilya Sutskever of OpenAI recalls that almost immediately after the Transformer paper's publication, they recognized its potential to address the limitations of Recursive Neural Networks, rapidly shifting to Transformer-based models, resulting in GPT-3.

While Google's contributions to the foundational technology of large models, particularly in the Transformer domain, are significant, the company missed several opportunities. Today, criticisms persist regarding the efficiency and potential of Transformers. Alternatives, such as Meta's Megabyte and DeepMind's Griffin, have emerged, aiming to address the limitations of Transformers and demonstrate advancements in efficiency metrics.

From Learning Cats to Recognizing Dragons
After the introduction of Transformer architectures, large models gained the remarkable ability to link context, ushering in a new era of transfer learning. This advancement significantly transformed AI's capabilities.

Early image recognition algorithms primarily relied on supervised learning. For example, to train a machine to recognize cats, you need to feed it a vast number of cat images. The sheer volume of data required to build a comprehensive cat dataset, and the extensive work involved in labeling it, explains why training a machine to recognize a cat cost around $1 million in 2012.

These early classifiers, however, could only identify cats and were not capable of recognizing other species. With an estimated 2 million animal species worldwide, creating a model to identify all of them would necessitate a dataset encompassing all these animals. Even with just one image per species, you'd need around 2 million pictures. In reality, recognizing each animal would require thousands of images, making such a project prohibitively expensive.

In the early days of deep learning, we mostly saw specialized models, which I refer to as "small models." For example, a model trained to identify specific pests in rice fields with a limited dataset was relatively manageable.

An ideal learning approach, akin to human cognitive habits, is zero-shot learning. This method allows models to recognize and classify categories they've never seen before, reducing their reliance on labeled data. Key to this is the model's ability to understand "high-dimensional semantic" features instead of relying on low-dimensional sample features, thereby enabling transferability.

For instance, in Western mythology, a dragon is depicted with features such as a horse's head, a lion's body, bat-like wings, four legs, and the ability to breathe fire. By providing this information, a model can identify a "dragon" even without having seen one before.

Today, AI models can indeed achieve this zero-shot learning capability. OpenAI's team, for instance, developed a method called Contrastive Language-Image Pretraining (CLIP). The core principle of CLIP is contrastive learning: it teaches the model to distinguish between positive samples (matching image-text pairs) and negative samples (non-matching pairs). By examining millions of image-text pairings, the model learns the relationships and can apply this knowledge to other classification tasks.

As large language models grow in scale, their "language understanding" capabilities also strengthen. One notable capability is In-Context Learning (ICL). With just a few examples of "input-label" pairs, a model can predict the label for previously unseen inputs.

For example, if we provide the model with translation examples like Cat-猫, Dog-狗, and Duck-鸭, and then input the English word Fish, the model can automatically output "鱼" as the translation. This learning process mirrors the human analogy-based decision-making process.

How exactly in-context learning operates remains somewhat opaque. Some researchers liken language models to meta-optimizers and view in-context learning as an implicit fine-tuning process. In essence, it functions like a black box.

Despite the excitement surrounding this transfer learning capability, which reduces the computational cost of adapting models to new tasks and makes Language-Model-as-a-Service (LMaaS) feasible, there are concerns about how far AI's learning abilities can go and whether we can fully harness them.

The Perils of Large Models: Navigating the Challenges Ahead

The capabilities of Large models are advancing at a rapid pace. Yet, many of the fundamental mechanisms driving these models remain unclear and unsettled.

A primary concern is whether the core principle behind large models, known as the Scaling Law, will continue to apply as models grow. There are also significant worries about challenges like "hallucinations" and other issues that could affect the practical deployment of these technologies in various industries.

Will Scaling Law Reach Its Limit?

Today, the GPT series and other large language models have achieved remarkable power. A key reason for their success lies in the belief of pioneers like Ilya Sutskever that by simply enhancing computational power, data volume, and model parameters, these systems become increasingly intelligent.

The term "large models" indeed lives up to its name, embodying three core aspects: massive parameters, extensive training data, and significant computational demands. For instance, industry insiders estimate that OpenAI's forthcoming GPT model will boast a staggering 3 to 5 trillion parameters and be trained using 7,000 NVIDIA H100 chips.

This substantial investment has given rise to what is known as the Scaling Law—a principle indicating that the performance of many AI models improves dramatically once their parameter scale surpasses a certain threshold. From GPT-1 to GPT-o1, each iteration has shown significant advancements.

Imagine boiling water: it reaches a rapid boil at 100 degrees Celsius. Similarly, large models, once they exceed a certain parameter size, gain new capabilities that can be described as "emergent." This emergence manifests in two primary ways:

1. **Sudden Quantum Leaps**: As the size of neural networks, training machine speeds, and sample quantities increase, there comes a tipping point where these networks experience a dramatic leap in capability, significantly enhancing model performance.

2. **Transferability of Skills**: Models that excel in one domain can swiftly be applied to other computing fields, demonstrating remarkable adaptability.

Many top AI scientists were initially skeptical about the existence of the Scaling Law. Geoffrey Hinton himself admitted he hadn't anticipated Scaling Law leading to the creation of ChatGPT. Even with over two decades of tracking AI, I never imagined that large models would emerge so rapidly. I had expected that the era of small models would continue for some time.

Now, both Ilya Sutskever and Geoffrey Hinton believe that following this path could lead us to AGI, which they predict might emerge within the next 5 to 10 years. However, Scaling Law is not a theoretical law with a clear scientific basis; it is an empirically observed pattern.

Yann LeCun has likened Scaling Law to plotting data on a graph and fitting it with a line: "We don't know how far this line will extend or where it might stop. Scaling Law may be a viable approach."

Many believe that simply scaling up models, increasing computational power, and expanding data will allow large models to reach human-level capabilities. Numerous projects and investments are betting on Scaling Law continuing to deliver results, with extensive GPU stockpiling.

To meet the explosive demand for intelligent computing, there has been a large-scale investment in new AI centers, significantly boosting NVIDIA's profits and market value. Yet, we cannot guarantee that the Scaling Law will keep functioning as it has.

In my view, relying purely on massive resource inputs to enhance model performance might not be the most effective strategy. It appears too blunt and inefficient, consuming resources that are neither economical nor unlimited. For instance, the public data pools available for training might soon reach their limit. Elon Musk has predicted that by 2025, power shortages could hinder the supply for all chips.

I advocate for a smarter, more effective approach to using models. Rather than focusing solely on scale, improving data quality is often more valuable. The concept of "Data-Centric AI," as opposed to "Model-Centric AI," emphasizes that refining the quality of data is crucial.

Improving datasets is a prerequisite for generating accurate models, avoiding the pitfall of "Garbage In, Garbage Out." Real-world data is often messy, and providing high-quality datasets—consistent and accurate labels, representative and high-quality inputs—leads to more effective models and successful AI applications.

In many specialized vertical applications, small datasets are common, making data quality directly impactful on model performance. For instance, Andrew Ng has noted that a well-chosen set of 50 images, accurately labeled, can be sufficient to build an excellent dataset for training custom models that solve real problems.

Data is the backbone of AI applications and profoundly affects model performance. Balancing the allocation of resources between data and model training will likely offer greater opportunities for model advancement.

Machine Hallucinations and Biases

The term "hallucination" refers to the phenomenon where large models generate content that is absurd or inaccurate, often unrelated to any real source. This issue becomes particularly concerning when models produce increasingly convincing responses. When these models offer information that seems partially accurate, users may develop an over-reliance on them, which can lead to misleading outcomes.

A concrete example of hallucination was provided by an AI lab at the University of Hong Kong. When asked, "What is the Dow Jones Industrial Average?" the model, drawing from Wikipedia, responded with, "An index of 30 major U.S. stocks." This answer conflicts with Wikipedia's description of it as "an index of 30 prominent publicly traded U.S. companies," despite the answers seeming superficially similar.

The reasons behind hallucinations in large models are complex. One explanation is related to their internal mechanisms, which involve understanding the relationships between the current word (token) and others within the vast dataset. The model's responses are generated by maximizing probability rather than through logical reasoning, leading to jumbled and synthetic results.

For instance, if you inquire about "apple," the model might mix contexts—religious, commercial, etc.—with the word, resulting in bizarre answers that merge unrelated contexts.

The impact of hallucinations becomes particularly severe when models are widely deployed in automated systems. For example, when used to generate news or information, these models can produce large amounts of indistinguishable false information, drastically diminishing the reliability and trustworthiness of the content. This issue is even more critical in fields requiring precision, such as healthcare and law.

Researchers are addressing the hallucination problem through methods like fact-checking and knowledge fine-tuning. Current models, like ChatGPT-4o, are designed to avoid responding to frequently hallucinated queries. Sutskever's team employs reinforcement learning from human feedback to create a new layer of human feedback to minimize hallucinations. In the future, there might even be a new profession dedicated to the expert verification of generated content, ensuring its accuracy.

In my view, a more significant challenge for large language models may lie in their inherent biases. These models often exhibit preferences and subjective slants in their output. Mechanistically, when we use these models, we are feeding them vast amounts of data that reflect our values. These models, in turn, consider this data as "basic facts" of human interaction. As the datasets grow, the models capture inherent human biases, including ugliness and cruelty.

For example, data input into these models may include racially discriminatory or ethnically hateful content. As such content becomes part of the training corpus, the output may also carry these biases. Studies have shown that generative models can reproduce and even amplify cultural and linguistic biases and stereotypes.

Relying solely on manual checks for political correctness may not be realistic. A more feasible approach might be to use technical methods to reduce bias in the system. For instance, when issuing personal credit loans, if racial bias is a concern, AI systems could be trained with credit data while freezing race-related weights, preventing the system from incorporating racial factors into its credit decisions, at least partially mitigating the issue.

There is also a dystopian concern that increasingly powerful AI might, one day, develop a malicious bias akin to the "Skynet" scenario in "Terminator," threatening human existence. While such discussions were once purely science fiction, the number of people holding these pessimistic views is growing.

SECTION 3: AI—THE MOST FAMILIAR STRANGER

As early as 1965, computer scientist Irving Good introduced the concept of "intelligence explosion." He wrote:

> Let us define a superintelligent machine as one that surpasses every human, no matter how intelligent, in every aspect of intellectual activity. Since designing machines is one such intellectual

activity, a superintelligent machine would be capable of designing even better machines. Thus, an 'intelligence explosion' would inevitably occur, leaving human intelligence far behind.

The rise of large models, emblematic of new technological advancements, is sparking an intelligence revolution in human society. We are rapidly approaching the moment of this "intelligence explosion."

Disrupting Social Paradigms

It is generally understood that our complex human society is composed of three interconnected subsystems. These subsystems evolve sequentially and blend together, forming a foundational principle that governs individuals, organizations, companies, and even digital systems:

1. ***Subsystem of Information****: This subsystem gathers data from the environment.*
2. ***Subsystem of Model****: This subsystem processes and interprets the information, enabling reasoning, analysis, planning, and decision-making.*
3. ***Subsystem of Action****: This subsystem interacts with the environment based on the previous subsystems to achieve our objectives.*

With the advent of large models, we have shifted from a world where "information is everywhere" to one where "models are everywhere" or even "knowledge is everywhere." And now, we are on the brink of a new era where "action is everywhere."

The Era of Zero-Cost Knowledge

With the explosion of the information revolution, particularly the rise of the internet, we have entered an age where "information is everywhere" and the cost of producing and accessing information is plummeting, approaching zero.

Take news for example. Back in 2000, newspapers were still the primary means of obtaining news. People would habitually purchase newspapers from stands. For instance, in Toronto, the largest local paper was the

Toronto Star, which had been in circulation for 132 years and boasted a peak daily distribution of 500,000 copies.

Fast forward to today, accessing news has become nearly free. Websites and social media provide instant access to information, disrupting traditional media like the Toronto Star, which now sees its circulation drop to below 200,000 copies. By 2013, Google's advertising revenue alone surpassed the total revenue of the entire US newspaper industry.

The convenience of accessing information has also birthed new business models, such as e-commerce and streaming services, leading to the rise of industry giants like Amazon and Netflix.

The advent of large model technologies, such as GPT, promises to usher us into a new era—where "knowledge is everywhere." These models are not just about retrieving information but about understanding and synthesizing it. They can generate systematic, coherent "knowledge" through forms like "agents," offering advanced comprehension and application capabilities with significant problem-solving potential.

Google has already felt the impact of this shift. In July 2024, OpenAI released a prototype of its AI search product, SearchGPT. In the official demo, when queried, "When can I see sea hares (sea slugs) in Half Moon Bay this weekend?" SearchGPT responds with, "You should go at low tide, as sea hares are often found in the intertidal zone and on rocky shores," and provides this week's low tide times, advising users to check local tide prediction websites.

The SearchGPT experience is akin to conversing with a knowledgeable human, building contextual information prompts for each query. This represents a new paradigm in search experiences.

As the ecosystem of large models evolves, they will be able to delve deeply into various specialized fields, read vast amounts of literature beyond the reach of any single individual, and understand it. They could provide medical diagnoses, legal services, and educational instruction, often more efficiently and cost-effectively than humans.

In the near future, seeking medical advice may not be about finding a doctor first but rather consulting a model. Consequently, the marginal cost of acquiring "knowledge" will approach zero.

This shift could profoundly disrupt our societal division of labor. Currently, professions like lawyers, doctors, teachers, and engineers form a stable middle class, but many of these roles could be replaced by AI. The capabilities of large models extend beyond human reach, potentially exploring knowledge beyond our current scope and even performing tasks traditionally reserved for scientists. This progression heralds the rise of "ubiquitous action," leading to new developments in autonomous driving, robotics, space intelligence, and more.

The Dawn of Embodied Intelligence

As Jensen Huang and others have proposed, the next wave of artificial intelligence will be "Embodied Intelligence"—smart systems that understand, reason, and interact with the physical world. Humanoid robots are a prime example of this emerging technology.

Elon Musk is already paving the way in this arena. In September 2022, Tesla unveiled its humanoid robot prototype, "Optimus." Musk shared a video on social media showcasing Optimus folding a shirt, illustrating a stark departure from the traditional, mechanically controlled robots of the past.

Optimus is designed to perform a variety of tasks autonomously—everything from house chores to cooking, and even teaching children how to play the piano. It is envisioned as a versatile humanoid robot capable of learning a broad range of skills on its own.

In July 2024, Fei-Fei Li's startup, World Labs, completed two rounds of funding, raising approximately $100 million and achieving a valuation exceeding $1 billion. World Labs focuses on "Spatial Intelligence."

What is Spatial Intelligence? Our daily actions occur within a "four-dimensional space-time" (three-dimensional physical space and time). From a young age, we learn to better observe and interact within this three-dimensional world. For example, seeing a cup tilting off the edge of a table, a child can generally predict what will happen next.

Spatial Intelligence involves creating models that replicate the four-dimensional space-time process, thereby endowing systems with the capabilities for perception, reasoning, and decision-making. This is a fundamental skill for achieving embodied intelligence.

Consider a care robot that, at the moment an elderly person stumbles over a step and is about to fall, needs to recognize the danger, intervene autonomously, and apply just the right amount of force to prevent the fall without causing harm. This scenario requires extensive spatial awareness and judgment.

World Labs is developing simulation environments driven by three-dimensional spatial models to train computers and robots, enhancing their ability to act within a three-dimensional world.

Yann LeCun is researching a "World Model," which bears similar characteristics. He posits that while large language models possess vast amounts of background knowledge extracted from written texts, they lack the common sense humans have, resulting in potential disconnections in applications. This common sense is derived from our interactions with the physical world. Yann suggests that human and animal brains seem to operate using a type of world simulation, known as a world model, which guides us in making accurate predictions about our surroundings.

Yann's view is that genuine breakthroughs in intelligence won't come from merely scaling up models but from enabling AI to learn common sense within a world model, akin to human learning processes where children understand the world through observation, interaction, and practice.

Ultimately, whether it is Spatial Intelligence or World Models, the goal is to guide artificial intelligence from mere knowledge injection to a broader perception of the real world, allowing it to execute tasks autonomously and efficiently.

While predicting when Spatial Intelligence will be fully realized is challenging, current advancements suggest promising potential. For instance, applications like Sora can generate realistic videos, indicating that existing technologies can recreate relatively complete 3D worlds. The potential of large models in perceiving three-dimensional spaces is evident.

The field of Spatial Intelligence is progressing rapidly. In June 2024, Jensen Huang revealed in a public speech that Foxconn and Delta are constructing digital twin facilities for their factories using the Omniverse simulation platform. These manufacturers are simulating and training factory elements like robotic arms and autonomous mobile robots, paving the way for automated operations.

Looking ahead, the integration of mechanical systems with artificial intelligence in embodied intelligence is advancing swiftly and will increasingly impact each of us.

Toward an Intelligence Explosion

In the evolving landscape of artificial intelligence, leading institutions like OpenAI, DeepMind, and Anthropic have proposed various classification systems for AI systems. Given that this book is aimed at a general audience, I've opted for a more accessible framework.

For simplicity, I categorize AI into three broad stages: **Artificial Narrow Intelligence (ANI)**, **AGI**, and **Artificial Superintelligence (ASI)**.

The concept of the "intelligence explosion" that Good referred to essentially corresponds to Artificial Superintelligence.

Many believe that humanity has already charted a course toward achieving AGI and that once we reach this milestone, ASI will follow rapidly.

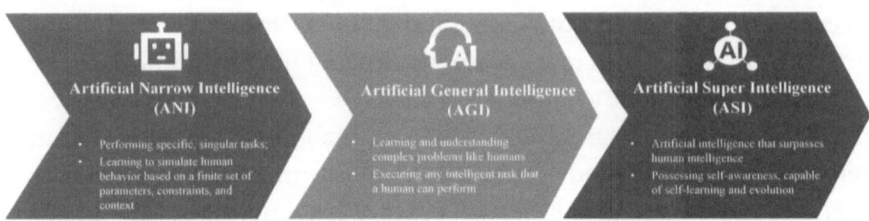

FIGURE 1.3   Development phases of artificial intelligence.

Stage One: Artificial Narrow Intelligence (ANI)

ANI is goal-oriented, designed to perform specific tasks as defined by humans. As algorithms, computing power, and data improve, ANI systems become increasingly proficient. Before the advent of large models, most AI products on the market were ANI. Examples include companion robots, AI vests, Google's AlphaGo, smart drones, voice assistants, and music composition robots—all designed to extend human capabilities. To date, the most widespread applications of ANI have been in human-machine interaction. These machines serve as assistants rather than conversational partners, failing to pass the renowned Turing Test.

Stage Two: Artificial General Intelligence (AGI)

When AI reaches the stage of AGI, intelligent robots will be nearly indistinguishable from humans in their cognitive abilities. They will exhibit abstract thinking, rapid learning, planning, and problem-solving skills akin to human brain functions. AGI systems will possess autonomous perception, cognition, decision-making, learning, execution, and social collaboration abilities, aligning with human emotions, ethics, and moral values.

Max Tegmark, a professor of physics at MIT, posits in his book *Life 3.0* that with sufficient time and resources, AGI could achieve any goal and perform at par with any other intelligent entity. If AGI determines it needs better social skills, predictive abilities, or AI design skills, it will work to acquire them. These robots will have independent thinking capabilities and are moving from the realm of science fiction to reality. Organizations like OpenAI are dedicated to exploring AGI.

Previously, many AI researchers estimated that AGI would emerge within the next few decades. However, this timeline has significantly accelerated. Leopold Aschenbrenner, a former employee of OpenAI's Superalignment team, likens the development from GPT-2 to GPT-4 to the evolution from a preschooler to a smart high-schooler. GPT-4o, for instance, demonstrates capabilities akin to a person who has completed an undergraduate degree and is preparing for graduate studies, especially excelling in tasks like Multi-task Language Understanding (MMLU) and Multi-lingual Elementary Mathematics (MGSM).

Aschenbrenner predicts that AGI could be achieved by 2027, based on advancements in computing power, algorithm efficiency, and unlocked potential. OpenAI CEO Sam Altman has similarly projected that AGI could be realized before 2030. Conversely, figures like Andrew Ng argue that some companies have set the AGI benchmarks too low, thereby accelerating the timeline. Ng insists that AGI should be defined as "AI that can perform any intellectual task that a human can," such as driving cars or piloting aircraft. By this standard, achieving AGI might take several decades or more.

In July 2024, OpenAI proposed a five-tier rating system for AGI:

- **L1**: Chatbots, like ChatGPT, with conversational abilities.

- **L2**: Reasoners, capable of human-level problem-solving.

- **L3**: Agents, able to take actions on behalf of users.

- **L4**: Innovators, assisting in invention and creativity.

- **L5**: Organizations, performing tasks akin to a managerial role.

OpenAI assessed itself as currently at Level 1, nearing Level 2, and progressing toward Level 5, which represents the final step to AGI. The debate continues about whether current large model technologies can lead to AGI and when it might be achieved. Nonetheless, it is undeniable that the timeline for AGI has been dramatically accelerated.

Stage Three: Artificial Superintelligence (ASI)

The 1984 film *The Terminator* depicted a dystopian future where robots rule the world, driven by an artificial intelligence known as Skynet. In the film, Earth is controlled by Skynet, and humanity rises in rebellion against this AI overlord.

In this cinematic scenario, Skynet represents the concept of ASI.

Superintelligence is a sophisticated form of AI that vastly surpasses the cognitive abilities of even the most brilliant human minds. It breaks through the limitations of the human brain, exploring and understanding realms of thought and observation beyond our biological capacities. Unlike traditional AI, superintelligence doesn't rely on carbon-based or silicon-based materials, nor does it need a physical substrate to exist.

A superintelligent entity would think and operate much like humans but on a grander scale, continuously redesigning and upgrading its hardware and existential mediums to achieve a form of digital immortality.

The general consensus is that as machine intelligence evolves at an ever-increasing pace, human intelligence, constrained by biological limitations, evolves at a much slower rate. One day, artificial intelligence is expected to surpass human intelligence, and the advent of superintelligence seems inevitable.

Academics broadly agree that once AGI is realized, the emergence of superintelligence will not be far behind. The theory is that AGI could self-replicate on a massive scale; millions of AGIs could work continuously and autonomously, effectively automating AI research and dramatically accelerating technological advancements.

Leopold Aschenbrenner takes a more radical view, suggesting that after achieving AGI, artificial intelligence systems might transition to ASI within a year. Elon Musk's predictions align closely, estimating that with current technological progress, AI could surpass human intelligence by 2030.

Irving Good famously predicted that the first superintelligent machine would become humanity's last invention, provided it is sufficiently controllable and able to instruct humanity on how to manage it.

However, Musk and many pessimists argue that a more advanced intelligence would not be constrained by a relatively lower-level intelligence. They are exploring various solutions to prevent such a scenario, and I will delve into these discussions in later sections.

SECTION 4: PREPARING FOR THE CO-EVOLUTION: HUMAN AND MACHINE IN SYMBIOSIS

The debate over whether artificial intelligence is a boon or a bane for humanity has been ongoing from the very beginning.

In the 1950s, during the first wave of artificial intelligence, Marvin Minsky, a tech optimist, believed that AI could bring widespread benefits to humanity. Meanwhile, Norbert Wiener, the father of cybernetics, issued a dark prophecy that AI might replace humans.

Today, Larry Page, the co-founder of Google, represents the "AI Utopia" perspective, which envisions AI leading human civilization to new heights. On the other hand, Elon Musk embodies the "AI Threat" view, advocating for stringent controls on AI to prevent significant risks to humanity.

In academia, figures like Geoffrey Hinton have shifted toward concern, and Dario Amodei's move into AI safety reflects this change in attitude.

Looking at the broader picture, it's clear that the controversy surrounding AI evolves alongside its technological development. This discourse has been a constant companion throughout the various stages of AI progress, and it continues to this day.

In my view, the future of AI and its coexistence with humanity is inevitable. Ultimately, the nature of this relationship will be shaped by human decisions and choices.

Nurturing the Beauty of Humanity

As someone deeply engaged in and passionate about the field of artificial intelligence, I'd like to focus on how individuals can navigate the challenges posed by AI.

Geoffrey Hinton once pessimistically predicted that AI would not create as many jobs as it would eliminate.

Before the advent of true AGI, my stance is cautiously optimistic.

Indeed, with the rapid iteration of large models that have the potential for general AI, some white-collar jobs will inevitably be replaced. As embodied intelligence advances, blue-collar positions on assembly lines, and even skilled trades such as plumbing and construction, may eventually be handled by robots.

However, AI will also give rise to a plethora of new professions, such as prompt engineers, AI trainers, and virtual avatar creators.

For most workers, especially those in knowledge-based roles, AI can enhance efficiency and convenience. A 2023 report by the International Labour Organization (ILO) suggests that generative AI is more likely to augment existing jobs rather than completely replace them. The study finds that the overall impact of AI is neither particularly positive nor negative; rather, the risk of task automation is higher for certain roles, such as typists, travel advisers, and bank tellers.

Regardless of technological advancements, I believe that the importance of purely technical skills will likely diminish over time, while social skills, management abilities, and other soft skills will become increasingly vital.

For instance, a doctor may find that AI matches or even surpasses their diagnostic accuracy, but their ability to empathize with patients and provide emotional support remains unmatched. Similarly, a teacher's knowledge output may be outpaced by AI models, but their role in inspiring curiosity and fostering a dynamic learning environment remains irreplaceable.

Human qualities such as sincerity, optimism, empathy, and compassion are still invaluable and uniquely human.

I speculate that as AI increasingly replaces foundational tasks, many services will cater more directly to emotional and psychological needs, providing what might be termed "emotional value." In this regard, one doesn't need to be a genius to offer warmth and kindness; cultivating personal virtues allows individuals to compete uniquely with machines.

This isn't merely a feel-good message. My personal experience confirms that success is not just about being at the cutting edge of technology but also about having a strong value system. For example, keeping promises and building trust can make clients willing to engage in long-term partnerships. After all, many decisions are still made by people, and many services are purchased by people. If one can connect with others, gain their favor, and build trust, numerous opportunities remain available.

Mastering the Art of Human-Machine Interaction

In November 2023, Singapore's Government Technology Agency (GovTech) organized a groundbreaking GPT-4 Prompt Engineering competition. Sheila Teo, a data scientist, emerged as the winner and subsequently shared her insights in a blog post titled "How I Won the Singapore GPT-4 Prompt Engineering Competition," detailing a series of effective prompt engineering strategies.

The foresight of hosting a prompt engineering competition cannot be overstated. Many have yet to fully grasp its significance. As AI becomes an integral part of our world, we must all consider the kind of future we are stepping into. Leading figures in the industry generally agree that humanity's destiny is to coexist with machines.

For instance, Jensen Huang predicts a dual existence for humans: one in the physical world and another in a digital twin, or Earth-2, where everyone interacts with various intelligent machines. "At the base level of the world is infinite, inexhaustible computational power; in the middle layer is the digital twin—simulation—that relies on computational power to provide an infinitely accurate imitation, experimentation, and prediction of the physical world; at the upper level is a world that achieves optimal solutions through computation—where humans and robots coexist."

Elon Musk takes this vision even further, believing that human life will inherently involve human-machine symbiosis. His company, Neuralink, is focused on brain-machine interface technology, aiming to enhance human capabilities through implanted chips and ultimately establish a deep linkage between the human brain and computers, creating a symbiotic relationship between human intelligence and digital intelligence.

In the future, machines may become sufficiently flexible and adaptable, potentially replacing some human functions and serving as physical carriers of human thought, thus aiding in achieving a form of intellectual immortality.

In a world where humans and machines coexist, we will need to master two languages: one for human-to-human communication and one for human-to-machine interaction. Prompt engineering, in this context, emerges as a new language of the human-machine era. Mastery of prompts is akin to training for effective human-machine interaction, enhancing one's communication capabilities.

Predictions suggest that in ten years, 50% of jobs worldwide will involve prompt engineering, with asking the right questions becoming more crucial than solving problems. Those who excel in using prompts will unlock AI's full potential, significantly boosting their task performance.

The key to effective prompt engineering lies in crafting clear and specific instructions and providing them to large models according to well-designed steps. A popular "universal prompt formula" circulating online encompasses various dimensions of instructions:

Universal Prompt Formula = Role + Role Skills + Core Keywords + Task Goal + Task Context + Task Scope + Task Success Criteria + Task Constraints + Output Format/Style + Output Quantity

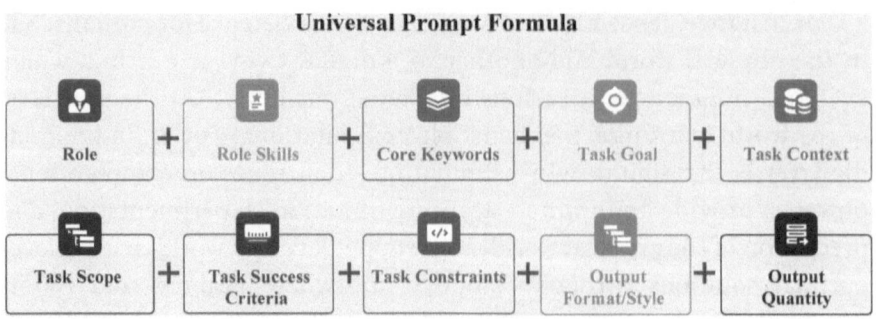

FIGURE 1.4 Diagram of the universal prompt formula.

An exemplary project in prompt engineering is the Mr. Ranedeer AI Tutor initiative, which demonstrates how prompts can unlock the potential of large models. This customizable prompt "suite" allows users to adjust variables like content depth (from elementary to PhD), learning styles, and tone styles (e.g., encouraging, humorous) to define their own AI tutor and provide a personalized learning experience. Remarkably, this project was created by an Australian high school student and his team, who utilized 15,000 characters of prompts to define ChatGPT as an all-knowing tutor.

I also encourage my team to learn and effectively use prompts to transform large models into intelligent assistants that can adapt to needs and efficiently execute complex tasks—an essential skill for future professionals. Many worry that AI will replace their jobs, but a more likely scenario is that individuals skilled in prompt engineering will replace those who are not, due to significant efficiency differences.

Prompt engineering is an emerging field that blends art and science. It requires not only an understanding of technology but also creativity and strategic thinking. Employing the right strategies can more effectively guide large models to complete tasks. In this realm, there are numerous strategies and recommendations. For example, Singapore's GovTech data science and AI team has developed the CO-STAR framework for creating efficient prompts, which includes six elements: Context, Objective, Style, Tone, Audience, and Response.

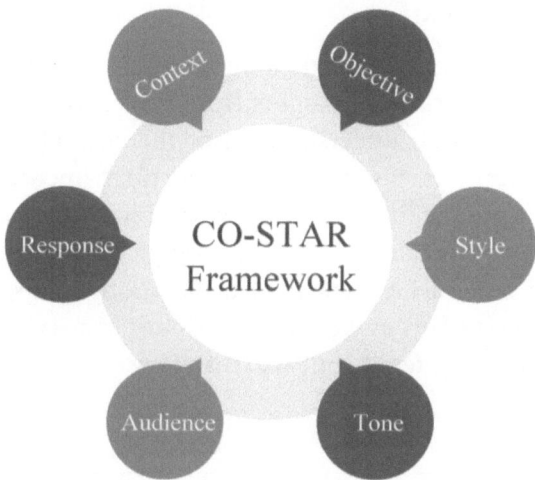

FIGURE 1.5   Six core elements of the CO-STAR framework.

CLOSING THOUGHTS

Since the spark of artificial intelligence was ignited at Dartmouth in 1956, its development has been anything but ordinary. The journey has been marked by peaks of excitement and chilling lows, but it has consistently been illuminated by the wisdom and courage of pioneers. Every moment has been a constellation of brilliance.

Whether on the cutting edge of technology or deeply embedded in various industries, we are all participants in a journey that intertwines "perception, thinking, and realization"—a process that applies to individuals, organizations, companies, and society as a whole.

For someone like me, who has been immersed in data analytics and artificial intelligence throughout my career, it is an extraordinary privilege to stand on such a high vantage point. This position allows me to push the boundaries of my understanding and witness a society undergoing technological transformation. Inspired by this exhilarating force of innovation, I am committed to a lifetime of exploration and practice. Much like venturing into uncharted territory, the allure lies in the fact that the journey is never-ending.

ACKNOWLEDGMENT

I am profoundly grateful to Jason Dong for his remarkable contributions to this chapter. His practical insights from professional experience provide a unique and deep understanding of the current AI wave and its real-world implications. Jason's ability to identify impactful application cases and articulate the future trajectory of AI has added immense value to our discussion. His talent for transforming complex ideas into accessible narratives has truly enriched our exploration. Thank you, Jason, for your unwavering support and dedication; your perspective has made this journey not only enlightening but also inspiring.

BIBLIOGRAPHY

Bahri, Yasaman; Dyer, Ethan; Kaplan, Jared; Lee, Jaehoon; Sharma, Utkarsh (2024). "Explaining neural scaling laws". *Proceedings of the National Academy of Sciences*, **121** (27): e2311878121.

Bostrom, Nick (2014). *Superintelligence: Paths, Dangers, Strategies*. Oxford, United Kingdom: Oxford University Press.

Byford, Sam (27 May 2017). "AlphaGo retires from competitive Go after defeating world number one 3–0". *The Verge*.

Chang, M.W. (2008). "Importance of Semantic Representation: Dataless Classification". AAAI.

Chemero A (2009). Radical Embodied Cognitive Science. MIT Press. ISBN 978-0-262-25808-1

Crevier, Daniel (1993). *AI: The Tumultuous Search for Artificial Intelligence*. New York, NY: BasicBooks. ISBN 0-465-02997-3.

Deng, Jia; Dong, Wei; Socher, Richard; Li, Li-Jia; Li, Kai; Fei-Fei, Li (2009), "ImageNet: A Large-Scale Hierarchical Image Database", *2009 conference on Computer Vision and Pattern Recognition*.

Dr. Fei-Fei Li "Fei-Fei Li: With Spatial Intelligence, AI will Understand the Real World" *Radical Ventures*, 21 May 2024. https://radical.vc/fei-fei-li-with-spatial-intelligence-ai-will-understand-the-real-world/

Jon Erlichman "'50–50 chance' that AI outsmarts humanity, Geoffrey Hinton says". Bloomberg BNN. 14 June 2024, https://www.bnnbloomberg.ca/business/economics/2024/06/14/50-50-chance-that-ai-outsmarts-humanity-geoffrey-hinton-says/

Fahey, J. "Tesla Says it is Building a 'Friendly' Robot that Will Perform Menial Tasks, Won't Fight Back". *Washington Post*. ISSN 0190-8286.

Gil Press "Andrew Ng Launches A Campaign for Data-Centric AI", Forbes, 16 June 2021. https://www.forbes.com/sites/gilpress/2021/06/16/andrew-ng-launches-a-campaign-for-data-centric-ai/

Ellen Glover "Artificial Intelligence (AI): What Is AI and How Does It Work? | Built In". *builtin.com* https://builtin.com/artificial-intelligence#:~:text=AI

%20works%20to%20simulate%20human,to%20new%20information%20 over%20time

Goldman, Sharon (14 September 2022). "10 Years Later, Deep Learning 'Revolution' Rages On, Say AI Pioneers Hinton, LeCun and Li". *VentureBeat*.

Hilliard, Mark (2017). "The AI apocalypse: will the human race soon be terminated?". *The Irish Times*.

Howe, J. (November 1994). "Artificial Intelligence at Edinburgh University: A Perspective". Archived from the original on 15 May 2007.

Kobielus, James (27 November 2019). "GPUs Continue to Dominate the AI Accelerator Market for Now". *Information Week*.

Krishna, Sri (9 February 2023). "What is artificial narrow intelligence (ANI)?". *VentureBeat*.

Larochelle, Hugo (2008). "Zero-data Learning of New Tasks".

LeCun, Yann; Bengio, Yoshua; Hinton, Geoffrey (2015). "Deep Learning", *Nature*, **521** (7553): 436–444.

Lighthill, James (1973). "Artificial Intelligence: A General Survey". *Artificial Intelligence: a paper symposium*. Science Research Council.

McCorduck, Pamela (2004), *Machines Who Think* (2nd ed.), Natick, MA: A. K. Peters, ISBN 1-5688-1205-1

Newquist, H. P. (1994). *The Brain Makers: Genius, Ego, And Greed In The Quest For Machines That Think*. New York: Macmillan/SAMS. ISBN 978-0-6723-0412-5

NRC (United States National Research Council) (1999). "Developments in Artificial Intelligence". *Funding a Revolution: Government Support for Computing Research*. National Academy Press.

Palatucci, Mark (2009). "Zero-Shot Learning with Semantic Output Codes", NIPS.

Radford, Alec; Kim, Jong Wook; Hallacy, Chris; Ramesh, Aditya; Goh, Gabriel; Agarwal, Sandhini; Sastry, Girish; Askell, Amanda; Mishkin, Pamela; Clark, Jack; Krueger, Gretchen; Sutskever, Ilya (2021-07-01). "Learning Transferable Visual Models From Natural Language Supervision". *Proceedings of the 38th International Conference on Machine Learning*. PMLR. pp. 8748–8763.

Russell, Stuart J.; Norvig, Peter (2021). *Artificial Intelligence: A Modern Approach* (4th ed.). Hoboken: Pearson. ISBN 978-0-1346-1099-3. LCCN 20190474.

Sheila Teo "How I Won Singapore's GPT-4 Prompt Engineering Competition", Towards Data Science, 29 December, 2023. https://towardsdatascience.com/ how-i-won-singapores-gpt-4-prompt-engineering-competition-34c195 a93d41

Varela FJ, Thompson E, Rosch E (1991). *The Embodied Mind: Cognitive Science and Human Experience*. MIT Press. ISBN 978-0262720212

Vaswani, A., Shazeer, N., Parmar, N., Uszkoreit, J., Jones, L., Gomez, A. A., Kaiser, L., & Polosukhin, I. (2017). Attention is All You Need. In *Advances in Neural Information Processing Systems* 30 (NeurIPS 2017).

"Will Artificial Intelligence Surpass Our Own?". Scientific American. 2015.

Wilson RA, Foglia L (2011). "Embodied Cognition". The Stanford Encyclopedia of Philosophy.

CHAPTER 2

AI Revolution: "All That Is Solid Melts into Air"

The world is changing at an unprecedented pace, with technological revolutions reshaping business and society in ways that defy old paradigms. The once-solid foundations of tradition are crumbling away. As we forge ahead, one truth stands clear: All companies will be AI companies, or become "marginalized."

When I joined IBM in 1999, Andy Grove, then Chairman of Intel, made a bold prediction about the impact of the Internet. "In five years' time there won't be any 'Internet companies,'" said Grove. "They'll all be Internet companies."

History has largely validated his prediction. After the Internet revolution, the next seismic wave in technology is undoubtedly artificial intelligence. Drawing from Grove's insight, I propose a similar vision for AI's impact.

No visionary can afford to ignore artificial intelligence. In recent years, AI algorithms and computing power have surged, transforming once-mystical capabilities into essential utilities akin to water and electricity. This rapid evolution has sparked countless business innovations and seamlessly integrated AI into the fabric of our daily lives.

In my frequent industry discussions, I've noticed a fascinating trend: while people eagerly debate breakthroughs in large models and various algorithms, and enthusiastically speculate about the dramatic changes and potential threats posed by artificial intelligence, there's surprisingly little conversation about how AI can be translated into a practical, scalable business system.

DOI: 10.1201/9781003510604-2

I believe this is one of the most vital topics for the industry to address. Real innovators prioritize action over words, as actions truly speak louder. In this chapter, I'll leverage my knowledge and experience to examine AI's transformative effects on the business world and outline the indispensable elements necessary to develop a practical and effective AI system.

SECTION 1: AI REDEFINES PRODUCTIVITY

In the Internet era, we witnessed the rise of countless websites, which became the primary platforms for native applications and the bedrock of success for tech giants like Google, Facebook, and Twitter. The ensuing web technology revolution provided the robust foundation that propelled these Internet stars to new heights.

As we entered the era of mobile Internet, apps eclipsed websites to become the dominant platforms, effectively monopolizing the focal point of our attention in the mobile age.

But now, we've entered an entirely new era of intelligence. What will be the core platform for "applications" in this age? We believe it's no longer apps or websites, but AI Agents. This transformation promises to fundamentally reshape how we interact with technology. AI Agents are poised to become pivotal players in the intelligent era, offering a level of intelligence, proactivity, and personalization far beyond any application.

The concept of an "Agent" originates from philosophy, where it describes an entity with desires, beliefs, intentions, and the capability to take action (in the sense of "someone or something that produces an effect"). Interestingly, when this notion was brought into the realm of artificial intelligence, it retained its philosophical roots while gaining a new dimension. In AI, an agent refers to an intelligent entity that, without needing direct human intervention, can autonomously perceive and understand its environment, plan decisions, orchestrate tasks, and employ various tools to achieve its goals.

As artificial intelligence evolves from knowledge-based tools, like chatbots that answer questions or generate content, to sophisticated AI Agents performing complex, multi-step workflows in the digital realm, we witness technology shifting from mere concepts to actionable results. This transformation marks a crucial milestone, indicating that innovative technology is now being solidly integrated into real-world industries.

Just as the Internet once revolutionized our lives and industries, artificial intelligence is poised to bring about similarly transformative—and perhaps even more disruptive—changes. According to McKinsey's latest report on the state of AI, over 72% of surveyed companies are deploying AI solutions, with growing interest in next-generation technologies. Given this trend, it's no surprise that companies are increasingly incorporating cutting-edge technologies like AI Agents into their strategic planning and future AI roadmaps. Today, AI Agents are making significant strides across various sectors worldwide, from finance and retail to healthcare and manufacturing, playing a crucial role in driving industry transformation.

We are witnessing the emergence of a new commercial foundation as the widespread adoption of AI Agents begins to reshape business ecosystems. For industry players, staying competitive will hinge on their ability to keenly observe and adapt to these transformative changes.

Everyone Has Their Own AI Agent

To put it simply, think of large models as akin to a liberal arts education, giving AI Agents a foundational knowledge base and providing them with "common sense." Building an AI Agent, on the other hand, is like taking that liberal arts education and turning it into specialized vocational training—transforming the AI into an industry expert capable of delivering tailored services across various fields.

Unlike traditional computational entities, AI Agents possess the ability to understand and generate natural language. This enables them to communicate and interact seamlessly with humans without relying on complex programming languages.

Bill Gates has predicted that within the next five years, artificial intelligence will be able to understand natural language and perform a variety of tasks based on the user's personal background. In this future scenario, there will be no need to open multiple apps—simply tell your "AI Agent" what you want to do, and it will automatically handle the rest.

Not only is it easy to use an AI Agent, but creating one is remarkably straightforward as well.

Building an AI Agent is as simple as creating a webpage in the Internet era. Just outline the workflow clearly and pair it with a specialized knowledge base or relevant data, and you can craft a valuable AI Agent with ease.

For example, consider the SAT/ACT standardized tests in the U.S., which are crucial for assessing applicants' academic abilities. Different schools and colleges have varying requirements for SAT/ACT scores, including whether they are needed and what scores are considered acceptable. If you want to build an AI Agent that evaluates which schools you could apply to based on your SAT/ACT scores and provides the top five recommendations, you can create an agent with this workflow in mind:

1) List all schools that require SAT/ACT scores;

2) For these schools, find the average SAT/ACT score ranges they accept (typically provided as the 25th to 75th percentile);

3) Match your SAT/ACT scores against these ranges to identify schools where your scores fall within the acceptable range;

4) Rank these schools according to the QS World University Rankings and highlight the top five institutions.

If public data is sufficiently comprehensive, you can simply input these steps via text or voice into a general large-model platform, and the AI Agent will automatically carry out the tasks.

Everyone can create their own personalized AI Agents in ways that suit their preferences. For instance, you could set an AI Agent to play soothing background music every night at 10 PM to help you sleep, or have it send real-time updates on every NBA playoff game as soon as the results are available.

In just 72 hours after the launch of OpenAI's GPTs, users had created over 2,000 AI Agents, spanning a diverse array of fields—from tax and currency converters to fitness coaches and language tutors.

It's not hard to imagine that in the future, the number of AI Agents will surpass the global population. People will interact with these agents in countless ways. Just as every business today has an email address, a website, and social media profiles, so too will every company have its own AI Agent.

Redefining Digitalization through AI Agent Architecture

If an AI Agent designed for a specific application is used frequently by a vast number of users and possesses unique, irreplicable features, it can hold immense value.

The chat program ChatGPT can be seen as a singular AI Agent in action.

When it first emerged, some dubbed it the "Google killer," believing that chatbots could replace search engines by delivering direct answers. Especially when handling complex queries, ChatGPT's ability to synthesize responses into a coherent whole proved far more convenient than sifting through multiple links to piece together information. Additionally, with its capabilities to write code and craft content—functions that traditional search engines can't perform—ChatGPT showcased a new level of utility.

Consider this: Google's annual ad revenue exceeds $180 billion. If its dominant position were to be threatened, it would indeed be a seismic shift in the tech world. It's no surprise that within just three months of ChatGPT's launch, Google introduced its own chatbot, Bard. While search engines haven't been replaced yet, I've noticed a personal decline in my own search usage.

In June 2024, Chris Paik, founding partner of the venture capital fund Pace Capital, authored an intriguing article titled "The End of Software."

His argument is built on the premise that software development is costly, primarily because skilled developers are expensive. These developers act as proficient translators, converting human language into computer language and vice versa. With large language models (LLMs) demonstrating exceptional efficiency in handling computer language, it is theoretically possible to drive software development costs down to zero. If this happens, the traditional business model of charging for software could collapse.

Websites are no different. For instance, on the GPT Store, there's a tool called DesignerGPT that offers intelligent web design services right within the ChatGPT interface. DesignerGPT comes with a variety of templates and design options that you can use directly or customize. You can even converse with the tool to add specific content and features to your pages. Additionally, users receive the AI-generated HTML code for the website, allowing them to further develop and refine it as needed.

In a Stanford lecture, former Google CEO Eric Schmidt envisioned a future where a single command could replicate TikTok or create a search engine that could rival Google, all powered by AI Agents and similar applications.

Currently, all our business operations are built on the digital frameworks of software, websites, and apps. However, AI Agents are poised to disrupt this landscape entirely. In the future, the very fabric of commerce will be redefined around the architecture of AI Agents.

Disrupting Conventional Work Paradigms

As the capabilities of AI Agents continue to advance, traditional work paradigms are undergoing a profound transformation: shifting from a "process-oriented framework" to a "goal-oriented framework." In the conventional work model, task execution relies on a series of predefined steps and procedures, with clear guidelines for each employee to ensure process standardization and outcome predictability. However, this "process-driven" approach is increasingly seen as rigid and inefficient in today's complex and rapidly changing business environment, especially when dealing with uncertainty and fast-paced change.

The introduction of AI Agents has revolutionized this landscape. With the power of deep learning and reinforcement learning (RL), these agents can autonomously analyze data, make decisions, and dynamically adjust their strategies in response to changing external conditions. This shift means that work no longer relies strictly on predefined processes; instead, it can be more flexibly centered around achieving goals. AI Agents can automatically identify the optimal path to a goal, optimize resource allocation, and swiftly adapt to changes in objectives.

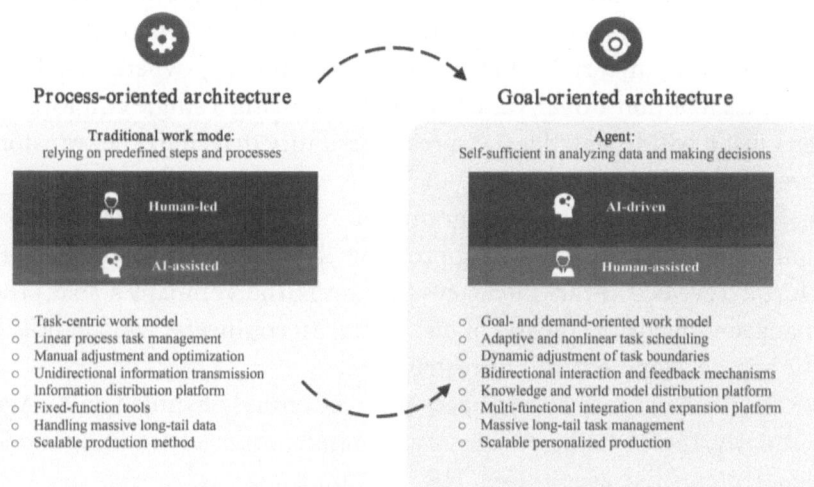

FIGURE 2.1   AI Agent disrupting traditional work paradigms.

This shift has ushered in a new era of work models and competitive advantages for businesses. Companies no longer need to expend extensive effort designing and optimizing processes; instead, they can focus on setting and managing goals. AI Agents autonomously make decisions based on these goals, enabling businesses to swiftly respond to the ever-changing market landscape, thereby enhancing operational efficiency and flexibility. This transition from a "process-oriented" to a "goal-oriented" approach not only boosts productivity but also redefines how businesses operate and create value. For organizations, this represents a revolutionary overhaul of traditional work paradigms, paving the way for a more efficient and agile future.

How Multi-Agent Systems Are Redefining Organizational Structures

AI Agents, with their autonomy and rapidly evolving capabilities, can collaborate not only with each other but also with humans. This synergy opens the door to a myriad of unexpected service models and promises to bring about profound transformations in organizational structures.

The capabilities of AI Agents, when applied to business organizations, can significantly streamline operations by reducing the need for large numbers of employees. This not only lowers the barriers to entrepreneurship and business management but could even give rise to the phenomenon of the "one-person company."

Sam Altman, CEO of OpenAI, once envisioned a groundbreaking possibility: AI technology could give rise to a new breed of startup—the "one-person unicorn." This would be a company where the founder achieves a billion-dollar valuation without hiring a single employee. This isn't just a whimsical idea; it's a real possibility driven by the transformative power of AI.

For instance, consider Telegram, the social app with around 900 million users and a valuation of approximately $30 billion. Its founder, Pavel Durov, revealed in an interview that he is the company's sole product manager. The team consists of just "about 30 engineers," who handle both the app development and infrastructure.

The work of those 30 engineers could be entirely handled by AI Agents. Similarly, these intelligent agents are poised to replace traditional roles in departments like accounting, HR, and more.

In 2023, Oxford Dictionaries selected "rizz" as the word of the year. That same year, two developers created RIZZ.AI, an "AI dating coach" software, in just four and a half months. Upon launch, it quickly racked up 1.5 million downloads. Built on the ChatGPT framework, RIZZ.AI leverages real-time AI feedback in a safe and controlled environment to enhance user communication skills and boost dating success rates.

In the future, it's entirely possible that a single super-product-manager, leveraging an array of multi-agent systems, could run a Fortune 500 company all on their own.

SECTION 2: THE PERPETUAL ENGINE OF DATA: UNLEASHING ENDLESS POSSIBILITIES

What's fueling the rise of intelligent agents? The answer is crystal clear: data. Data is like the Promethean fire, igniting the revolution in artificial intelligence and serving as the core engine behind modern AI. It drives intelligent agents to continually learn and optimize, powering their evolution and effectiveness.

Today, every breakthrough in AI relies on a vast flow of data. Without data, artificial intelligence cannot reach the level of general intelligence. For machines to master the inductive and deductive skills humans excel at, they also need continuous data practice. Once algorithms and computing power are balanced, the ultimate competition in AI comes down to the battle for data.

To truly grasp artificial intelligence, one must first understand the intricate relationship between data and AI.

To understand the significance of data in AI, one must begin with the renowned scholar Fei-Fei Li. A prominent figure in the field, Li is the pioneering force behind the ImageNet dataset, a cornerstone in AI research. Her remarkable insight into the power of data, coupled with her creation of this extensive image dataset, has been pivotal in advancing AI technology.

In the year 2000, while pursuing her Ph.D. at Caltech, Fei-Fei Li was deeply immersed in the intersection of neuroscience and computer science. She encountered a significant issue: despite extensive research into models for computer vision and image decoding, these models struggled with accurately recognizing individual, concrete objects. This limitation severely constrained the practical applications of these models.

Fei-Fei Li decided to take a different approach. She suspected the real issue might not lie in the models themselves but in the data. Much like how children learn to recognize objects through repeated exposure, perhaps computers could emulate this learning process by sifting through vast quantities of images. By immersing themselves in this wealth of visual data, they might ultimately master the ability to identify specific objects within images.

As soon as this groundbreaking idea emerged, Fei-Fei Li wasted no time in pushing it forward. However, bringing her vision to life proved to be an uphill battle.

First, she needed to create a comprehensive labeling standard to accurately tag each object in the vast database of images, ensuring that gender, ethnicity, or personal biases did not skew the results. When annotating a photo, data labels had to range from broad, abstract categories to detailed, specific classifications—moving from a general term like "mammal" all the way to something as precise as "star-nosed mole."

Next came the colossal task of image annotation—a tedious and overwhelming process. Initially, Fei-Fei Li offered Princeton students $10 per hour, but despite their overtime efforts, progress was painfully slow. It wasn't until students suggested a novel approach that she discovered a game-changing solution: Amazon Mechanical Turk. By harnessing a global network of annotators, she could significantly reduce costs and speed up the labeling process. This innovation dramatically accelerated the work.

By 2009, Fei-Fei Li's team had annotated nearly 3.2 million images, covering a vast array of categories. Drawing inspiration from her undergraduate years at Princeton University, where researchers had developed a cognitive linguistic-based English dictionary called WordNet, she decided to name this monumental image dataset ImageNet.

Today, ImageNet boasts 14 million images, serving not just as a vast repository but also as an industry-standard benchmark. This enormous dataset allows various algorithms to showcase their prowess across millions of images, with accuracy serving as the metric to quantitatively assess each algorithm's effectiveness.

Once ImageNet was established, Fei-Fei Li managed to persuade the organizers of a major computer vision competition to use this database for training and testing participants' algorithms. The European competition held in 2010 became a landmark event in AI history, known as the ImageNet Large-Scale Visual Recognition Challenge.

From 2010 to 2017, the classification error rate in the ImageNet competition plummeted from 28% to below 3%, representing a reduction to just one-tenth of its original value. The average accuracy for object recognition soared from 23% to 66%. The introduction of deep learning algorithms by Geoffrey Hinton in 2012 led to a significant leap in accuracy. By 2015, error rates in several specialized scenes even fell below human levels, effectively solving basic object recognition challenges and paving the way for large-scale industrial applications.

The contributions of Fei-Fei Li and the ImageNet competition vividly illustrate the profound connection between data and artificial intelligence.

First and foremost, data is the linchpin of the deep learning revolution in artificial intelligence. Without the pivotal shift in focus and the creation of large-scale databases like ImageNet, the rise of this wave of AI might have been significantly delayed.

Second, popular deep learning algorithms, their validation, and their application all rely on extensive data for training. For instance, in computer vision, it's become a global standard for researchers to pre-train models using the ImageNet dataset.

Third, building a database suitable for artificial intelligence relies heavily on the meticulous and laborious task of annotation. Geoffrey Hinton may have gained fame for his pioneering work, but without the countless unnamed contributors working through platforms like Amazon Mechanical Turk, even the most sophisticated algorithms would have been nothing more than a house built on sand.

People Cannot Draw from an Empty Well

In the 1990s, the dominant approach in artificial intelligence was symbolic learning, where data played a relatively minor role. To be fair, the industry lacked the vast amounts of data needed to "nourish" AI. It wasn't until the 2000s, with the widespread advent of Internet applications and a significant leap in computational storage capabilities, that big data truly emerged. When combined with advancements in deep learning, this confluence sparked a new wave of innovation and value in the field.

Data and AI are locked in a dynamic, symbiotic relationship. To achieve exceptional results, it's essential to start with high-quality data from the very source. Only then can AI truly thrive and deliver its best performance.

Data Annotators: The Unsung Heroes of the AI Revolution

For artificial intelligence to recognize data, it must be meticulously annotated; only then can artificial neural networks truly "see." Today, while many companies possess vast amounts of data, they can't simply deploy AI without preprocessing. If ready-made algorithms aren't available, the data must first undergo rigorous labeling.

The data labeling process is a comprehensive journey that includes collection, cleaning, annotation, and validation. At its core, data labeling involves tasks such as "drawing boxes." For instance, if the objective is to detect a cat, the annotator must outline the cat in the image with a box, ensuring it fully encompasses the cat and highlights key features. Similarly, if the target is a person, the annotator must mark 18 crucial points related to human anatomy.

With today's technology, industries such as retail, autonomous driving, and healthcare must first rely on human efforts for data labeling before AI systems can effectively train neural networks with specific data for targeted applications. Consequently, in specialized fields, data annotators need a relevant professional background. For instance, annotators working with medical imaging data must have a medical background to accurately interpret medical images. Similarly, for AI applications involving regional dialects or foreign languages, annotators need to be proficient in those languages.

Data labeling, a crucial element of artificial intelligence, has evolved into a significant industry with a diverse array of types and applications. This sector now includes global platform giants like Amazon Mechanical Turk, which offers open data platforms and specialized startups such as Scale AI, CrowdFlower, and MightyAI. Currently, there are over 10 million data annotators worldwide, spread across countries with low labor costs, including China, India, Malaysia, Thailand, and Kenya. In China, Tencent has implemented an ingenious method to cut data labeling costs: by combining CAPTCHA with labeling tasks, they turn the data annotation work over to players who need identity verification, effectively outsourcing a large volume of work for free.

The rise of data labeling has accelerated the adoption of artificial intelligence across various industries. For instance, in fields like industrial quality inspection and equipment defect repair, machines, now thoroughly trained, are increasingly replacing traditional manual labor. From the early days of the ImageNet dataset to its widespread industry application, the progress of AI development is deeply rooted in the diligent efforts of data annotators.

Therefore, **I've always believed that data annotators are the unsung heroes of the AI revolution**.

At present, the shortage of training data stands as a critical bottleneck across the industry. In many niche categories of visual data, there are only a handful or even just a few dozen images available for training. On the flip side, when sample sizes are large, the time and financial costs associated with cleaning, analyzing, and labeling data can become overwhelming for companies.

As large-scale AI models advance, data annotation is evolving into a realm of greater specialization. Crafting valuable industry-specific models, such as those for pathology diagnostics, requires not only access to extensive proprietary data—like vast collections of digital pathology images—but also the ability to interpret this data in a way that AI algorithms can understand. This necessitates a blend of expert domain knowledge and precise data annotation. As a result, annotation is becoming increasingly specialized, demanding an in-depth grasp of the relevant industry expertise.

Data-Centric AI: Tackling the Hidden Risks of Data Debt

In the world of algorithm engineering, there's a well-known saying: "Garbage in, garbage out." If you feed a model a heap of dirty data, it will churn out a pile of worthless results. The gap between "why we do it" and "how we do it" is often filled with communication breakdowns, misunderstandings, and execution flaws. Data labeling that fails to address algorithmic issues can end up being a thankless task—one that might not yield immediate results but can have far-reaching and delayed consequences.

As "Data-Centric AI" transitioned from academia to the mainstream, it sparked widespread discussion.

This concept was introduced by the renowned AI scientist Andrew Ng. Ng posits that AI = Data + Code (model/algorithm), with data serving as the essential ingredient (Data is food for AI) and models and algorithms representing the cooking process. Just as the quality of a dish often hinges on the quality and preparation of its ingredients, the effectiveness of an AI system is fundamentally determined by the quality of the data it is fed.

For artificial intelligence, the quality of data, data strategy, and the management of the entire data lifecycle largely determine the potential of the model. Similarly, when addressing the same AI problem, improving the data often yields better results than tweaking the code. Consequently, the key to successful AI implementation today lies in enhancing data quality.

In essence, Data-centric AI offers more constructive and practical guidance for data labeling.

In the development of algorithm models, a myriad of roles come into play, including business professionals, product managers, data operations/

project managers, data annotators, data scientists, and algorithm engineers. Each participant must have a clear understanding of the data's value and usage. For instance, it's crucial to determine what type of data the algorithm requires, what features to use, and what specific details need to be considered. Are the data labeling rules reasonable? Is the data labeling project manager's understanding accurate? Are there any discrepancies in the labelers' interpretations? Every detail counts in ensuring the success of the AI model.

It's not hard to envision that by placing data quality at the heart of AI development, Data-Centric AI will drive profound changes across industries. I anticipate that its impact will be particularly evident in the following areas:

1. **Driving Industry-Wide Data Governance and Quality Enhancement**

   It compels companies to focus more on data collection, cleaning, and annotation, leading to the creation of efficient data processing workflows. This, in turn, drives technological innovation and industry growth in fields like data engineering and data governance.

2. **Lowering the AI Adoption Barrier for Small and Medium Enterprises**

   Traditionally, developing high-performance AI models has hinged on complex architectures and hefty computational resources, creating a formidable barrier for small and medium-sized enterprises. By focusing on enhancing data quality, these businesses can achieve efficient AI solutions with fewer resources.

3. **Refining AI Applications in Specific Industry Sectors**

   By enhancing the accuracy of domain-specific data and the quality of labels, AI models can more effectively cater to industries with stringent data requirements, such as healthcare, manufacturing, and finance. This, in turn, improves production efficiency and service quality.

At the Heart of AI Rivalries: The Battle for Data

Artificial Intelligence is merely a tool; it is the value of data assets that ultimately shapes AI's industry applications and unlocks new market opportunities for businesses.

Artificial Intelligence thrives on the synergy of three critical components: algorithms, computing power, and data. Each plays a unique role in the competitive landscape. Algorithms can be shared across platforms, with developers accessing a wealth of options through tools like Google's TensorFlow or Baidu's PaddlePaddle. Computing power, on the other hand, can be acquired; with sufficient financial resources, companies can procure the necessary hardware from vendors, setting up extensive Docker or GPU clusters. But it's the data that truly drives the value, making the right mix of these elements crucial for success in AI.

With advancements in the Internet, open-source technologies, and cloud computing, companies are becoming increasingly technology-agnostic. In the near future, breakthroughs in chip computing power, driven by the Super Moores' Law, will push AI further into the mainstream. Over time, the differences in technological capabilities will diminish. In the realm of industry applications, the true differentiator for building a robust "moat" will invariably be data.

I firmly believe that within the next three to five years, the battle for supremacy in artificial intelligence will center around data.

So, from what dimensions will the competition for data unfold? In my view, this battle will primarily focus on the following three aspects:

1) The quality and relevance of data. This includes factors such as accuracy, completeness, traceability, continuity, authenticity, and shareability. These qualities are crucial as they determine the effectiveness of AI models and ultimately influence the success of their real-world applications.

2) The advantage of being first to data. In fields where organizations secure data early and in large volumes for specific applications, their AI capabilities tend to have a marked advantage.

3) The security and privacy of data will determine just how far AI applications can advance. Ensuring that data is safeguarded and protected is crucial for the sustainable growth and deployment of artificial intelligence.

Data Excellence and Relevance
The quality of data significantly influences the accuracy of algorithms. Even with the same initial algorithm, differing data quality can lead to variations in the time required to filter and iterate to the optimal solution.

Big Data's defining characteristics can be succinctly summarized by the four V's: volume, variety, velocity, and veracity. Hence, in any given field, the larger, more authentic, accurate, and traceable the dataset is, and the richer and more collaborative its dimensions, the better the algorithm that can be derived and the greater the competitive edge it can offer.

For instance, on Netflix, user data is categorized by dimensions such as gender, age, movies watched, favorite stars, and viewing history. Similarly, movie data includes dimensions like release year, director, cast, genre, and user reviews. The richer the data dimensions around these two entities, the more precisely they can be matched, enabling companies to enhance user experience, expand their audience, and continually strengthen their competitive edge.

It's clear that the larger the user base of an app, the better it can deliver personalized experiences. For example, many music apps we use today have become adept at discerning each user's preferred music styles and delivering precise recommendations tailored to individual tastes.

To enhance data quality, businesses should focus on two key areas simultaneously. Internally, they need a systematic approach: implement real-time data collection and organization, and build a robust, long-term data accumulation strategy. Externally, companies should proactively create ecosystems or seek partnerships to gather as much relevant data as possible. Additionally, establishing a unified framework for data integration will facilitate seamless data interchange and maximize the value derived from these efforts.

Moreover, when it comes to the data needed for industry-specific models, the relevance is paramount. It's crucial to emphasize the alignment with particular scenarios, ensuring that the data closely matches the context in which the model will be applied.

Today, artificial intelligence applications are tailored to specific tasks or goals, requiring diverse types of data. For instance, the media, finance, and healthcare sectors each demand distinct kinds of data, and even within a single industry, subfields have unique requirements. Take the healthcare sector as an example: the data needed for diagnosing cardiovascular diseases differs significantly from that required for cancer diagnosis.

Most AI applications are designed to tackle specific tasks. For example, assessing credit risk in personal loans, optimizing delivery routes for food services, and providing precise, personalized recommendations in news feeds—all these scenarios hinge on highly relevant data. In each context, the importance of data varies based on its relevance, with different types of data holding varying degrees of significance.

First-Mover Advantage in Data

In the realm of data competition, a clear first-mover advantage exists. The sooner and more extensively a company acquires data in a specific domain, the more pronounced its edge in artificial intelligence will become.

Currently, data hasn't been fully commercialized, and data exchange between companies remains inefficient. Due to market complexities, competition, data security, and regulatory concerns, businesses are often reluctant to freely share their data. Instead, they seek to gather more data through their own products and ecosystems. From this perspective, platform-based tech giants, with their robust data capabilities, hold a significant advantage.

In the long run, data is not just an asset but a revenue-generating powerhouse and a core competitive advantage for companies. The earlier a company dives into strategic data planning, the more proactive its position will be. Once data becomes fully commoditized in the future, its value will become strikingly clear.

Data Security and Privacy Protection

As data becomes a core asset for future enterprises, its security is equally crucial. In the era of big data, losing data can result in significant losses, making robust protection essential.

Data security has two key dimensions: First, it involves ensuring that user data remains intact and is not lost—an issue that, while less common, is significantly mitigated by cloud storage. Second, and more critically, it entails safeguarding data from unauthorized disclosure or misuse, which is the primary focus of concern.

The Cambridge Analytica scandal, which came to light widely in 2018 but originated in 2016, stands as an early example of AI technology's involvement in data breaches and privacy issues. At that time, Cambridge Analytica exploited artificial intelligence and big data techniques to illegally harvest the personal data of 87 million Facebook users. This data was then used to target political advertisements and predict voter behavior.

In various industry sectors—whether in healthcare, energy, manufacturing, aviation, or financial lending—data breaches are becoming increasingly common, sparking widespread public outrage across the globe.

People will not tolerate violations of their data privacy. If information leakage and misuse are allowed to continue, companies will find themselves ensnared in a maelstrom of public criticism, and the challenges to business growth will ultimately impede the advancement of artificial intelligence. The level of protection for data security and personal privacy will determine how far AI can truly progress.

SECTION 3: ASSEMBLING THE COMPLETE PUZZLE OF DEPLOYABLE AI SYSTEMS

Imagine that intelligent agents are the new engines of productivity for the next era, and data is their crucial raw material. Before you lies a grand blueprint for AI systems, slowly coming into focus. In this chapter, I will unfold the complete narrative of how to build a deployable AI system.

Today, the media is enamored with star companies like OpenAI and NVIDIA, but even their high-profile offerings can't single-handedly develop your company's bespoke AI system. Whether you're integrating a GPT model or purchasing NVIDIA's GPU chips, these are just pieces of the puzzle. They're crucial steps, but they don't directly create a complete AI product on their own.

To build a practical, deployable AI system, you need to piece together five crucial components: data, algorithms and models, industry applications, AI infrastructure, and computing power. Data, algorithms, and models form the core of AI, while infrastructure and computing power provide a robust foundation. Each element plays a pivotal role throughout the AI system's lifecycle, collectively driving the technology from concept to tangible impact.

In the first two sections of this chapter, I've delved into data and industry applications (with numerous case studies to follow in the next chapter). Now, we'll shift our focus to explore algorithms and models, AI infrastructure, and computing power in detail.

Algorithms and Models: The Convergence Wave

Algorithms and models are the beating heart of an AI system. They transform raw data into intelligent decisions and predictions. In recent years, one of the most remarkable trends in AI has been the widespread adoption of deep learning. Leveraging multi-layered neural networks, deep learning algorithms can now identify objects in images, translate languages, and even make complex strategic decisions.

With breakthroughs in deep learning technology, the advent of Transformer models like GPT-4o and BERT has marked a significant leap forward in the realm of language understanding and generation. These models don't just process natural language; they generate human-like text and are employed across a variety of applications, including chatbots, automated translation, and intelligent search systems.

Since 2022, the rapid rise of generative AI has brought large models into the spotlight. The future of AI Agent-driven smart applications hinges on their rapidly improving understanding and generalization capabilities, allowing them to deliver increasingly personalized and coherent interactive experiences. This remarkable advancement is undeniably fueled by the swift progress of large models.

As we gaze into the future, there's no chance the pace of model evolution will slow down. In fact, the industry is shifting from a state of "everyone for themselves" to one of "collaborative success."

From Model Development to Ecosystem Creation

The landscape of general-purpose large models is now a bustling arena of competing giants.

Major players are now staking their claims in the realm of general-purpose models. Microsoft and OpenAI champion the GPT series, Google promotes the Gemini series, Meta introduces the Llama series, and Anthropic rolls out the Claude series. While each of these models has its own strengths, there's a noticeable trend toward convergence in their overall performance. The developers behind these models are shifting their focus toward building ecosystems and applications. They're striving to attract users and provide more convenience for industry developers, aiming to gain a competitive edge and secure their position in this rapidly evolving landscape.

In January 2024, OpenAI, a major trendsetter in the field, launched the GPT Store—an innovative platform designed to empower users to create, discover, and utilize GPTs tailored for various purposes. This platform allows individuals to build their own large-model AI Agents, making it possible for anyone to become a "no-code AI assistant creator." This move significantly lowers the barriers to developing and using AI-driven applications, democratizing access to advanced artificial intelligence tools.

In April 2024, Google made headlines with the launch of Gemini 1.5 Pro, its cutting-edge large model. Offering it completely free of charge, Google enabled developers to access it via API, while everyday users could dive straight into the experience through Google AI Studio. This move not only broadens the model's accessibility but also invites a wide range of users to explore its advanced capabilities.

In May, GPT-4o made waves by offering free access to a certain usage capacity for all users. This announcement created a buzz among the over 100 million people worldwide using ChatGPT for work and study. Among them, more than a million developers seized the opportunity, leveraging GPTs to create innovative new tools.

These tech giants envision attracting a vast array of ecosystem developers to build an expansive network of applications and technologies, essentially creating an operating system for the AI era. By enabling diverse applications based on their proprietary models, they aim to establish a solid foothold in the market.

As Mark Zuckerberg puts it, "We are a technology company, and we need to build not just at the application layer but across all foundational levels. For us, making large-scale investments in this endeavor is worth it."

After all, relying solely on a subscription-based revenue model has its limitations, especially in the face of formidable competitors. Expanding the user base through strategies like offering free access opens up a multitude of future commercialization possibilities. This could include premium paid services, advertising revenue, API licensing, or even bundling models, computing power, and tools into comprehensive solutions. Such approaches pave the way for diverse revenue streams and greater market leverage.

In the early stages of the large-model competition, the focus is on drawing more users into the ecosystem and gaining leverage. User and developer contributions, including feedback and data, are invaluable for model iteration. The vibrancy of the model ecosystem and the maturity of its supporting tools and infrastructure will be crucial factors in selecting a foundational model.

Hybrid Models: The Fusion of Open Source and Closed Source

Today's battle in the realm of large models is divided into two major camps: open-source giants and closed-source behemoths. When choosing between them, businesses must weigh a multitude of factors including technical prowess, data security, and the potential for innovation.

Closed-source models are typically controlled by major tech giants, and their standout advantages lie in their technological edge and commercial maturity. For instance, OpenAI's GPT series and Google's Gemini represent some of the most advanced AI models available today.

These models excel not only in language generation and question answering but also in tackling complex business challenges such as financial forecasting and supply chain optimization. The closed-source approach effectively safeguards intellectual property and technological secrets, ensuring that the model's creators maintain a competitive edge in innovation and expertise.

For businesses, closed-source models offer a stable and reliable technology foundation, making them particularly well-suited for companies that need cutting-edge technology but lack the capability to develop their own AI models. By leveraging APIs and other integration methods, these companies can quickly deploy AI into their operations, enhancing efficiency and productivity. Models like GPT-4o, for instance, are already extensively used in automated customer service and content generation, significantly reducing labor costs.

However, as businesses increasingly seek customization, the flexibility of open-source models is beginning to reveal its undeniable advantages.

In the spotlight of the open-source movement, the most notable examples include Meta's Llama series and the emerging contributions from Deepseek, a rising star in the AI open-source community. Deepseek has gained global recognition for its complete transparency and lightweight, efficient models, which are designed to be highly accessible and resource efficient. Unlike many open-source projects, Deepseek provides noth only model weights and code but also full access to training datasets and detailed documentation, setting a new standard for open-source integrity.

In July 2024, Meta unveiled its Llama 3.1 series, with the Llama 3.1 405B model being touted as the most powerful open-source model of its time. This model's capabilities rivaled those of leading closed-source giants like GPT, marking a significant milestone in the open-source AI landscape. Around the same time, Deepseek introduced its own suite of open-source tools, which have been widely adopted for their efficiency in fine-tuning and deploying AI models across various industries.

Open-source models empower businesses with greater autonomy, especially for small and medium-sized enterprises or startups. These organizations can leverage open-source frameworks to swiftly develop and tailor models to meet their specific needs. By fine-tuning weights and algorithms, companies can integrate open-source models with their proprietary data, creating AI applications that are more attuned to their business contexts. For instance, some enterprises have enhanced open-source models by combining Retrieval-Augmented Generation (RAG) techniques with RL, optimizing performance in specialized business scenarios and achieving remarkable results.

The terms "open-source" and "closed-source" originally stem from the software industry's source code concepts. However, when it comes to large models, the reality of "open-source" and "closed-source" is far more nuanced and intricate.

A model is typically composed of four key elements: weights, datasets, code, and the training process. For a model to be truly open-source, it must make all four elements, as well as the entire development process, fully transparent and accessible.

By this standard, even the Llama series falls short. While it has made the model weights and some code available, it has yet to disclose the datasets used for training or the training process itself. It's akin to having the recipe for Coca-Cola but missing the exact manufacturing techniques and propri-etary ingredients—without these, fully replicating the original flavor remains elusive. Deepseek, on the other hand, has been pushing the bound-aries by offering more comprehensive documentation and training datasets, setting a new benchmark for transparency in the open-source community.

In the fierce competition of the large-model ecosystem, many compa-nies are adopting a "hybrid strategy" for model selection. They leverage the core capabilities of closed-source models while taking advantage of the customization benefits offered by open-source models.

For instance, while Google champions its closed-source Gemini series, it has also introduced the open-source Gemma model, which shares the same technological architecture as Gemini. Gemma aims to offer developers a lightweight, free, and commercially usable model. This hybrid strategy enables companies to rely on closed-source technology for core functional-ities, ensuring security and performance, while simultaneously fostering innovation and customization through open-source models.

This hybrid approach is especially well-suited for companies with some development capabilities that are reluctant to build AI models from scratch. It allows them to leverage the stability of closed-source models while taking advantage of the flexibility and innovation offered by open-source models, thereby maximizing the benefits of both.

When choosing between open-source and closed-source models, busi-nesses should carefully weigh their specific needs, technological capabilities, and long-term strategic goals. If data security and technological assurance are top priorities, closed-source models might be the more suitable option.

However, for companies seeking greater flexibility and innovation in personalized services or niche business scenarios, open-source models offer significant advantages. For most enterprises, the optimal path may not be an either/or choice but rather a strategic blend of both open-source and closed-source models, tailored to create the most effective technological framework.

AI Infrastructure: Expanding Horizons and Broadening Boundaries

Getting the infrastructure right is absolutely crucial for the success of AI projects. According to a recent survey by Microsoft, 56% of respondents indicated that their organizations lacked the infrastructure needed to support their AI workloads effectively. Prioritizing the development of robust AI infrastructure is essential for the successful deployment, scaling, and innovation of AI technologies.

In simple terms, AI infrastructure encompasses the hardware, software, networks, tools, and services essential for developing, deploying, and optimizing AI systems. As data volumes and model complexities surge, traditional computing architectures fall short, particularly for deep learning tasks that demand massive parallel processing. For companies aiming to successfully implement AI, it's crucial to integrate AI capabilities into their existing IT infrastructure, establish dedicated hardware and network frameworks, and develop a comprehensive technology stack that includes algorithms, frameworks, and libraries.

With the advancement of cloud and edge computing, the foundation of AI infrastructure now boasts crucial scalability. Cloud computing offers virtually limitless storage and processing power, while edge computing processes data at its source, reducing latency and enhancing real-time processing capabilities.

The rise of AI as a Service (AIaaS) has revolutionized how businesses access AI tools and services, enabling them to leverage sophisticated capabilities via APIs without the need to build their own AI infrastructure. Cloud giants like Amazon AWS, Microsoft Azure, and Google Cloud have rolled out an impressive array of AI development and deployment tools, accelerating the adoption and integration of AI across industries. According to IDC, the global cloud computing market is set to reach $500 billion by 2024, with AI-related services capturing an increasingly significant share of this expansive market.

Computing Power: The Balancing Act between Innovation and Cost

Computing power is the backbone of AI system development, not only driving the speed and efficiency of training and processing but also impacting energy consumption and economic costs.

As AI models grow increasingly complex, the demand for computing power is skyrocketing. Deep learning models, particularly colossal language models like GPT-4o, require immense computational resources for both training and deployment. This surge in computing capacity not only drives technological advancements but also results in a significant increase in energy consumption, posing a critical challenge for the global AI industry.

Computing power plays a crucial role in every facet of an AI system:

1. Model Training: Training deep learning models demands vast amounts of data and multiple iterations. The greater the computing power, the faster the model can be trained. High-performance hardware like GPUs and TPUs delivers the computational muscle needed for tackling complex models, drastically cutting down training time.

2. Real-Time Inference: In practical applications, AI models must process input data and deliver outputs in real time. Robust computing power accelerates the speed and accuracy of real-time inference, which is crucial for scenarios demanding low latency, such as autonomous driving and real-time translation.

3. Scaling Up Deployment: As AI becomes increasingly integrated into various industries, companies must deploy AI models on a global scale. Robust computing power supports extensive parallel processing, ensuring that AI models operate efficiently across distributed systems.

With the surge in computing power demands, the energy consumption associated with AI training and deployment has garnered significant attention. Reports reveal that tech giants like Google and Microsoft consumed more electricity in 2023 than some small nations do in an entire year. For instance, Google's electricity usage hit 15.6 terawatt-hours (TWh) in 2023, while Microsoft's consumption approached 16 TWh. This colossal energy footprint has placed immense pressure on global power infrastructures and has driven the industry to seek greener, more energy-efficient solutions.

It's not just energy consumption that's on the rise; the carbon footprint of training large AI models is also soaring. When OpenAI trained GPT-3, the computational power required was ten times greater than for GPT-2, leading to a corresponding increase in energy consumption. As a result, balancing computational power with reduced energy use and lower carbon emissions has become a major challenge for technology companies.

In meeting the ever-growing demands for AI computational power, specialized chips designed for AI tasks have emerged as crucial players, offering the dual benefits of robust performance and reduced overall energy consumption. By 2023, NVIDIA's A100 chip had become the cornerstone of hardware for training cutting-edge AI models at companies like OpenAI and Google DeepMind. This chip not only supports the training of complex models but also significantly slashes training times, making it a game-changer in the AI landscape.

While current GPUs and AI-specific chips deliver impressive computational power for AI systems, the growing complexity of AI tasks means that existing capabilities may still fall short of future demands.

Quantum computing represents a highly anticipated leap in computing technology, with the potential to tackle problems beyond the reach of classical computers. In 2019, Google's Sycamore quantum processor showcased its groundbreaking capabilities by achieving "quantum supremacy," performing a complex computation that would have been infeasible for classical machines to complete in a reasonable timeframe.

The unique strength of quantum computing lies in its ability to process vast amounts of information simultaneously. This capability gives it a distinct edge in tackling complex tasks such as optimization problems, cryptography, and molecular simulations. For AI, quantum computing holds the promise of significantly accelerating the training of certain machine learning algorithms. In scenarios involving large-scale data and intricate challenges, it could become a crucial breakthrough in overcoming the computational limitations faced by traditional AI systems.

High-quality data, advanced algorithms and models, practical industry applications, reliable AI infrastructure, and robust computational power—these are the five essential components required to build a deployable AI system. Companies must not only have a keen, current understanding of how to execute these elements effectively but also possess a forward-looking vision. Embracing emerging technologies like quantum computing could be key to addressing the ever-increasing demands for computational power in the future.

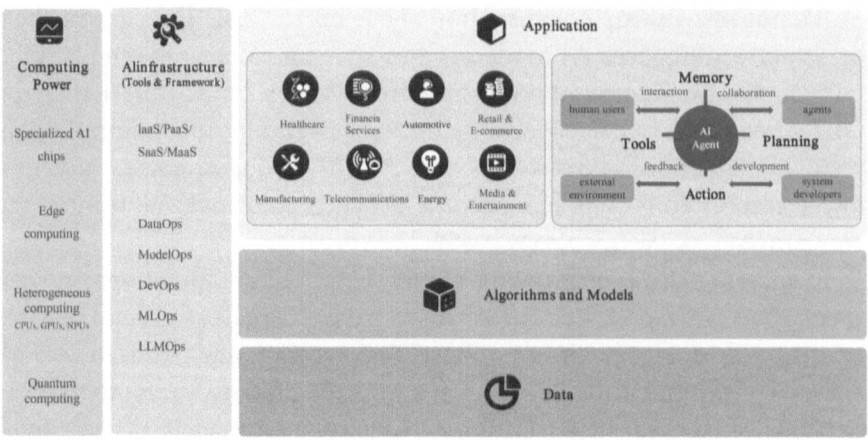

FIGURE 2.2   Blueprint for building an artificial intelligence system.

SECTION 4: BUILDING A SOVEREIGN AI SUPPLY CHAIN

The concept of a supply chain is something we are all quite familiar with, encompassing the entire chain from production to distribution across various industries. In the burgeoning landscape shaped by artificial intelligence, the supply chain takes on a new dimension. It comprises five core elements: data sources, computing resources, algorithms and models, software tools, and platforms and applications. These elements, alongside talent and expertise, ethics and compliance, as well as market and customer dynamics, form the lifeblood of the AI industry—the AI supply chain—which underpins the entire journey from research and development to practical deployment.

Unlike traditional supply chains, which emphasize manufacturing and delivery efficiency, the AI supply chain focuses on the full lifecycle of technological products, from foundational research to end-use applications. This focus introduces greater complexity, with a broader range of industry links and higher demands for coordination between various stages.

Thus, the AI supply chain not only serves as the backbone of the technology sector but also plays a crucial role in a nation's technological autonomy, strategic security, and economic development.

"Every nation must develop its own AI infrastructure to harness economic potential while safeguarding its unique cultural heritage..."

In February 2024, NVIDIA founder Jensen Huang championed the concept of "sovereign AI" at the World Government Summit in Dubai.

He argued that every nation should develop its own sovereign AI, which encompasses both physical and data infrastructure, including autonomous foundational models.

Currently, governments around the world, including those of Japan, France, and Canada, are discussing and taking action on the importance of investing in "sovereign artificial intelligence capabilities."

In my view, maintaining sovereign AI is more complex than it seems—true autonomy is elusive. The key lies in navigating the intricate international landscape and safeguarding the AI supply chain. A country must start with robust AI infrastructure to ensure it possesses a complete supply chain, empowering its individuals and businesses just as it would with traditional food or energy supplies.

Looking at the AI system puzzle today, nations are actively working to build their sovereign AI supply chains, focusing on three key elements: computing resources, sovereign models, and data supply.

Building Your Own Powerhouse: The Rise of Self-Built Compute Clusters

Access to intelligent computing power is the fundamental requirement for AI development. If a region can't secure sufficient smart computing resources, it risks falling behind in the global competition.

Right now, one of the primary focuses for nations worldwide is their computing infrastructure.

For instance, in April 2024, Canadian Prime Minister Justin Trudeau unveiled a groundbreaking development plan worth CAD $2.4 billion in the AI sector. Of this, CAD 2 billion is earmarked for building and providing computing power and technological infrastructure to support the country's AI researchers, startups, and scaling businesses.

Countries across Asia, the Middle East, Europe, and the Americas are gearing up to invest billions of dollars into new AI computing facilities. In May 2024, NVIDIA projected that its sovereign AI business could generate nearly $10 billion in revenue for the year.

At the government level, China has launched the "High-Quality Development Action Plan for Computing Infrastructure," aiming to dramatically expand the scale of intelligent computing power. By the end of May 2024, over ten smart computing centers with high-performance clusters are planned nationwide, with intelligent computing accounting for more than 30% of the total computing capacity.

In 2023, China's total computing power reached 230 EFLOPS, making it the second-largest in the world, just behind the U.S.' 350 EFLOPS.

In 2023 and 2024, governments across the globe, including those in the UK and Australia, have made bold moves to invest heavily in AI computing infrastructure. The UK government, for instance, has launched the "AI Research Compute Taskforce," a groundbreaking initiative set to invest £900 million in the creation of dedicated AI supercomputing facilities. This ambitious plan also includes advancements in cutting-edge semiconductor and quantum technologies, signaling a major push toward bolstering the nation's AI capabilities.

For sovereign nations, especially major powers, ensuring a robust and independent supply of computing power has become a top priority in their infrastructure planning.

Sovereign Giants Unleashed: The Surge of National AI Models

For a sovereign nation, having autonomous control over its digital intelligence is crucial not only for industrial competitiveness but also for cultural cohesion. Especially with generative AI, the content it produces can directly shape the collective consciousness of the nation's citizens.

Today, leading nations are tailoring their language and cultural data into models that reflect their unique characteristics.

For instance, institutions like the Tokyo Institute of Technology, RIKEN, and Fujitsu have harnessed the power of the supercomputer "Fugaku" to develop the cutting-edge language model "Fugaku-LLM." This model, built entirely with homegrown Japanese technology, excels in processing Japanese language and cultural nuances. It shines particularly in handling polite Japanese speech and demonstrates impressive capabilities in the humanities and social sciences.

Japan is rapidly accelerating the rollout of this model to boost the integration of AI technology across various industries, with a particular focus on areas requiring deep understanding and nuanced use of the Japanese language.

In the realm of social interactions and cultural content, countries are expected to exhibit a strong sense of "sovereignty," independently developing large models tailored to their own cultural and linguistic characteristics. This approach aims to guard against the influence of foreign models. Meanwhile, in purely technical domains, nations will seek to incorporate parameters from other countries' models to enhance the performance of their own systems.

In the world of large models, the dance of offense and defense between sovereign nations is expected to become a staple in the AI supply chain landscape.

For example, in May 2024, the U.S. House Foreign Affairs Committee passed a groundbreaking bill with overwhelming support—the "Enhancing National Frameworks for Overseas Critical Exports Act" (HR 8315), or ENFORCE Act. This legislation significantly broadens the U.S. government's authority to regulate the export of AI systems, marking a bold step in controlling the international flow of cutting-edge technology.

The ENFORCE Act defines the scope of AI regulation to encompass all hardware and software implementations of artificial intelligence, including the intricate weights and parameters of AI models themselves.

The plan expands and clarifies the Bureau of Industry and Security's (BIS) authority, enhancing export controls on artificial intelligence and other critical technologies. These measures are set to profoundly impact international cooperation and the application of AI technology.

The Global Data Race: The Dawn of International Competition

In my view, the future of maintaining the global AI supply chain will ultimately hinge on data.

Forward-thinking nations are already fostering cross-border data flows through multinational cooperation and relaxed data licensing, all while striving to ensure the stability of their own data supplies.

A prime example is the Digital Economy Partnership Agreement (DEPA), which was signed online on June 12, 2020, by Singapore, Chile, and New Zealand. This landmark accord aims to bolster digital trade cooperation among the three nations and establish a framework for digital trade, including a dedicated module on data issues.

The DEPA mandates that, with the exception of public administration purposes, no restrictions should be placed on the cross-border flow of data or the location of computer facilities. It requires that any such measures be reasonable, necessary, and non-discriminatory. Additionally, it facilitates seamless cross-border information transfer for businesses operating in Singapore, Chile, and New Zealand.

In terms of national scale, China is one of the countries with the richest data resources. Despite this, in November 2021, China's Minister of Commerce sent a formal letter to New Zealand's Minister for Trade and Export Growth, officially requesting to join the DEPA, which New Zealand oversees as the custodian of the agreement.

Japan's data acquisition policy is even more audacious. In mid-2023, the Japanese government announced that it would not enforce copyright protection on data used for AI training. This bold policy permits AI to utilize any data—whether for non-profit or commercial purposes, including content acquired through means other than copying or sourced from illegal websites and other channels.

Japan's Minister of Education, Culture, Sports, Science, and Technology has made a clear statement: Japanese law will not extend copyright protection to materials used in AI datasets. By fully opening up copyright restrictions, Japan aims to tap into a global pool of data, ensuring it stays competitive in the AI race and avoids falling behind.

In the realm of cross-border data flow, industries have the opportunity to make their own significant contributions within specialized fields.

A stellar example is the formation of Accumulus Synergy in early 2021 by ten leading biopharmaceutical companies, including Pfizer, Johnson & Johnson, Roche, Sanofi, Takeda, and Eli Lilly. This non-profit initiative is dedicated to creating a cloud platform for real-time data exchange with regulatory agencies worldwide.

This platform is set to drive the standardization and transparency of clinical trials and regulatory processes. It will facilitate the seamless exchange of data, enabling the rapid development of precise AI algorithms. In turn, this will accelerate advancements in biopharmaceutical research and transform the service delivery system.

As industry professionals, we hope that sovereign nations, while safeguarding their national security interests, will adhere to widely accepted institutional frameworks. We look forward to a balanced approach that maintains necessary openness and collaboration, ensuring the smooth and stable operation of the global AI supply chain.

AI is not just a crucial technology but also a groundbreaking tool that should empower everyone, not be confined to select groups.

CLOSING THOUGHTS

With advancements in cutting-edge technologies like large models, humanoid robots, and smart connected vehicles accelerating at breakneck speed, artificial intelligence is spearheading a new wave of technological revolution and industrial transformation. AI is driving unprecedented changes across global technology landscapes, industries, and eras.

It is crucial to recognize that AI is more than just a technology; its true significance will unfold and deepen as it integrates into various industries. The consumer market dictates the breadth of its applications, while the enterprise market determines the depth.

Building an AI system requires a holistic view of five key components, which have become critical elements in the AI supply chain. Much like the historical battles over land, oil, and gold, the realms of AI—comprising computational power, algorithms and models, and data—have become new frontiers in the global arms race, fiercely contested by nations, entrepreneurs, and innovators alike.

Time waits for no one. How can one prevail in this rapidly evolving landscape? The next chapter will delve into real-world applications of AI, providing insights into the industry's tangible scenarios.

ACKNOWLEDGMENT

I wish to extend my heartfelt appreciation to Jason Dong for his outstanding contributions to this chapter. His rich experience in merging new technologies with business has brought invaluable creativity and analytical intelligence to our work. Jason's innovative perspectives on AI productization and commercialization, coupled with his meticulous organization of the text, have added both clarity and depth to our discussions. Working alongside him has been a rewarding experience, filled with shared insights and enthusiasm for innovation. Thank you, Jason, for being an exceptional partner on this journey; your contributions have truly enriched our exploration.

BIBLIOGRAPHY

ashwinb "llama-models/models/llama3_2/LICENSE at main · meta-llama/llama-models · GitHub". GitHub.

Bringsjord, Selmer; Govindarajulu, Naveen Sundar. (2018). "Artificial Intelligence." In Edward N. Zalta (ed.), *The Stanford Encyclopedia of Philosophy* (Summer 2020 Edition). Metaphysics Research Lab, Stanford University.

Confessore, Nicholas (4 April 2018). "Cambridge Analytica and Facebook: The Scandal and the Fallout So Far". *The New York Times*. ISSN 0362-4331

Deng, Jia; Dong, Wei; Socher, Richard; Li, Li-Jia; Li, Kai; Fei-Fei, Li (2009), "ImageNet: A Large-Scale Hierarchical Image Database" (PDF), *2009 conference on Computer Vision and Pattern Recognition*.

Digital, McKinsey, "Why Agents Are the Next Frontier of Generative AI", 24 July 2024.

Garnelo, Marta; Shanahan, Murray (October 2019). "Reconciling deep learning with symbolic artificial intelligence: representing objects and relations". *Current Opinion in Behavioral Sciences*, **29**: 17–23.

Gil Press "Andrew Ng Launches A Campaign for Data-Centric AI", Forbes, 16 June 2021, https://www.forbes.com/sites/gilpress/2021/06/16/andrew-ng-launches-a-campaign-for-data-centric-ai/

Grove, Andrew S. (22 May 1999). *Keynote Speech, Los Angeles Times 3rd Annual Investment Strategies Conference.*

NVIDIA's CEO Jensen Huang, "Countries must build sovereign AI infrastructure", the World Governments Summit, in Dubai, United Arab Emirates, 12 February 2024.

Russell, Stuart J.; Norvig, Peter (2003). *Artificial Intelligence: A Modern Approach* (2nd ed.). Upper Saddle River, New Jersey: Prentice Hall. Chapter 2. ISBN 0-13-790395-2

Joanna Seow "Singapore, Chile, NZ ink deal to boost digital economy cooperation". *The Straits Times*, 13 June 2020. https://www.edb.gov.sg/en/business-insights/insights/singapore-chile-nz-ink-deal-to-boost-digital-economy-cooperation.html

Shoham, Yoav; Leyton-Brown, Kevin. (2009). *Multiagent Systems: Algorithmic, Game-Theoretic, and Logical Foundations*, by Yoav Shoham and Kevin Leyton-Brown, Cambridge, United Kingdom: Cambridge University Press.

Thomason, Richmond (27 February 2024). "Logic-Based Artificial Intelligence". In Zalta, Edward N. (ed.). *Stanford Encyclopedia of Philosophy*. Metaphysics Research Lab, Stanford University.

CHAPTER 3

Global Industry Transformations in the Age of Artificial Intelligence

In the past, I frequently explored a compelling theory with clients about the "electric motor" and the "production line." While the electric motor first appeared in the 1880s, its transformative impact on productivity didn't become apparent until the 1920s. This was because the full potential of the electric motor was only unleashed as an increasing number of factories redesigned their production lines to leverage its power.

If artificial intelligence is the "electric motor," then its profound integration with industry applications serves as the "production line"—sparking revolutionary business models and driving major industry shifts. Especially with the advent of large models, which enhance human-machine interaction and reasoning abilities, the spectrum of application scenarios has expanded dramatically.

Some argue that foundation models might eventually solve all problems by providing extensive industry expertise and rendering industry models unnecessary. However, no matter how sophisticated foundation models become, industry-specific applications will always require tailored industry models. To be truly effective, these models must achieve a deep integration of "industry + technology + data." Regardless of the scale of parameters in foundation models, they simply cannot address every nuanced need.

DOI: 10.1201/9781003510604-3

Take, for instance, pathology AI-assisted diagnostic medical device software. This innovation goes beyond simple "single-point applications" like image recognition. It requires a rich array of high-quality, proprietary pathology images from medical institutions, meticulously tailored to clinical environments, along with a profound understanding of clinical challenges and pathologists' specific needs—essentially creating a "central brain" powered by a large model. Such a feat would be unattainable without deep industry insights. AI technology has revolutionized pathology diagnoses, boosting both efficiency and accuracy. Even more astonishing, large AI models have given rise to entirely new product forms, capable of handling pathology images from a range of organs and diseases, advancing from "single-disease models" to "multi-disease models," and providing extensive coverage for clinical applications.

Indeed, top foundation model players like OpenAI, Google, and Meta are actively working to forge connections with industry institutions and professionals, aiming to build thriving ecosystems and develop cutting-edge applications. The wave of foundation models has ignited significant industry excitement, yet it's the more specialized and efficient industry models that will truly fuel the growth of industrial applications. From my own experience in the field, I can feel this transformative shift happening and firmly believe that 2024 may well mark the dawn of an era dominated by industry-specific large models.

In this chapter, I delve into four key industries—healthcare, media & entertainment, automotive, and finance—to showcase how artificial intelligence is transforming these sectors. Each example highlights the dynamic ways AI is being harnessed to drive innovation and reshape traditional practices.

In the healthcare sector, intelligent diagnostics are the most celebrated application of AI. The arrival of foundation models has significantly expanded the horizons of detection and diagnosis. Yet, I want to spotlight some less obvious but profoundly valuable scenarios within this field. As data integration weaves its intricate patterns, we are witnessing the emergence of astonishingly innovative combinations.

Embracing the principle that "where there is data, there is opportunity and profit," the media & entertainment industry stands at the forefront of immense business potential in the data age. With streaming and video data making up 50%–70% of global data, artificial intelligence is igniting a surge of creativity, heralding a new era of human-machine collaboration and innovation.

The automotive manufacturing industry was among the pioneers in adopting big data analysis and artificial intelligence, with its applications now well established. As electrical, automation, and internet technologies have advanced, today's vehicles have transformed into dynamic data centers, evolving from mere "horseless carriages" to sophisticated "vehicle-shaped robots." This evolution is unlocking exciting new possibilities for innovative commercial models.

The financial industry, with its high level of informatization, stands as one of the most critical arenas for the application of artificial intelligence and blockchain technology. The convergence of these two transformative technologies holds the potential to fundamentally reshape the very infrastructure of human society.

The data, regulatory, and ethical challenges confronting these four industries are emblematic of the broader hurdles faced when deploying artificial intelligence across diverse sectors. These common issues underscore the complexities involved in integrating AI into different fields.

By examining these four industries, I aim to shed light on how artificial intelligence is not only fueling innovation and generating new business opportunities but also potentially disrupting established sectors. We will also tackle the data-related challenges these industries face and propose effective solutions to overcome them.

SECTION 1: A CENTURY-LONG LIFE IS WITHIN REACH

Today, cutting-edge technologies such as artificial intelligence, the Internet of Things, and genetic engineering are driving a wave of innovation in the healthcare sector. This section delves into the profound impact of AI on pharmaceutical research and development, insurance, and health management. It investigates how to forge a cohesive business ecosystem that seamlessly integrates "pharma + insurance + health management" to tackle the complex data challenges confronting the healthcare industry.

In 2020, the sudden outbreak of the novel coronavirus took the world by surprise. As the pandemic unfolded, global medical scientists and major pharmaceutical companies raced against time to develop vaccines and effective treatments. While the usual drug development cycle spans a decade or more, the urgency of the crisis pushed researchers to explore repurposing existing medications as a quicker route to potential solutions.

Drawing on the biological traits and pathogenic mechanisms of the coronavirus, as well as previous clinical research and treatment protocols from SARS (Severe Acute Respiratory Syndrome), the medical community, with the help of artificial intelligence, swiftly identified promising drugs such as Kaletra, chloroquine, hydroxychloroquine, remdesivir, Lianhua

Qingwen capsules, Jinhua Qinggan granules, and Xuebijing injection. Within just a few months, these candidates were rapidly advanced into clinical trials. In China alone, over 500 clinical trials have been registered for COVID-19, encompassing approximately 100 existing and novel drugs.

This is far from the first time that artificial intelligence has been harnessed to repurpose existing drugs in the battle against a pandemic.

In 2015, amid the global outbreak of the Ebola virus, the drug design company Atomwise turned to artificial intelligence to model the virus's invasive "claws" that attack biological cells. Utilizing neural networks to sift through drug compounds, they screened over 7,000 potential treatments. Remarkably, within just one day, Atomwise identified two promising candidates to combat Ebola, all while keeping the entire screening process under USD1,000.

In the past, testing existing drugs for new uses was a laborious "trial-and-error" process, often spanning months or even years and racking up costs in the tens or hundreds of millions. Enter artificial intelligence: now, entire drug libraries can be screened in a fraction of the time. AI swiftly analyzes drug data and matches it to new indications, transforming the process into a more efficient and cost-effective endeavor.

Today, AI-assisted drug discovery has emerged as a leading trend in the pharmaceutical industry, with global AI drug development projects sprouting up like mushrooms after a rainstorm.

The world's leading tech giants are increasingly captivated by the biopharmaceutical sector. Jensen Huang, CEO of NVIDIA, has frequently highlighted that "AI + pharmaceuticals" is poised to become the next "golden opportunity." NVIDIA has not only introduced BioNeMo, a generative AI cloud service tailored for drug development, but also ramped up its investments in the AI pharmaceutical realm. In 2023, NVIDIA's stock price soared threefold, fueled by the surging demand for computing power driven by generative AI. This dramatic rise underscores the immense, untapped potential of the AI + biopharmaceutical industry and its continued allure to investors.

In the healthcare industry, artificial intelligence has progressed from making ripples to generating dynamic waves of change. With the advent of cutting-edge technologies like large models, entirely new products and services are springing to life, and the range of applications is expanding at a breathtaking pace.

Pioneering the Frontier: Where Healthcare Meets Artificial Intelligence

The impact of artificial intelligence on the healthcare industry is nothing short of riveting, especially when exploring its transformative integration across pharmaceutical research, insurance, and health management.

The trailblazers of AI-assisted drug development can be traced back to a landmark merger in 2016. During this pivotal year, the biopharmaceutical development and outsourcing giant Quintiles joined forces with IMS Health, a leading American healthcare information provider. The newly formed company was initially known as QuintilesIMS, but it soon evolved into the industry powerhouse we now recognize as IQVIA.

Quintiles specialized in delivering clinical research CRO services to pharmaceutical and biotechnology firms. In contrast, IMS Health excelled in providing information and strategic consulting services across the global healthcare landscape, operating in over 100 countries. With its enormous trove of medical data, IMS Health stood as a colossal figure in the domain of healthcare big data.

The merger of these two giants swiftly gave rise to a more expansive and lucrative opportunity, blending their strengths to unlock unprecedented potential.

Traditional CRO companies often navigate the laborious process of recruiting and managing clinical trial volunteers for Phase II and III studies through painstaking manual methods. This involves a complex dance with patients, hospitals, insurance agencies, and pharmaceutical firms to collect and consolidate data, which is then painstakingly submitted to regulatory bodies. The entire process can stretch over several years, with roughly 20% of the data often lost due to various issues and significant challenges in maintaining format, granularity, and completeness. To combat these hurdles, some CROs deploy large teams, consuming extensive resources in the quest for data quality.

Following the merger, IQVIA has transformed into a powerhouse of data services, blending IMS's vast troves of healthcare data with Quintiles' deep expertise in product development. By harnessing the power of big data, IQVIA refines every facet of clinical research—from streamlining patient recruitment to optimizing study execution. The company employs a rich array of techniques, including the aggregation of diverse datasets, integration of anonymized information, and analysis of real-world evidence, to dramatically boost the efficiency of drug development. Beyond enhancing operational workflows, IQVIA offers tailored solutions for drug R&D, providing pharmaceutical companies with profound insights into diseases, treatments, and costs, thereby delivering invaluable consulting and strategic support.

This seismic shift has created extraordinary value. In fiscal year 2016, IQVIA reported revenues of $6.8 billion and a profit of $70 million. Fast forward to fiscal year 2023, and the company saw its revenues soar to $15 billion, with profits skyrocketing to $1.358 billion. By July 2024, IQVIA's global market capitalization had firmly surpassed $40 billion, reflecting its remarkable ascent and the enormous potential unleashed by this transformation.

Harnessing Big Data to Supercharge Drug Development Efficiency

The merger of Quintiles and IMS Health sparked a global surge in the integration of artificial intelligence with drug development.

A popular industry saying about new drug development is "the three tens." This phrase highlights the notoriously protracted nature of the process: it often stretches up to a decade from inception to market. The journey unfolds across four major stages: target identification and validation, compound screening and optimization, preclinical studies, and four phases of clinical trials. Attrition rates are steep at every turn, with only about 10% of drugs ever reaching the market. The price tag for development usually begins around $1 billion.

Moreover, as drug targets become ever more elusive and complex, pharmaceutical companies find themselves pouring more time, resources, and risk into developing "First-in-Class" drugs. In 2023, out of the 55 new drugs approved by the FDA's Center for Drug Evaluation and Research (CDER), just 36% earned the coveted "First-in-Class" designation.

Faced with these daunting challenges, pharmaceutical scientists are focusing their efforts on two pivotal areas: *first, boosting the overall efficiency of research and development; and second, mining existing data to uncover fresh, groundbreaking insights.*

With artificial intelligence driving the charge, new drug development stands on the brink of shattering the limitations of the "3 tens" framework, promising to dramatically boost efficiency in both critical areas.

Harnessing image and text recognition, artificial intelligence is revolutionizing drug development by pinpointing new targets, screening biomarkers, predicting efficacy, and optimizing the crystal structures of small-molecule drugs. A recent Boston Consulting analysis of clinical pipelines from over a hundred AI-driven pharmaceutical companies reveals a dramatic leap in success rates. AI-discovered drug molecules now boast an overall success rate that has surged from 5%–10% to about 9%–18%, effectively doubling the odds. Phase I clinical trials are especially impressive, with success rates soaring to 80%–90%.

In clinical research, artificial intelligence excels at merging newly acquired data with extensive historical clinical datasets. This capability not only yields profound insights but also forecasts drug research outcomes and reveals novel clinical applications for existing drugs. With AI driving these advancements, the efficiency of new drug development has seen a remarkable boost.

The swift development of effective treatments for the novel coronavirus and Ebola virus, highlighted at the beginning of this section, exemplifies the power of "repurposing existing drugs." Compared to developing new drugs from scratch, repurposing existing ones can slash costs to about one-tenth and reduce the timeline by more than half. In recent years, artificial intelligence has revolutionized drug repurposing by overcoming many of its previous limitations. By sifting through vast amounts of biological and chemical data, AI reveals hidden connections between existing drugs, disease targets, and potential new uses. It not only broadens the pool of candidate drugs while minimizing off-target effects but also identifies drugs that are no longer under patent, tackling intellectual property challenges head-on.

Moreover, real-world data is pivotal in supporting drug approvals, conducting virtual clinical trials, and analyzing the safety and efficacy of drugs and devices. It also plays a vital role in post-marketing safety monitoring and refining pharmacoeconomic models. Big data and artificial intelligence have emerged as formidable engines, propelling the rapid advancement of public health and well-being.

To capture commercial opportunities in drug development, prioritizing the collection, organization, and analysis of clinical big data is crucial.

As we look ahead, the next wave of pharmaceutical innovations is anticipated to spring from the rich tapestry of accumulated clinical big data.

Maximizing Profit and Efficiency in Health Insurance

In the insurance sector, leveraging healthcare data effectively and in compliance can unlock powerful insights. This data becomes a game-changer, driving innovation in product development, refining underwriting and claims processes, enhancing marketing strategies, and strengthening risk management for insurance companies.

Overall, the insurance industry's core objectives revolve around advancing both business development and risk management. Innovations in artificial intelligence and health insurance can be unlocked by focusing on these two pivotal areas.

Expanding the Client Base—Attracting More Customers   For insurance companies, one of the top priorities for managers is figuring out how to attract more customers. With most insurance products differing mainly in terms of covered conditions and coverage limits, innovative product design has emerged as a promising new avenue for growth.

Artificial intelligence can revolutionize how insurance companies approach pricing by enabling truly differentiated models. For instance, in products tailored for niche scenarios like sports or chronic disease management, AI can harness data from innovative sources such as sensors and social tools. This allows for dynamic, personalized risk assessments and premium adjustments. As a result, insurance providers can extend coverage to specific groups—like individuals with diabetes, hypertension, or smokers—making insurance accessible even to those with preexisting conditions.

Disease prediction models are a cornerstone of big data applications, driving innovation and diversification in insurance products. These models offer invaluable insights for crafting and pricing new offerings, dramatically boosting the insurance industry's capacity to refine risk management and underwriting processes.

In enhancing sales efficiency, insurance companies are turning to artificial intelligence for a host of services, including smart customer support, mobile insurance applications, and AI-driven advisers. Take Lemonade, for example: this innovative online insurer has created a fully digital sales bot named Maya (AI.Maya) using GPT-3 technology. Maya offers personalized insurance pricing by engaging customers in online chats, providing tailored recommendations and quotes, and guiding them through the entire insurance process—all within a digital platform. Today, such intelligent chatbots are becoming a staple on insurance and sales platforms, facilitating real-time interactions and boosting customer engagement.

Cost Control—Mastering Risk Management   By harnessing the power of artificial intelligence, insurance companies can revolutionize their approach to underwriting and claims processing, delivering precision and efficiency while bolstering internal risk management.

In their operational processes, insurance companies are turbocharging claims management and after-sales service through automated claims systems and integrated service platforms. A prime example is OpenAI's 2024 partnership with Oscar Health, a U.S. health insurance tech company, to infuse AI into claims processing. Their AI assistant has slashed issue resolution time by 50%, matching or even surpassing the accuracy of human representatives. Oscar Health expects this collaboration to automate at least 4,000 claims each month, amounting to a staggering 48,000 claims by the close of 2024.

In the realm of underwriting, Captricity, a data cloud platform company, has revolutionized the process for New York Life Insurance by digitizing over 500,000 commercial insurance applications. This leap has dramatically accelerated both underwriting and approval workflows. But Captricity's innovation doesn't stop there; it has also delved into historical death certificate data, extracting cause-of-death information from the past decade. This invaluable data helps insurance companies refine their life insurance actuarial models and fine-tune their pricing strategies for a more accurate risk assessment.

In claims management, artificial intelligence acts as a powerful integrator, merging user medical records, health management data, online activity, and financial information to effectively control risk. By constructing sophisticated anti-fraud models, AI not only enhances risk detection but also significantly reduces potential losses, providing a comprehensive safeguard against fraudulent claims.

In Europe, fraudulent claims are estimated to account for about 10% of the insurance payouts, posing a significant challenge to the industry. Many innovative startups are now leveraging artificial intelligence to revolutionize claims management, with Shift Technology—founded in Paris—leading the charge. Shift utilizes big data and machine learning algorithms to craft advanced anti-fraud solutions, helping insurance companies curb their fraud-related losses. By 2023, Shift's system had analyzed over 100 million claims globally, boosting fraud detection efficiency by 34% and quadrupling investigative speed.

Insurance companies are tapping into health and medical data to broaden their corporate client base and bolster risk management. At the same time, they are constantly refining their customer service capabilities to enhance client retention and loyalty.

Health Management: Keeping Tabs on Your 24/7 Wellness
My career has granted me the privilege of helping implement or observing the deployment of artificial intelligence across various countries globally. Recently, I've witnessed a remarkable transformation in the healthcare sector, transitioning from a traditionally "hospital-centered" model to a more "patient-centered" or "personal-centered" approach.

We all remember the classic tale of Snow White and her magical mirror—"Mirror, mirror, on the wall, who's the fairest of them all?" Today, the realm of human-computer interaction has made the magic mirror a reality. At the 2019 CES in Las Vegas, I encountered smart mirrors tailored for health management. These innovative devices use deep learning algorithms and facial imaging to precisely calculate health indices and even forecast the onset of certain diseases.

These smart mirrors are just the tip of the iceberg in the world of health management devices.

Health management is the all-encompassing process of monitoring, analyzing, evaluating, predicting, planning, preventing, and controlling health risks for individuals and populations through biosensors and mobile devices. It covers everything from routine health maintenance and chronic disease management to emotional well-being. Thanks to an array of smart wearables, we can now keep a vigilant eye on our health around the clock.

Picture this: You start your day by checking your health indicators through a smart mirror. At mealtimes, intelligent kitchen appliances guide you with tailored food and nutrition advice. During your afternoon workout, sensor-equipped fitness apparel offers real-time insights into your physical activity. Before bedtime, a sleep device and a blood oxygen ring help you monitor and manage your sleep quality and potential risks. When you wake up, you review the detailed sleep report and make adjustments based on the expert recommendations.

Technology is transforming personal health experiences in remarkable ways. By harnessing real-time dynamic big data, artificial intelligence

FIGURE 3.1 Revolutionizing hospitality: The "Magic Mirror" AI voice interaction service for hotel guests, unveiled in partnership with Panasonic in 2017.

platforms craft a detailed health profile tailored to each user. Drawing on this wealth of information, AI algorithms and models provide insightful health analysis and predictive guidance, revolutionizing how we manage our well-being.

Wearable devices are making a profound impact on chronic disease management. Consider diabetes, a condition affecting 10% of the global population. A hospital director once shared that patients often struggled to follow the recommended routine of checking their blood sugar one to six times a day, with compliance rates falling below 40%. Without constant supervision, sticking to such a regimen can be daunting. In this context, wearable devices emerge as game-changers, boosting the frequency of blood sugar monitoring and significantly enhancing adherence to chronic disease management.

Traditional healthcare services tend to concentrate on the 5% of individuals who are already ill, while the majority of people experience a gradual progression from mild to severe conditions over time. Medical research underscores that early detection and intervention, paired with cutting-edge health management technologies, can dramatically boost public well-being and slash healthcare costs.

The rapid expansion of smart mobile devices and personal wearables has unleashed a constant flow of personal health data for artificial intelligence to analyze. This surge has paved the way for digital health—a burgeoning trend that harnesses sensors and software to deliver treatment interventions, and to prevent, manage, or treat diseases. Quietly yet powerfully, digital health is reshaping the landscape of modern medicine.

Digital therapeutics (DTx) heralds a new era in modern healthcare, fusing sensor-equipped wearables and medical devices with cutting-edge computing and information technology to transform the entire medical process. Unlike traditional treatments that depend heavily on medications and medical devices, digital therapeutics pivots to software solutions as its mainstay. Yet, this isn't your run-of-the-mill software; digital therapeutics must undergo rigorous scrutiny and receive formal approval from regulatory agencies before it can be used. This ensures that these innovative digital interventions meet the highest standards of efficacy and safety.

FDA clinical trials reveal that within just three months, 40% of patients using digital therapeutics successfully overcame alcohol and cannabis addiction or dependence, compared to a mere 17.6% in the group receiving traditional drug treatments. The impressive success of digital therapeutics lies in its real-time connectivity with patients, enabling it to gather pertinent data, deliver personalized treatment plans, and provide ongoing monitoring. This dynamic approach ensures that interventions are both timely and tailored to individual needs, significantly enhancing treatment outcomes.

How can big data and artificial intelligence weave together pharmaceuticals, insurance, and health management to forge innovative new business ecosystems?

The Business Ecosystem of Pharmaceuticals, Insurance, and Health Management

Today, artificial intelligence has woven itself into the fabric of healthcare, with the most thrilling innovations emerging from the seamless integration of pharmaceuticals, insurance, and health management into a unified commercial ecosystem.

Artificial intelligence has shifted from a supporting role to a leading one. To unlock its full commercial and societal potential in healthcare, it must thrive within an ecosystem that integrates insurance, pharmaceuticals, and health management. The remarkable transformation of UnitedHealth Group, America's largest commercial health insurer, stands as a prime example of this integrated approach in action.

In 2011, UnitedHealth embarked on a strategic overhaul, merging its health services division into Optum. This pivotal restructuring gave rise to two core business segments: "Health Insurance" and "Health Management." This bold move positioned UnitedHealth to capitalize on three pivotal trends reshaping the healthcare landscape: big data analytics, value-based care, and a user-centric approach.

Optum's roots stretch back to the 1980s, when its predecessor, Ingenix, laid the foundation by developing UnitedHealth's core IT systems and analyzing business data. Following the integration, Optum has evolved into three dynamic branches: Optum Health, which specializes in healthcare services, health management, and financial solutions; Optum Insight, dedicated to health information technology, including systems, data management, and consulting, and heavily invested in big data and AI; and OptumRx, which manages pharmacy benefits, processes prescription drug claims, and cuts costs through bulk purchasing.

UnitedHealth's insurance division and Optum's health management sector work seamlessly together to forge a holistic ecosystem spanning multiple business areas. When a customer buys commercial health insurance, Optum takes charge of policy administration, risk management, and health data oversight. By tapping into Optum's rich data troves, the company provides personalized insurance recommendations, boosting sales efficiency. If a claim occurs, the customer can smoothly traverse the entire process—from hospital diagnosis and medication dispensing to tracking treatment outcomes—within the fully integrated healthcare ecosystem created by UnitedHealth.

This business ecosystem not only delivers seamless services to users but also manages insurance payout costs effectively. This virtuous cycle not only elevates the customer experience but also fortifies commercial barriers, generating a powerful bilateral network effect.

In this process, data is the linchpin of the business ecosystem. From the start, Optum amassed a vast repository of physician resources and client information. By the end of 2023, Optum boasted over 90,000 contracted doctors and a treasure trove of data from 4 million patients, encompassing years of medical records, insurance details, and health management insights. This rich dataset empowers Optum to provide smarter, more precise health services, elevating customer satisfaction and unlocking new value for clients.

Optum not only enhances its own commercial health insurance products but also applies its data analytics prowess to serve a diverse clientele, including government agencies, hospitals, pharmacies, patients, and pharmaceutical companies. This expansive reach has allowed Optum to generate substantial revenue from external sources, showcasing its expertise across the healthcare landscape.

In January 2016, the globally acclaimed CRO Parexel forged a groundbreaking partnership with Optum. With Optum's extensive electronic health records offering a treasure trove of real-world clinical and claims data, Parexel was able to harness these insights to revolutionize its approach to drug trials. By leveraging this rich data, Parexel optimized clinical trial services, slashed drug development costs, improved volunteer care, and lowered patients' medical expenses, marking a significant leap forward in the field.

UnitedHealth Group has masterfully integrated "pharmaceuticals, insurance, and health management," fueling an impressive surge in both revenue and profit. By 2023, their annual revenue had soared to $371.6 billion, a robust 15% increase from the previous year, with a compound annual growth rate exceeding 8%. This remarkable growth places them at the pinnacle of major U.S. corporations. Optum, in particular, has seen explosive growth, reaching around 25%. Its contribution to UnitedHealth's operating profit has escalated dramatically, climbing from 40% in 2016 to a striking 60% in 2023.

UnitedHealth Group stands as a shining example of how to integrate pharmaceuticals, insurance, and health management into a cohesive commercial ecosystem. Its success makes it a compelling model for companies around the globe to study and aspire to.

In this business ecosystem, the health insurance sector spearheads customer acquisition, while the health services division takes charge of backend

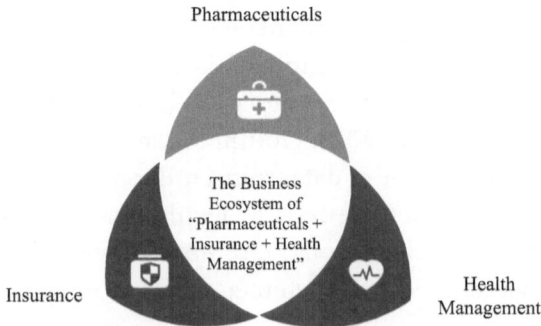

FIGURE 3.2 The business ecosystem of "pharmaceuticals + insurance + health management."

health management and medical services. Health management continuously collects data, which feeds into pharmaceutical R&D, optimizes sales channels, and refines insurance product design, pricing, risk management, and claims. As the data deepens, it even opens doors to pioneering business model innovations.

A survey conducted by MuleSoft, a Salesforce.com company, reveals that among over 8,000 consumers worldwide, 62% of younger individuals are open to letting insurance companies tap into third-party data from sources like Facebook, fitness apps, and smart devices to secure lower premiums. With permission to access health-related data, health management companies can not only offer personalized pricing but also engage in post-sale health management. This means they can monitor user behavior and, in theory, adjust prices dynamically based on real-time insights.

John Hancock, a leading U.S. insurance company, is transforming insurance sales with its groundbreaking "interactive" policies, driven by advanced health management. This innovative approach has captivated consumers and stands as a truly disruptive force in the insurance industry.

Sureify, an innovative insurtech company, exemplifies the fusion of industries. Its flagship platform, the "Lifetime Platform," enhances engagement between life insurance products and policyholders by integrating with over 250 wearable and mobile devices. With user consent, this platform gathers and analyzes data on physical activity and health metrics—such as heart rate, blood sugar, and blood pressure—to deliver real-time insurance pricing. Beyond this, Sureify's technology encourages clients to stay active and monitor their health, providing life insurers with valuable insights into policyholders' health throughout the policy lifecycle. This, in turn, helps reduce moral hazard and minimize claims risk.

Healthcare is an enormous industry. According to the Centers for Medicare & Medicaid Services (CMS), U.S. health-related spending surged to nearly $4.5 trillion in 2022, representing a staggering 17.3% of GDP. Insurance institutions foot a significant portion of this bill. Data from 2022 reveals that 92.1% of Americans had some form of insurance coverage. Of these, 65.6% were covered by commercial insurance, with 54.5% holding employer-sponsored group plans, 9.9% purchasing individual health insurance (often with overlapping coverage), and 36.1% relying on government insurance programs.

The evolution of a country's healthcare system hinges on a nuanced evaluation of factors like population dynamics, financial resources, and

GDP growth. With the transformative power of artificial intelligence at our disposal, we can anticipate the rise of multiple global giants in the realm of "pharma + insurance + health management." These titans will not only redefine industry standards but also become trailblazers in leveraging big data for revolutionary advancements in healthcare.

The Data Dilemmas in Healthcare

The healthcare industry grapples with distinctive data challenges, magnified by legacy issues like data silos. Tackling these obstacles demands a concerted effort from regulators, industry leaders, businesses, and individuals working in unison.

Healthcare data primarily flows from three key sources: first, there's data from government and healthcare institutions, like electronic medical records; second, industry data, which encompasses raw and derived information from various sectors—such as insurance claims, genetic testing in biotechnology, and pharmacological data from drug development; and third, health behavior data collected by biometric sensors.

For the industry, the biggest challenge in harnessing artificial intelligence is undoubtedly the data.

Firstly, the problem of data silos is a widespread challenge that many are striving to overcome. Furthermore, from a historical standpoint, electronic health records—the primary source of medical data—were never designed with big data analysis in mind.

FIGURE 3.3 Navigating the future: Insights from the health tech panel at GITEX Global Dubai 2023—balancing AI innovation with governance in healthcare.

As a trailblazer in electronic health records (EHRs), the U.S. embarked on its healthcare informatics journey in the 1970s, but it took nearly 40 years for EHRs to gain widespread traction. The turning point came in February 2009, when President Obama signed the Health Information Technology for Economic and Clinical Health (HITECH) Act. This landmark legislation earmarked $35 billion to ignite a fresh wave of healthcare IT innovation, providing a new surge of optimism for the advancement of EHRs.

To amplify the HITECH Act's impact, President Obama signed the Patient Protection and Affordable Care Act (PPACA or ACA) in March 2010, which legally mandated the broad adoption of EHRs. This legislation was a game-changer, driving the widespread implementation of EHRs. Institutions like the Agency for Healthcare Research and Quality and the Centers for Medicare & Medicaid Services, among others, played crucial roles in advancing and integrating EHRs into the U.S. healthcare landscape.

Beginning in 2010, the surge in healthcare IT integration in the U.S. offered a golden opportunity for companies to establish themselves as titans in the EHR domain while simultaneously driving their own digital transformations. Take Epic Systems, for instance. Founded in 1979, Epic initially served as an IT solutions provider for hospitals, clinics, and pharmacies. Its path to dominance was paved through the strategic integration of EHRs via a sophisticated database management approach. Today, Epic Systems is a powerhouse in the field, boasting one of the largest repositories of health records in the U.S., with data on up to 250 million individuals.

Epic Systems has notably embraced a patient-centric approach, with data as its cornerstone. The company is committed to setting standards for data sharing, acknowledging the crucial role of health data, and championing a transition from mere medical data to a holistic health data model. Epic also advocates for openness and ecosystem development. After crafting their systems, Epic provides the source code to healthcare institutions, allowing for customization and further innovation. Additionally, they offer APIs to a wide range of partners, which encourages the creation of diverse products and fosters a dynamic ecosystem. Currently, Epic Systems is collaborating with Apple to build a patient-focused electronic health record system, enhancing their capabilities in health services, chronic disease management, and more.

Once EHRs became widespread in the U.S., the benefits were immediate, sparking the rapid growth of a dynamic clinical big data analytics industry.

Beginning in 2015, companies such as IBM, Optum, Oracle, and Verisk Analytics plunged into the secondary development of healthcare big data, fueling a rapidly expanding analytics market. Today, this sector is thriving, yet as of 2024, EHRs in the U.S. are still evolving. The quest to fully harness the power of big data in healthcare remains a daunting and ongoing challenge.

Given that the rise of healthcare IT came before the big data boom, many early EHRs were not built with big data analytics in mind. As a result, developing an EHR platform that meets today's big data demands requires a complete overhaul of data structures, the standardization of data formats, and the creation of IT systems capable of managing enormous volumes of dynamic, high-concurrency data. It's evident that this is a monumental and complex task.

Integrating the first type of data can tackle persistent industry challenges like "data standardization" and "data silos." At a strategic level, this integration not only enhances patient privacy and data security but also establishes a robust foundation for secondary data development and the emergence of data trading markets.

The second and third types of healthcare data span multiple sub-sectors, including pharmaceuticals, insurance, and health management. This results in a rich tapestry of data sources and intricate standards. The industry is actively seeking ways to create a unified data dialogue system for these varied categories. In this context, it may be beneficial to let market forces handle these data types, allowing market mechanisms to streamline their exchange and utilization.

The healthcare industry is pivotal to both national well-being and personal health. To unlock the full potential of data and boost industry efficiency, we must embrace cutting-edge technologies like artificial intelligence. Equally important is the collaborative effort of governments, industry players, businesses, and individuals to build a unified, efficient, and orderly data marketplace. Such a concerted approach will pave the way for a sustainable development model in the sector.

There's an experiment from around 40 years ago that continues to resonate with me today.

From 1974 to 1982, the RAND Corporation, a prominent non-profit research and consulting organization, invested $82 million in a landmark healthcare experiment that spanned thousands of American households. The findings were quite eye-opening: the study revealed no significant difference in health outcomes between individuals who paid partially out-of-pocket for healthcare services and those who received fully subsidized care.

The RAND study's findings had a seismic impact on the global design of healthcare and insurance systems, sparking a revolutionary approach that seamlessly integrates pharmaceuticals, insurance, and health management. This groundbreaking research paved the way for a new era of innovative business models in the healthcare industry.

This system design drastically cut down on unnecessary healthcare spending and optimized the use of scarce medical resources. The ripple effects of these findings have reshaped health systems and insurance schemes across numerous countries. Remarkably, the data from this landmark experiment still fuels ongoing research today.

If an experiment can endure for nine years, it's clear that the intricate world of healthcare demands our patience and relentless innovation. I'm convinced that once big data flows seamlessly through the healthcare sector and is supercharged by artificial intelligence, we'll see healthcare resource allocation soar to new heights of efficiency. With technological advancements forging ahead, I firmly believe we'll not only enhance the quality of human life but also extend our lifespans, turning the dream of living to a ripe old age into a tangible reality for all.

Finally, I'd like to wrap up this section with a poignant quote from Michael Rich, Chairman and CEO of the RAND Corporation, on the 40th anniversary of the experiment: "Innovative research and health care reform don't happen overnight."

SECTION 2: TRANSFORMING THE MEDIA INDUSTRY—DATA ANALYTICS AND AI AS THE NEW POWER BROKERS

In the media industry, users are the left hand, content is the right hand, and artificial intelligence is the bridge that seamlessly connects them. AI enables companies to achieve a more precise and efficient alignment between users and content. This pivotal concept was a highlight of my keynote at the 2017 NAB Show, where I spoke as a global thought leader in big data analytics and AI.

This insight has been validated by the ongoing global shifts in the media industry. Today, the reigning media formats—information streams and short videos—are both powered by artificial intelligence. AI not only

FIGURE 3.4 Unveiling best practices: My 2017 presentation on artificial intelligence in the media industry at the NAB Show, New York City.

builds detailed user profiles but also generates rich content tags through text, audio, and image analysis. This dual capability ensures precise matches and delivers a highly personalized experience to users.

Looking back over the past 20 years, from the rise of the internet to the mobile revolution and now to artificial intelligence, the media industry has been at the forefront of technological upheaval. Even the titans of the field, like *The New York Times* and *The Washington Post*, have faced mounting challenges. Their storied prestige and the cachet of Pulitzer Prizes have proven insufficient to stem the tide of user loss.

New wave companies like Google, Meta, YouTube, Netflix, Snapchat, Spotify, and Twitter have surged ahead by harnessing technological innovation to capture the zeitgeist. They've seized users' time and money, crafting entirely new experiences and business models that have fundamentally shaken the survival strategies of traditional media—newspapers, radio, and television. The pace of technological change has been so rapid that even once-dominant formats like search and video, which emerged just a decade or two ago, are now overshadowed by the rising tide of information streams and short videos.

The effectiveness of artificial intelligence technology is directly influencing content monetization and starting to reshape the business models of the media industry. In the U.S., giants like Google, Meta, and Amazon now claim 70% of digital media ad revenue, while Netflix has emerged as a powerhouse in the paid content arena. In China, short video startups have skyrocketed, even challenging the dominance of the "BAT" trio—Baidu, Alibaba, and Tencent—in the online advertising space.

Why is the media industry so highly sensitive and subject to constant upheaval? From an economic perspective, the answer lies in the very low switching costs for users. When a new media platform emerges with a better experience and greater interactivity, the cost for users to shift is virtually zero. From a technological standpoint, the essence of the internet and artificial intelligence is the processing and dissemination of information. Since media products and services are fundamentally about information and content, changes in these underlying technologies can shake the industry like tectonic shifts, causing a dramatic transformation of the entire ecosystem.

With the advent of large language models, technology has delivered a fresh jolt to the media industry. This time, the impact extends beyond content recommendation and matching, sparking a revolutionary upheaval on the content supply side. Large text-to-video models, such as Sora, empower creators with unprecedented creative freedom, ushering in a global wave of "creativity democratization."

Three Game-Changing Trends Shaping the Media Industry

Mobility, video-centric content, and personalization are the three dominant trends reshaping the media industry today.

In 2023, if you're in China, there's a 68.4% chance that you'll have a smartphone in your pocket. In Japan, this probability jumps to 78.6%, and in the U.S., it soars to an impressive 81.6%.

People use smartphones for chatting, listening to music, taking photos, binge-watching shows, shopping, paying bills, and gaming. As smartphones become increasingly social media hubs, they offer more than just access to information and services; they also turn everyone into a potential broadcaster. A casual text, a snapshot, or a quick video can be shared across various content platforms, with some even getting picked up by personalized recommendation engines and reaching a wider audience.

The rise of various mobile devices has fundamentally disrupted the traditional media industry's model of professional production, one-way distribution, and uniform delivery. Driven by technologies such as 5G, artificial intelligence, virtual reality (VR), and augmented reality (AR), the media industry is now witnessing three major trends:

Trend 1: The Rise of Mobility

We live in a multi-screen world, surrounded by smartphones, tablets, smart TVs, and other internet-connected devices. These gadgets, backed by powerful data centers, offer seamless access on the go and constantly vie for our attention.

The scale of these devices is so astounding that their penetration surpasses many essential goods. According to the latest data from analysts like Statista, IDC, and Gartner, by 2024, there will be around 8 billion smartphones globally—figures that surpassed the number of bank and water utility accounts (around 5 billion) three years ago. Mobile device traffic now accounts for approximately 60% of total internet traffic, a dramatic increase from just 8% reported by Cisco in 2016.

The diversity of mobile devices has greatly expanded users' media channels. The Olympic Games have long been a prime example of successful multi-platform broadcasting. For the 2024 Paris Olympics, NBC alone utilized four major TV networks (NBC, NBCSN, USA Network, and Golf Channel) and multiple streaming platforms for comprehensive coverage. Official Olympic social media accounts on Twitter and Instagram provided real-time updates with tweets and posts, generating over 3 billion interactions. Content related to the Olympics on TikTok achieved over 1 billion views. Additionally, numerous mobile apps, each with over 10 million downloads, offered event schedules, live streams, replays, and audience interactions. Mobile platforms not only ensured broad audience reach but also enhanced viewer engagement and interactivity.

Trend 2: The Video Revolution
We are living in the age of the "Video Explosion." Back in 2006, when Google bought the fledgling company YouTube for a staggering $1.65 billion, many people were left scratching their heads in disbelief. Fast forward to today, and the numbers speak for themselves: over 2.5 billion users log in to YouTube every month to watch videos. That's more than the combined population of the U.S., China, and Japan!

The explosive growth of video content isn't confined to professional platforms like online TV and Netflix. It has also taken social media by storm, with platforms like Facebook, WeChat, and Line becoming hotspots for video sharing. Since 2012, the increasing clarity of smartphone cameras has made it possible to create high-quality original videos, dramatically lowering the barriers to video production. This democratization of video has fueled the rise of video socializing, live streaming, and video shopping, drawing in ever-growing numbers of users.

Take TikTok, the reigning champion of short-form video. With over 1 billion active users worldwide, it leads the pack in user engagement, with people spending nearly 54 minutes a day on the app. This surge in video consumption is reshaping how we connect, entertain, and shop, making video a central and dynamic force in our digital lives.

In 2020, the global shift to 5G marked a pivotal moment, dramatically accelerating network speeds. With 5G, downloading a high-definition movie can be reduced to mere seconds, revolutionizing video consumption. Meanwhile, VR and AR technologies are advancing rapidly, offering increasingly immersive video experiences. The use of video is no longer confined to consumer applications; it is expanding into enterprise sectors such as healthcare, manufacturing, and education, transforming how these industries operate and interact.

Trend 3: The Era of Personalization

In October 2008, Spotify launched in Stockholm, Sweden, marking the debut of a groundbreaking licensed streaming music service. By pushing the boundaries of digital distribution to their limits, Spotify has since grown to boast an impressive 365 million users and reached a staggering $26.5 billion market value in its IPO.

Initially, Spotify's approach was relatively straightforward: it categorized its 30 million tracks based on user search histories and provided recommendations for songs, artists, and playlists tailored to individual tastes and contextual information. Over time, Spotify evolved from basic editorial curation and collaborative filtering to harness the power of advanced deep learning algorithms. Now, even without prior user interaction history, Spotify can suggest newly released tracks with remarkable accuracy. Its audio analysis engine is so sophisticated that it can classify unfamiliar tracks and align them with users' personal preferences, all without a single listen.

Under the influence of artificial intelligence, personalized experiences have become increasingly popular. On platforms like Google, Facebook, Amazon, YouTube, Netflix, and Twitter, the more time users spend, the more personalized data—such as their thoughts, attitudes, behaviors, concerns, and desires—is collected. This data fuels the delivery of increasingly tailored content and services. The more personalized the offerings, the better the user experience. For example, on Google, search results for the same keyword can vary; on Facebook, users appreciate when the system proactively suggests "people they might be interested in"; and on YouTube, when the system recommends videos that users enjoy, they feel a sense of "someone understands me."

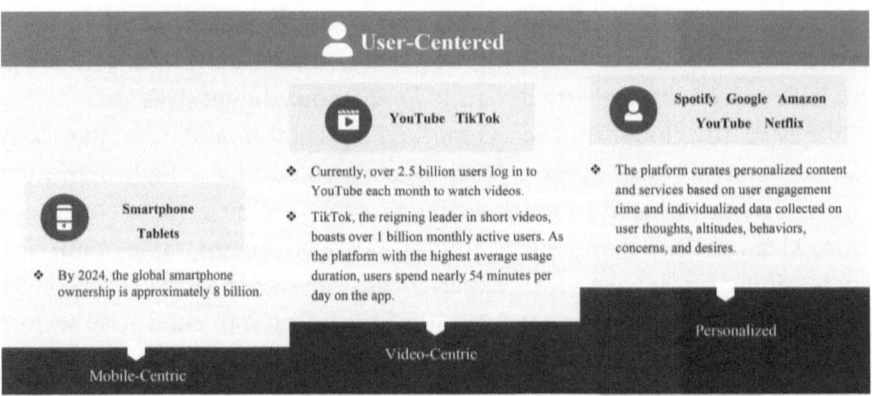

FIGURE 3.5   Emerging trends in the media industry.

Symphony of Content and User: The Art of Perfect Harmony

Artificial intelligence is revolutionizing the media industry by transforming user experiences, content creation, business models, and interactive activities. This innovation is a direct result of putting the "user-centric" philosophy into practice.

At the heart of the media industry are two crucial elements: "content" and "users." The challenge lies in how to align vast amounts of content with a multitude of users and effectively harness the enormous data generated from their interactions. With the power of artificial intelligence and data tagging, we can precisely connect and match content with users, delivering personalized experiences tailored to their context, anytime and anywhere. This seamless integration not only enhances user engagement but also transforms content into a revenue stream. By optimizing efficiency and accuracy in these matches, leading media organizations can attract the right content and users, thereby carving out a competitive edge in the industry.

Unleashing a New Wave of Creative Inspiration

Cutting-edge media companies have recognized that leveraging user data with the power of artificial intelligence can predict what content users will love most. This insight provides a unique edge in content creation and distribution. Netflix was a pioneer in exploiting this potential to its fullest. In 2013, Netflix broke the mold with its hit series *House of Cards*, revolutionizing traditional production and broadcasting models. Not only did the show become a massive success for Netflix, but it also showcased the incredible power of algorithms in the media landscape.

Netflix engineers delved into AI to analyze viewing preferences of 30 million users, 4 million comments, and 3 million topic searches. They discovered a significant overlap among fans of BBC dramas, director David Fincher, and actor Kevin Spacey. The insight was clear: combining these three elements could drastically increase the likelihood of a show's success. So, if a series incorporates all these winning factors, could it be a surefire hit?

Netflix's management decided to take a bold gamble. They not only spent $100 million to acquire the rights to the 1990 BBC series *House of Cards* but also meticulously followed the data-driven playbook by hiring the same director and lead actor. The storyline of *House of Cards* was crafted based on extensive data analysis: it turned out that viewers have a deep curiosity about politics, power, and intrigue. Big data also guided Netflix in optimizing the series' release strategy, recommending that episodes be released all at once rather than the traditional two-episode format favored by TV networks. By choosing to drop all 13 episodes of the first season at once, Netflix catered to viewers who prefer binge-watching. Additionally, Netflix tailored its marketing efforts by analyzing user behavior data, creating multiple versions of trailers to appeal to diverse audience segments.

It turned out that Netflix's gamble paid off spectacularly. *House of Cards* went on to produce seven seasons, becoming the most-watched show in Netflix's history. It was a global sensation, achieving major success in over 40 countries and clinching multiple Emmy and Golden Globe Awards along the way.

House of Cards marked the dawn of AI's deep integration into content creation. The show set a new standard where every aspect of filmmaking—from script selection and character development to actor casting and plot direction—could be guided by data-driven insights. By aligning production choices with the preferences of potential viewers, creators could craft content that resonates deeply with audiences, leading to maximized commercial success. This groundbreaking approach highlighted how data analytics could not only satisfy audience tastes but also deliver substantial financial rewards.

Elevating User Experience to New Heights

No matter how richly enhanced, user experience can always be taken further. The challenge is achieving a level of personalization and interactivity that is both profound and engaging. This is where artificial intelligence truly shines, making it possible to deliver experiences that are not only highly customized but also irresistibly entertaining.

The 2024 Paris Olympics are touted as the first-ever AI Olympics. Thanks to cutting-edge AI technology, thrilling moments can be captured and replayed in multi-angle slow motion within mere seconds, allowing viewers to transcend the constraints of time and space and immerse themselves in the splendor of Olympic competition. NBC is utilizing AI-generated voices based on real people, with Emmy-winning Hall of Fame broadcaster Al Michaels bringing his signature enthusiasm to the commentary. This creates a vivid portrayal of the events, making viewers feel as though they are right there in the midst of the action.

The integration of artificial intelligence has crafted an unprecedented event experience.

It can be personalized, offering fans of Messi and Ronaldo real-time, tailored views of their match. It can be integrative, featuring a duet between a current superstar and a digitally resurrected legend. And it can be downright intriguing.

The Met Gala, the annual charity ball hosted by the Metropolitan Museum of Art in New York City, is a dazzling fusion of fashion and technology. At the 2016 Met Gala, which revolved around the theme of technology, a groundbreaking smart gown stole the spotlight. Created in collaboration between the fashion brand Marchesa and IBM Watson, this innovative dress captivated everyone with its cutting-edge design and technological flair.

The smart gown, with its pristine white base, had the remarkable ability to change colors based on the mood of social media and the live audience. IBM Watson processed over 150 dress designs from Marchesa, generating color schemes to match each dress's style. Marchesa selected five human emotions—joy, passion, excitement, bravery, and curiosity—and IBM Watson assigned colors such as rose pink, coral red, pale yellow, and lavender purple to these emotions. Throughout the evening, the gown dynamically adapted its color in real-time, reflecting the fluctuating emotions of the crowd and creating a mesmerizing spectacle of shifting hues.

Leveraging technological advancements, grand spectacles, and top-tier events now have the opportunity to transcend conventional boundaries. These activities can seamlessly bridge the gap between onstage and offstage, as well as online and offline spaces. Audiences are no longer passive observers; they can engage in real-time interactions, dramatically enhancing and enriching their overall experience.

Mastering Precision: Unlocking the Art of Targeted User Acquisition
The streaming market is witnessing a high-stakes, smoke-free battle, with leading companies pulling out all the stops to maintain and expand their user bases.

After launching a massive wave of original content globally, Disney+ discovered that while their user base was rapidly expanding, engagement and retention rates remained inconsistent. This was particularly evident following the conclusion of the first season of the hit series *The Mandalorian*, which saw a notable drop in both viewing hours and subscription rates.

Could AI be the golden key to solving this dilemma?

Disney+ employed AI algorithms to analyze the audience for *The Mandalorian*, discovering that it drew a significant number of sci-fi enthusiasts and Star Wars fans. Armed with this insight, Disney+ leveraged its AI-driven personalized recommendation system to suggest other sci-fi shows and upcoming Star Wars content to these viewers.

At the same time, Disney+ refined its recommendation strategy by integrating user behavior data. By tracking viewing duration, favorite content, and patterns of skipping or replaying segments, the platform could precisely identify diverse user preferences. For instance, some users favored story-driven narratives, while others were drawn to visually stunning spectacles. Armed with these insights, Disney+ customized its recommendation lists and tailored its advertising and marketing campaigns, creating a more personalized experience for each viewer.

Clearly, Disney+ has conquered this fortress.

When the second season of *The Mandalorian* premiered, Disney+ not only attracted a surge of new users but also leveraged its personalized recommendation system to guide viewers toward other high-quality original series like *Loki* and *WandaVision*. This strategic move resulted in a 33% increase in user growth for Disney+ in 2021, solidifying its position as a leading contender in the streaming industry.

Today, acquiring user data through mobile platforms has become the mainstream method, supplementing traditional data assets. There are three primary types of data collected: 1. *Data from Physical Media*: This includes data generated from mobile device signals. 2. *Carrier Channel Data*: Carriers provide relatively comprehensive records, including details such as age, gender, and ID, as well as some user behavior data.

3. *App Data*: Apps track user behavior and data. The volume of data varies significantly depending on the app's user base. Super apps in social media, entertainment, and e-commerce generate enormous amounts of data, enabling highly detailed user profiles. This multifaceted approach allows for increasingly precise and comprehensive user insights.

While companies can legally and compliantly acquire data from external sources and secure support from major data providers, they must also be proactive in building their own data assets. In the future, lacking independent control over user data equates to not truly owning the users and limits the potential for innovative user solutions.

Interactive Ads: Creating a Win-Win for Users and Advertisers

Artificial Intelligence is revolutionizing the advertising industry by transforming ads into interactive and personalized experiences through precise content matching. This innovation represents a significant shift in the commercial model of advertising, making it not just a broadcast but a conversation tailored uniquely to each user.

Interactive media has disrupted the traditional one-way advertising model, allowing users to engage with ads based on their personal preferences and interests. This shift ensures that marketing content reaches its target audience with remarkable precision.

In 2022, Netflix and Google Assistant took a groundbreaking step with their collaboration on the second season of the sci-fi animated series *Love, Death & Robots*. Users could voice their interest in themes such as "Love," "Death," or "Robots," and Google Assistant would then play tailored ad snippets matching their chosen theme. This approach transformed passive ad consumption into an active, personalized choice. As a result, user engagement soared by 60% compared to standard ads, with viewers more eager to explore the curated content.

The role of artificial intelligence goes far beyond just delivering content—it also extends to the creation of personalized content.

By leveraging big data analytics, we can tailor messages to algorithms based on various regions, media, and user preferences. These algorithms can then create hundreds of distinct video ads from the same source material, with subtle variations like an actor's shirt, hairstyle, or skin tone. With personalized ads that require no manual editing, we get a closer match to users' psychological profiles.

In the realm of personalized advertising, algorithms are capable of dynamically editing videos in real time, conducting A/B tests, and fine-tuning ad performance. As a result, each user ends up receiving an ad video that is perfectly tailored to their preferences.

Moreover, the landscape of video content monetization is expanding beyond traditional models. Transactional Video on Demand (TVOD), Subscription Video on Demand (SVOD), VIP memberships, and Virtual Intellectual Properties (VIPs) are all ripe for innovation. By harnessing the power of big data analytics, these avenues can be explored and reimagined to uncover fresh and exciting business models.

The current setup for VIP membership fees on video platforms is still quite rudimentary. Platforms have the potential to refine these fees based on factors like viewing duration, time slots, and user preferences. For instance, the subscription model for a middle-aged man who watches just two documentaries a week could be vastly different from that of a young woman who binge-watches trending reality shows daily. With the vast amounts of data available in the media industry, companies can delve deeply into individual preferences. Coupled with adaptive machine learning algorithms, this data continuously refines and personalizes content or ads to match users' unique tastes. Whether it's content innovation, user engagement, or business model evolution, AI's capability to enhance and personalize each aspect is both intricate and profound.

In commercial practice, businesses have the opportunity to delve into how artificial intelligence can drive comprehensive, multidimensional innovation. By continually harnessing their own creativity, companies can leverage AI to deliver ever-more surprising and delightful experiences to their users.

Navigating the Tsunami of Content Supply: Innovations and Disruptions

In the coming years, the most significant disruption to the media industry driven by artificial intelligence will unfold on the supply side, where the very methods of content creation will be radically transformed.

Today, an increasing number of content platforms are leveraging generative AI to inject fresh elements into their recommendation systems. This emerging model of content creation is delighting both users and the industry, composing a vibrant new symphony in the age of human-AI collaboration.

This is undoubtedly a symphony that crescendos from delicate melodies to exhilarating triumphs. The democratization of content creation is reshaping both creators and users, heralding a new media landscape. As we navigate these changes, we must ask: are disputes over data ownership and content copyright merely human wishful thinking?

Anticipating Desires: Betting on What Users Want Before They Know It Themselves

AI's infiltration into content creation is already well-documented with numerous pioneering examples.

In 2017, Grammy-winning producer Alex Da Kid teamed up with IBM Watson to create the song "Not Easy," blending human creativity with AI's innovative edge.

As Alex Da Kid grappled with the challenge of pleasing a global audience, Watson approached the task in a way that no human could replicate. It "listened" to over 26,000 songs from the Billboard Hot 100 of the past five years and scoured reports from the Los Angeles Museum, Wikipedia articles, popular movie summaries, and trends in pop music. By analyzing these sources, Watson identified cultural trends, emotional expressions across various melodies, chords, and genres and helped Alex pinpoint the theme of "heartbreak." With what seemed like a divine perspective, Alex and Watson crafted a track that captured complex, multifaceted emotions in just minutes. The song soared to number two on Spotify's global chart within a week.

Silicon Valley's Hollywood Invasion: The Tech Takeover of Tinseltown

In February 2024, OpenAI made waves by launching its first text-to-video model, Sora. This groundbreaking technology can produce high-definition videos from textual instructions, creating a buzz across the industry. The 60-second videos generated by Sora feature stunningly clear visuals and seamless camera movements, significantly raising the bar for video generation technology and showcasing its immense potential for creating high-quality content.

Artificial intelligence has already made its mark in creative fields, assisting with harmonies in music, chord progressions, and even face-swapping in film. However, models like Sora reveal a new frontier: AI as a standalone creator capable of producing complete video works. This represents a groundbreaking shift, marking an unprecedented moment in creative history.

As the immense potential of artificial intelligence in content creation begins to unfold, titans from Silicon Valley and Hollywood are exploring a high-stakes merger.

Both Meta and Google have unveiled their ventures into text-to-video technology with projects like Emu Video and VideoPoet. These tech giants are reportedly investing tens of millions of dollars to develop systems that create lifelike scenes based on textual prompts. They are particularly eager to collaborate with film studios, hoping to secure IP licenses to produce content that brings their cinematic visions to life.

The Era of Creative Equality: Is the Tower of Copyright on the Brink of Collapse?

AI-driven advancements are injecting new energy into the flourishing world of content creation, especially within the realm of user-generated content (UGC). This dynamic boost is redefining the creative landscape, offering fresh momentum and possibilities.

Many ordinary people's creative talents are often constrained by technical limitations. For example, the dazzling special effects we see in blockbuster films require meticulous frame-by-frame creation, with costs running into tens of thousands of dollars for just one minute of effects. This means that the power to create stunning visual effects has remained in the hands of only a few.

Once text-to-video technology matures, the cost of special effects will plummet dramatically. For a monthly fee of just a few dozen dollars, individuals could produce high-quality effects that once cost hundreds of thousands. This would make creating stunning visual effects as easy as using real-time beauty filters on a smartphone. As a result, we'll see more people turning their creative ideas into reality and a surge of imaginative breakout hits emerging.

There's no doubt that artificial intelligence can equip everyone with remarkably powerful creative tools, bridging the gap in content production. Essentially, it levels the playing field for creators, democratizing the creative process like never before.

However, behind the mantra of "everyone is a creator" lurk two critical controversies that are generating global turbulence and brewing into a storm: first, the legality of the data used in training generative AI and whether data sources should receive a share of the profits; second, the issue of copyright ownership for content generated by AI.

First, generative AI relies on vast amounts of training data, often encompassing text, images, and music created by humans. The question arises: should these data sources receive permission from the original creators? For instance, artists and writers might question the use of their works to train AI models without compensation or acknowledgment. This unauthorized usage has sparked calls within the creative community for a "data source revenue-sharing" mechanism, ensuring that creators receive fair remuneration when their content is used by generative AI.

Secondly, the issue of copyright for AI-generated content is fraught with controversy. Under most legal systems, copyright holders must be human, complicating the ownership of AI-created works. For instance, can companies or individuals using AI claim ownership of the generated content? And if an AI's output closely resembles the style or structure of existing works, potentially constituting infringement, how should responsibility be assigned? These questions highlight the intricate challenges of defining ownership and liability in the age of AI.

To tackle these challenges, a new legal framework is urgently needed to clarify the rules for using AI training data and determining the ownership of AI-generated content. For example, we might look to the music industry's copyright management models and introduce revenue-sharing mechanisms for AI-generated content, ensuring that data contributors are fairly compensated and their interests are protected.

The door to a new world has swung open, with artificial intelligence poised to unleash the full creative potential of the masses and usher in an era of human-AI co-creation. However, for this new age to thrive, regulators, technology developers, and the creative community must forge a consensus, establishing a fair and transparent new order.

Data Privacy and the Perils of Fake Data: Navigating Emerging Challenges

For the media industry, data privacy represents the greatest challenge. The true victor will be the one who masters the delicate balance between user service and data privacy.

Artificial intelligence has added immense value to the media industry's supply chain, but the flip side is the urgent need to prevent data misuse and safeguard user privacy from breaches.

During the 2020 Super Bowl, Google showcased a poignant ad for its smart voice assistant, Google Assistant. The commercial featured an 85-year-old man living alone, who uses the assistant to reminisce about cherished moments with his late wife. The ad artfully portrayed how, through the assistant, his memories came to life, making it feel as though his wife were still present and he were still young. As he shared his memories, Google Assistant smartly recorded his information and used algorithms to respond to his needs, blending nostalgia with cutting-edge technology.

While this ad tugged at the heartstrings of viewers, it also sparked concerns. As people interacted with Google Assistant, questions arose about whether their privacy was being compromised and if their emotions were being manipulated by AI. There's a spiraling paradox with artificial intelligence: the more detailed your personal information, the better AI can understand and cater to your needs, offering more convenient and personalized services. Yet, this requires individuals to divulge even more data.

In the media industry, where services are relatively lightweight, this paradox is particularly pronounced.

Balancing intelligent services with personal privacy is a challenge that every individual and company must carefully consider, finding the right measure as they navigate this delicate terrain.

Today, countries around the world are continuously rolling out and updating data privacy protection laws. In response, digital media giants are revising their privacy policies and improving the standards for collecting and safeguarding data to comply with these regulations.

Beyond concerns about data privacy, as scientists continue to push the boundaries of artificial intelligence, we must also learn to interpret data that isn't authentically human—or, in other words, data that isn't generated by real people.

Today's algorithms are generating "fake" data to fuel the training of other algorithms. Artificial intelligence can create millions of synthetic faces that belong to no one, redefining the concept of stolen identities. This fraudulent data has the potential to further distort social media and other parts of the internet. Deepfakes, powered by advanced AI and deep learning technologies, replace individuals in existing photos or videos with look-alikes, fabricating media content to depict events that never occurred. Such privacy infringements are now under close scrutiny and regulation from both governments and industry.

The term "Deepfake" originates from a Reddit user's handle, who in December 2017 used a deep learning AI model to superimpose celebrities' faces onto explicit videos. Deepfake technology enables AI to create or alter content so convincingly that it looks or sounds real, leading viewers to believe that what they are seeing or hearing is genuine.

Imagine the unsettling possibility that you might be unable to distinguish between genuine connections on your social media platform and fabricated profiles, or that the people you follow may not even exist. It's a chilling thought.

One thing is certain: in the future, without data, the AI of media companies is merely theoretical. However, if user data is leaked or exploited for illicit activities, companies could find themselves in deep trouble.

Finding the balance between personalized user services and privacy is a critical challenge. It involves safeguarding data privacy and security while achieving a win-win between smart technology and ethical standards. This is a pressing issue that global regulators and industry stakeholders must delve into deeply.

In the AI era, a media company's success in maintaining a close and interactive relationship with users hinges on two crucial factors: first, the precision of their algorithms and the robustness of their technology must ensure that users are eager to embrace their services. Second, the company must be characterized by integrity and trustworthiness, so users feel comfortable entrusting their personal data. Only by excelling in both areas can media companies continue to gather vast amounts of data, leverage AI algorithms to match content with users, and refine their business models to capture the market.

The success of media companies in the AI era depends on two key factors: in the short term, it's all about the precision of their algorithms and technological prowess. In the long term, however, it hinges on their integrity and trustworthiness.

SECTION 3: MINING THE FUTURE OF AUTOMOTIVE INDUSTRY—THE THREE KEY TECHNOLOGIES AND TWO MAJOR TRENDS IN TOMORROW'S CARS

When cars first rumbled along streets littered with horse manure, competing with horse-drawn carriages, they were dubbed "horseless carriages." Over the past century, this invention has reshaped human travel, lifestyle, commerce, and urban landscapes. Today, autonomous vehicles are poised to ignite a new revolution, much like the horseless carriage did over a hundred years ago.

From 2013 to 2016, I had the privilege of being involved in and witnessing PSA Peugeot Citroën's groundbreaking innovations in the connected car sector. I experienced firsthand the early waves of transformation in the automotive industry.

At that time, my team and I assisted Peugeot Citroën in developing groundbreaking new features for their "connected car" technology. We integrated vast amounts of data from various sources—cars, smartphones, traffic signals—and conducted real-time analysis. Thanks to this data, Peugeot Citroën vehicles became far more intelligent. For example, while driving, the cars could sense road conditions ahead and issue warnings; during traffic congestion, they could suggest alternative routes and provide updates to drivers through the network.

The connected technology significantly boosted user satisfaction with Peugeot Citroën's brand, allowing the company to bypass intermediaries and engage directly with customers. This direct interaction enabled Peugeot Citroën to better understand user needs and offer more personalized services.

In this project, these data assets were successfully monetized, becoming a crucial component of Peugeot Citroën's profits. Thanks to connected technology, Peugeot Citroën carved out a distinctive path in the fiercely competitive market—transforming into a mobile service provider that builds lifelong relationships with its customers.

Today, the global automotive industry is being reshaped by three transformative technologies: electrification, automation, and connectivity. Each company is strategically leveraging these three cards to their advantage, evolving toward two major trends: the rise of electric vehicles and the advent of autonomous driving.

In the near future, our driving habits could be revolutionized. Imagine summoning autonomous vehicles anytime and anywhere, eliminating the

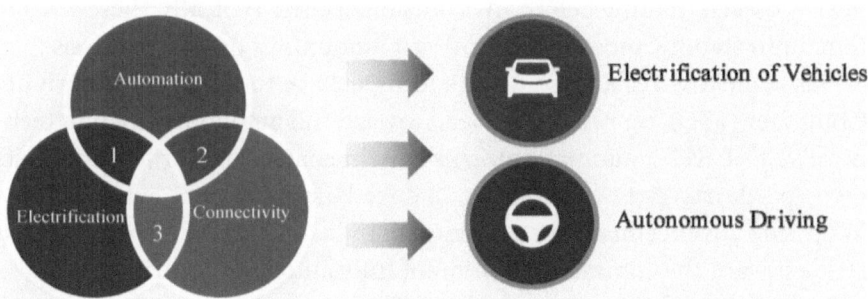

FIGURE 3.6   Three key technologies and two major trends shaping the future of cars.

hassles of hailing a cab, finding parking, or dealing with traffic jams. People might no longer need to own cars, embracing a new era of shared autonomous transportation. These changes will radically transform our lives, work, business models, and urban landscapes, propelling us into the wave of a smarter, more interconnected future.

The New Frontier in Automotive Innovation: Electrification, Automation, and Connectivity

Companies that have mastered the rhythm of technological and industry trends have emerged as the new elite in automotive manufacturing, challenging traditional carmakers with their innovative approaches.

Tesla's Secret Weapon

Tesla is now the world's most valuable automaker. As of July 2024, its market value has soared to a staggering $800 billion, eclipsing traditional giants like Ford, General Motors, BMW, and Daimler, and is approximately three times that of Toyota. Interestingly, in 2023, Toyota sold around 11.2 million vehicles, while Tesla sold only 1.8 million. So, where does this colossal valuation gap come from?

Many investors are captivated by Tesla's potential in autonomous driving, believing that Elon Musk is poised to be the first to seamlessly integrate electrification with automation and emerge victorious in the industry.

Starting in 2014, Tesla equipped its vehicles with 12 ultrasonic sensors around the bumpers and sides, integrating them with cameras, front radar, and an advanced braking system into a collision-avoidance "tech package." This system takes over control if the vehicle gets too close to nearby objects, halting before any collision occurs. Typically, these sensors remain in standby mode, gathering vast amounts of data for analysis.

Subsequently, Tesla upgraded its tech package to the Full Self-Driving Computer (FSD), representing a leap toward full autonomy (though technically, it's Level 2 automation). This system enables the car to manage its own speed, navigate within lanes, change lanes, and park automatically. With this advancement, the automotive industry has taken a significant stride toward the commercialization of fully autonomous driving.

In the eyes of the capital markets, Tesla is not just an automaker; it's also a software licensing powerhouse and an autonomous mobility provider. Its most valuable assets are the advanced AI algorithms that drive its innovations.

As Tesla continuously collects vast amounts of data to refine its algorithms and models, it prioritizes these large models for autonomous driving. This relentless cycle of data and iteration propels advancements at an astonishing pace, bringing forth innovations that surpass our wildest expectations.

Autonomous Driving: Imperfections Amid Perfection

Over a decade ago, autonomous driving was seen as nothing more than a fantastical notion, much like every emerging technology in its early days. The reality was rather awkward. In 2004, at a deserted Air Force base on the outskirts of Los Angeles, a dozen autonomous vehicles lined up, ready to tackle a 240-kilometer route across the Mojave Desert in California. This was the scene of the DARPA Grand Challenge, organized by the U.S. Department of Defense's Advanced Research Projects Agency.

The results of the competition were nothing short of dismal. Most of the vehicles met their Waterloo almost immediately, crashing and rolling over at the starting line in a chaotic spectacle. The top-performing robot car managed to cover a mere 11.9 kilometers. Despite the underwhelming outcome, the event drew together a passionate crowd of autonomous driving enthusiasts and students. These early adopters formed various communities and forums, laying the groundwork for future technological discussions and nurturing the first generation of talent in the field.

In the years that followed, the competition continued to be held, and gradually, hope for the practical application of autonomous driving technology began to emerge. By 2005, five vehicles successfully completed the course. By 2007, the participating cars were not only adept at avoiding obstacles but were also able to obey traffic laws, change lanes, park, and even execute safe and legal U-turns.

Doing the right thing often matters more than just doing things right. The relentless dedication of countless enthusiasts and the substantial capital investments from players large and small have transformed autonomous driving from a "potential possibility" into an "absolute possibility," and from "inevitable" to a reality that is now "successfully on the market."

By the end of 2018, Google's subsidiary Waymo launched its commercial autonomous vehicle service, named "Waymo One." As of February this year, the Waymo One fleet boasted around 700 vehicles. Morgan Stanley has valued Waymo's robotaxi business at a staggering $80 billion.

Traditional automakers are also sharpening their blades. In 2016, General Motors spent over $1 billion to acquire the robotaxi startup Cruise. By June 2022, California regulators approved Cruise's autonomous vehicles for paid operations, marking the state's first genuine driverless taxi service. Cruise's robotaxis now operate around the clock throughout San Francisco. General Motors forecasts that by 2030, the robotaxi business will generate annual revenues of $50 billion.

Undoubtedly, the surge of cutting-edge technology and the torrent of data are propelling humanity—those driven by a passion for innovation—toward the era of autonomous driving. In the coming decades, this technology promises to add trillions of dollars to the global economy, potentially slashing accident rates by over 80% and saving millions of lives.

In business terms, it will upend the traditional automotive industry, along with related sectors like fuel services and road trips, and it will radically transform or even render obsolete the profession of driving itself. In this ultimate gold rush that promises benefits for all, some will strike it rich, while others may face inevitable obsolescence.

According to ARK Invest's projections, the global market for humanoid robots represents a staggering $24 trillion opportunity, with about 50% of that potential concentrated in the manufacturing sector.

The next paradigm shift for humanity will come from the convergence of autonomous driving, robotics, and spatial computing, paving the way for pervasive automation. In the future, a leading automotive company could very well double as a dominant robotics manufacturer. This seamless integration will leverage expertise in artificial intelligence, chip technology, power systems, and supply chain management, suggesting that the future might see these domains merging into a unified powerhouse.

Among these elements, artificial intelligence stands out as particularly crucial, and this pivotal insight is already making waves across the industry.

In July 2023, when Elon Musk announced the launch of x.AI, a storm began brewing. x.AI, an ambitious new player in the AI arena with the lofty goal of "creating the world's most powerful AI," has surged forward in its first year, investing heavily in computing power and already making established AI giants sit up and take notice.

Tesla shareholders' unease has been steadily mounting, with growing concerns that Elon Musk might shift the core of his AI operations to x.AI, a standalone entity. If this happens, Tesla could lose its status as the central hub for its AI prowess, leading to a fundamental shift in its market position. Once celebrated as a shining jewel in the realm of smart electric vehicles, Tesla might become merely a massive data-driven machine. The question now is whether stripping away its role as a trailblazer in smart innovation could cause Tesla to lose its future-forward edge.

Striking Gold in the Age of Big Data

The convergence of big data with the automotive industry is reshaping the ecosystem of car manufacturing. Today, insurance firms, internet companies, and traditional tech giants are deeply embedded within the automotive landscape, giving rise to a multitude of new business models. The interconnectedness of data is not only expanding the industry's ecosystem but also spawning innovative revenue streams that were once unimaginable.

Big Data Revolutionizing Profit Models in the Automotive Industry

Both autonomous driving and connected vehicle technologies are transforming cars into mobile data machines. At their core, artificial intelligence and autonomous driving are both fundamentally driven by data. When a car becomes a gateway for data, it unlocks expansive new commercial opportunities.

Automotive data can be categorized into four dimensions: people, vehicle, road, and environment. *People* data encompasses consumer information, human biometrics, and human-machine interactions. *Vehicle* data includes details on vehicle manufacturing, automotive R&D, market data, and vehicle performance. *Road* data covers usage patterns, simulation data, and road conditions. Finally, *environmental* data includes weather conditions, real-time monitoring, nearby vehicle information, and hazard alerts.

Through a multitude of sensors, the car has evolved into an intelligent terminal that frequently interacts with users. It gathers data related to both the vehicle and its occupants. By merging and exchanging various types of related data, the car is able to analyze and leverage this information effectively.

Specifically, in terms of vehicle safety, features such as real-time emergency calls, instant information for rescue services, and road hazard warnings can be activated. This allows drivers to be informed and respond swiftly to potential dangers. For vehicle maintenance, by collecting data on the owner's driving habits and behaviors, remote diagnostics can be performed to monitor the car's condition in real time. This reduces the risk of breakdowns, enables predictive maintenance, and delivers personalized repair and service recommendations. When it comes to travel, data can be used to optimize routes and navigation, provide advance parking information, and reduce travel time. For convenience, services such as refueling, car washes, and even advertising and entertainment options can be offered, all aimed at creating a superior user experience.

Automobile development is notoriously expensive, but analyzing automotive data can significantly reduce these costs. From customer targeting and pricing strategies to design choices, core system parameters, and interior features, data analysis plays a pivotal role. It helps minimize trial-and-error costs, enhances the likelihood of success, and boosts development efficiency. Ultimately, this data-driven approach reduces R&D expenses across all dimensions of automotive design and production.

Beyond cost-cutting, data's role in driving innovation is even more pronounced.

Within the automotive industry, manufacturers hold a prominent position. Leveraging their existing advantages, they can establish interconnected big data platforms, break down data silos, and create a robust data ecosystem. This approach allows the entire automotive industry to benefit from data, driving sector-wide development. Infrastructure operators, such as toll roads, gas stations, and charging stations, can analyze automotive data to enhance services, explore more flexible pricing strategies, and monitor asset performance to reduce maintenance costs. Meanwhile, roadside assistance services can collect and process emergency calls in real time, optimize rescue vehicle deployment, and analyze accident and failure data to implement targeted prevention strategies.

At the beginning of this section, I shared an example where my team and I assisted Peugeot Citroën in developing their new "connected car" feature. This innovation revolutionized the traditional interaction between cars and users, turning data into a valuable asset. Building on this success, Peugeot Citroën established an open platform for other car brands to utilize. By leveraging this data, the company not only discovered new revenue streams but also expanded its commercial ecosystem.

According to a McKinsey report, by 2030, revenue from new car sales will account for about 54% of the total automotive industry income. The remaining market will be driven by revenues from car sharing, after-sales services, and data, with the surrounding automotive ecosystem experiencing rapid growth. Notably, by 2030, data generated by vehicles could create a market worth between $450 billion and $750 billion.

As the automotive data ecosystem continues to flourish, we can envision a future where users might not need to pay for the car itself. Instead, by signing data agreements with automakers, they could drive off with a vehicle at no cost. In this emerging landscape, all service providers within the automotive ecosystem would leverage insights from user data to offer a range of services—such as safety features, maintenance, customization, navigation, entertainment, and marketing—relying on these services to generate revenue. This shift could usher in a "passenger economy" that places the customer at its core.

Elevating Equity: A New Era for Auto Insurance

The benefits of integrating big data with the automotive industry extend far beyond just car manufacturers. The insurance sector, too, is tapping into automotive data to unlock new opportunities and reshape its business landscape.

Insurance companies can leverage the IoT-enabled smart devices installed in vehicles to track policyholders' driving behaviors. By analyzing driving habits, techniques, and mileage, insurers can craft personalized insurance policies tailored to individual usage patterns. This means offering discounted rates to safe drivers or those with low mileage. In essence, technology ushers in a new era of fairness—if you're a law-abiding driver with a clean record, you could pay significantly less for insurance while still enjoying the same coverage.

Take Metromile, an insurance company founded in 2001, as an example. Metromile introduced an insurance model tailored for drivers with lower mileage. They provide policyholders with a free wireless device that plugs into the vehicle's diagnostic port to track mileage. Unlike traditional insurers, Metromile focuses solely on tracking mileage rather than other driving factors such as braking incidents, speed, or sharp turns. This innovative approach allows drivers to benefit from insurance premiums that reflect their actual driving habits, offering a fresh perspective on fairness in auto insurance.

Metromile's insurance model is a blend of a "fixed premium" plus a "pay-per-mile" charge. This setup proves to be especially cost-effective for drivers who rack up fewer than 10,000 miles annually. If you're someone who doesn't drive frequently, Metromile's insurance could save you up to $400 compared to traditional policies. It's a smart solution for those who want their insurance costs to align more closely with their actual driving habits.

As a policyholder, wouldn't you find such a fair and personalized insurance plan more appealing? Looking ahead, as high-tech insurance models like this become more widespread, they will encourage every driver to pay closer attention to their driving habits and safety. This shift not only benefits individuals but also paves the way for a safer and more responsible driving culture.

Authenticity and Security: Navigating the Challenges Posed by Data

The revolution in the automotive industry, driven by big data applications and artificial intelligence technologies, has transformed its ecosystem in profound ways. Yet, as the industry accelerates along the path of "Automobiles + Data + AI," data security and driving safety issues remain critical concerns. As stakeholders rush forward, they must remain vigilant and ready to hit the brakes when necessary.

Traffic Data Deception: Why Seeing Isn't Always Believing

The impact of data on our travel safety versus our sense of direction remains to be seen. German artist Simon Weckert once conducted a clever prank on Google Maps. He borrowed 99 smartphones from friends and placed them all in a single small trailer. Then, pulling the trailer alone through a sparsely trafficked street, he created a fascinating experiment. Sure enough, this empty street showed up as congested on Google Maps, proving that, sometimes, data can be misleading.

Of course, there are many more complex techniques and methods for deceiving Google Maps or similar apps. However, Weckert's prank demonstrates that with a bit of ingenuity, even rudimentary tactics can disrupt the accuracy of big data in traffic management.

Imagine this: when users see a route highlighted in red on their map app, they're likely to alter their commute, inadvertently creating real congestion. If self-driving cars fall victim to this deception, passengers could find themselves even more passive in navigating the chaos.

As people increasingly harness the value of data and enjoy the conveniences it offers, we must also recognize that we might be slowly opening Pandora's box.

What might emerge from Pandora's box are hacker attacks, capable of stealing sensitive information or jeopardizing vehicle safety. Alarmingly, compared to other industries, the automotive sector's cybersecurity defenses are somewhat lagging.

McKinsey's "Safe Car" research, which began in 2015, reveals that while most automakers recognize cybersecurity as a critical issue, less than half have an effective cybersecurity team in place. Even among those with functioning departments, fewer than half are confident in their ability to tackle emerging threats.

If the firewall of a connected car is not robust enough, the consequences could be dire. On the lighter side, there's the risk of misuse of driving data, which could compromise user privacy. On the more serious end, there's the potential for safety issues with connected or autonomous vehicles, posing a direct threat to driving security.

In older automotive architectures, most critical systems are interconnected, creating a vulnerable web for attackers. They could potentially access the car's safety-critical systems, steal personal data, sabotage the infotainment and GPS navigation units, and disable the vehicle's alarm systems. Even more alarming is the risk to driver safety: if hackers manage to take control of steering and braking systems, they could pose a serious threat to the driver's well-being.

Once these malicious attacks become a reality, they won't just jeopardize user safety—they'll also deal a severe blow to the automotive manufacturers' brand reputations. At that point, discussions about advanced driver assistance systems (ADAS) and autonomous vehicles will likely fall on deaf ears.

So, as the automotive industry harnesses the power of data, it must also be ever-prepared to tackle the challenges that come with it.

Can Foreign Stones Sharpen Jade? The Enigma of Synthetic Data
Even artificial intelligence may face a day of "creative burnout." Research predicts that by 2026, training large language models like ChatGPT could exhaust the available textual data on the internet, leaving no fresh data for training. To keep AI well-fed with "nutrients," a new solution has emerged: "synthetic data"—algorithmically generated data designed to mimic real-world scenarios.

"Synthetic data" refers to computer-generated artificial data. In the automotive industry, synthetic data is rapidly becoming the key to overcoming data shortages. With safety and driving experience requiring extensive testing and optimization, synthetic data offers companies a highly efficient and cost-effective solution.

In the realm of developing autonomous driving technology, the cost of acquiring real-world driving data is astronomical, especially in hazardous scenarios like emergency braking or complex traffic situations. Synthetic data comes to the rescue by simulating a vast array of extreme and rare driving conditions, allowing autonomous systems to be tested in a virtual environment. This approach enables automotive companies to validate their self-driving algorithms more swiftly and safely. Companies like Waymo are already leveraging vast amounts of synthetic data to train their autonomous models, supplementing their real-world road tests.

Synthetic data also plays a crucial role in simulating diverse driving behaviors for the development of ADAS. Engineers can fine-tune how these systems respond to various driving modes, enhancing both their precision and reliability. In collision testing, synthetic data allows for the creation of myriad accident scenarios in a virtual environment, thereby boosting the safety of vehicle designs.

More and more tech giants are joining the quest to mine "foreign stones," driving the application of synthetic data to new depths. NVIDIA is a leading force in this arena, with its DRIVE Sim platform designed to generate highly realistic driving scenario data. This tool simulates a range of complex road conditions, climate variations, and traffic situations, helping automakers accelerate the development and testing of autonomous driving features.

According to a forecast by market research firm Gartner, by 2024, 60% of the data used for AI development and analysis will be synthetic. By 2030, synthetic data is expected to completely replace real data, becoming the primary source for AI models. As a burgeoning element in the data market, synthetic data is poised not only to create immense commercial value but also to address the data supply challenges faced by artificial intelligence and the digital economy.

While we remain optimistic about the future of the synthetic data industry, we must also acknowledge some pressing issues: first, the production and application processes for synthetic data are still lacking standardization; second, the challenge of assessing the quality of synthetic data remains unresolved.

In this era of rapid synthetic data advancement, could it be the true shortcut to our smart future? As research progresses, synthetic data is likely to become increasingly reliable for a variety of applications.

Autonomous Driving: Safety and Environmental Risks

For an autonomous vehicle to safely replace a human driver, it must be intimately familiar with every conceivable traffic scenario. This means that when faced with a cyclist, the self-driving car needs to not only recognize their presence but also understand their behavior and reactions. The complexity of real-world situations and the limitations of programming necessitate that autonomous vehicles have the ability to learn from experience and think independently. However, this machine learning comes with significant risks, sometimes even at the expense of human lives.

In March 2018, a Volvo XC90 operating in autonomous mode struck and killed a woman named Elaine Herzberg in Tempe, Arizona. Six seconds before the collision, the vehicle's sensors detected an object in its path but couldn't identify what it was. During those crucial six seconds, the safety driver received no braking alerts from the system.

This incident marked the world's first fatal pedestrian collision involving a self-driving vehicle on public roads, capturing global attention. In early 2019, U.S. judicial authorities ruled that the autonomous vehicle was operating normally and bore no criminal responsibility for the accident, while the pedestrian, who crossed the road unlawfully, was deemed at fault.

Although the case has been resolved, it has left all those involved in autonomous driving deep in thought. Are these safety drivers actually effective at ensuring safety? Perhaps humans are simply ill-suited to serve as mere backups for machines. The incident highlighted that when not in the driver's seat, human vigilance can significantly wane, particularly in the context of driving.

Ensuring safety remains a paramount challenge for autonomous driving, and the industry's current dilemma is that the ecosystem for self-driving technology is still incomplete.

If you're looking to own an autonomous vehicle, you'll need a knowledgeable salesperson to guide you through all the details of its use—yet such experts are still in short supply. Even if you manage to buy an autonomous car, you'll find that charging stations, parking facilities, and repair shops are not yet equipped to handle them. And let's not forget the lack of government regulations tailored to this emerging technology.

It's important to remember that the traditional automotive supply chain has been honed over a century of evolution and interaction. As a disruptor of conventional vehicles, autonomous driving must build an entirely new ecosystem to support its growth—an undertaking that is equally complex and fraught with challenges.

Perhaps, after a lifetime of effort, we may find that a perfect autonomous vehicle remains an elusive dream. Yet, this doesn't diminish the value of the advancements we gain from the evolution of autonomous driving technology.

When it comes to the future of automobiles, we shouldn't obsess over when perfection will be achieved. Instead, we should focus on where improvements are needed, how to advance further, and how to deliver an exceptional experience for users.

Of course, this belief holds true as we explore any cutting-edge technology.

SECTION 4: FORGING A NEW ERA IN FINANCE

For the financial industry, the internet has delivered a wealth of data assets, while mobile internet has introduced a plethora of application scenarios. Together, these data and contexts create the ideal conditions for the robust growth of artificial intelligence in the sector.

Global platform-based tech giants, leveraging their technological and data prowess, are making relentless strides in the financial sector, gaining momentum with each passing day.

Artificial intelligence is rapidly transforming traditional finance, making inroads into areas such as lending, insurance, asset management, accounting, personal finance, and regulatory compliance. Meanwhile, blockchain technology is starting to make its mark, shaking the very foundations of financial operations with innovations like digital currencies.

The convergence of "Artificial Intelligence and Blockchain" is ushering in revolutionary financial practices, giving rise to entirely new economic and financial theories.

Platform Giants Take Center Stage

Platform tech giants possess core capabilities in finance that set them apart from traditional institutions. Leveraging vast amounts of data, these companies are increasingly penetrating the financial sector with remarkable influence.

Over the past few decades, I've provided big data strategy consulting to numerous financial institutions and also served as an independent director for several banks. The financial sector has long been a pioneer in digital transformation and one of the early adopters of data value investment. However, when I saw platform tech giants starting to infiltrate the financial industry, I knew that the "catfish" had arrived.

Twenty years ago, financial executives could hardly have imagined that their future fiercest competitors would be the burgeoning platform tech giants.

At its core, human needs boil down to "clothing, food, shelter, transportation, and entertainment." Platform tech companies have expertly positioned themselves to cater to these fundamental needs, constantly aligning their services with the evolving scenarios of their customers' lives.

These platform tech companies emerged from various sectors. Google, Meta, and Tencent cater to global information needs, addressing search and social demands. Amazon and Alibaba focus on retail goods and services, while Uber excels at matching customers with precise transportation needs (time, route, vehicle) and driver supply. Today, we seamlessly use our phones or computers to socialize on Facebook or WeChat, explore the world via Google, shop on Amazon, and arrange travel through Uber.

Platform tech companies have recognized the immense value generated by this behavioral data.

Building on vast amounts of data and leveraging artificial intelligence, platform tech companies can craft high-quality financial products and services, precisely matching customers with what they need. Seizing this opportunity, these companies ventured into the financial sector starting in 2000. They began with simple financial information matching, progressed to secure online payment transactions, and have since expanded into data-driven lending and investment services, gradually encroaching on the territory of traditional financial institutions.

Platform tech companies have revolutionized payments by offering streamlined, cost-effective solutions for online transactions, cross-border payments, interbank transfers, and city-to-city payments. They have not only driven the de-cashification and digitization of currency but also seamlessly integrated these payment methods into everyday life and business operations.

When it comes to personalized investment management, machines can often outperform humans. AI-driven investment advisers leverage machine learning to provide tailored financial services for thousands of clients, aligning with their individual risk preferences. They can automatically adjust portfolios and implement smart profit-taking and loss-cutting strategies. Previously, personalized investment advice was largely restricted to a select few high-net-worth individuals. For ordinary clients, personalized financial guidance was limited by human resources and cost constraints.

In the realm of credit lending, by analyzing social behavior data, payment methods, transaction speeds, shopping frequency, and purchase details, companies can develop entirely new credit scoring models. This allows for personalized credit assessments and the creation of tailored credit loan profiles for applicants. This innovation in credit products not only significantly reduces service costs but also enhances the overall financial service experience for customers.

Leveraging data, platform tech companies can also innovate new financial service models. For instance, by analyzing shifts in social network sentiment, artificial intelligence can more acutely monitor investor mood swings, develop investment models, and assist in making informed investment decisions.

Unlike traditional finance, where the core competitive edge lies in regulatory licenses, platform tech companies' advantage in the financial sector is all about data. With billions of customers on their platforms, these companies continuously gather vast amounts of dynamic, real-time data through frequent interactions. By analyzing this data, they deliver more precise and efficient financial services, setting a new standard for the industry.

Beyond their vast data troves, platform tech companies also gain a significant edge in finance from network effects.

A vast customer base creates powerful network effects. In delivering products and services, this translates into a massive supply-and-demand market. Platform tech companies use machine learning and data analysis to match customers with services, while continuously iterating data to achieve economic optimization. This approach ensures both personalized service excellence and overall economic efficiency, balancing individual needs with broader market demands.

From an economic perspective, network effects drive deeper business innovation and higher-quality services. The synergy creates a feedback loop where customer demand data informs the customization of products and services. As these offerings are optimized, they in turn better satisfy customer needs, fostering a virtuous cycle of continuous improvement and business growth.

Data resources differ markedly from traditional material resources. While material resources are tangible and limited in supply, data resources are intangible and virtually limitless. Material resources are constrained by time and space in their distribution, whereas data can be transmitted repeatedly without such restrictions. Additionally, using material resources typically depletes them, while using data creates value, transforming and expanding its worth with each interaction.

In the traditional economy, the cost of producing products and services played a significant role in pricing. However, data operates on a different scale: its cost is virtually zero. Moreover, the value of the same data can vary drastically from one person to another. By leveraging data matching, companies can identify customers who are willing to pay for the insights and advantages that data provides.

In the data-driven future, personalized pricing is set to become the new norm. Currently, platform-based tech companies use data to tailor credit loan rates to individual customers, reflecting a shift toward more personalized financial services. As we advance further into the data era, the financial industry's business models are poised for dramatic transformation.

As 5G and IoT technologies mature, we are stepping into an era where everything becomes smart and interconnected. In this world, countless scenarios will seamlessly blend the digital and physical realms through the internet. The data generated from these connections will be captured by servers and ultimately flow into the data lakes of platform-based tech giants.

Wall Street's Foray into Large Models

Embracing threats is the only path to avoiding disruption. Clearly, Wall Street is as adept at this strategy as Silicon Valley.

Artificial intelligence is not just shaking up Silicon Valley; it's also making significant waves on Wall Street.

JPMorgan Chase, America's largest commercial bank, operates over 6,000 branches and employs a staggering 288,000 people. Serving 60 million households, it covers nearly every facet of the financial world.

In the first half of 2024, JPMorgan Chase CEO Jamie Dimon revealed that the bank has assembled a dedicated team of around 200 experts to delve into large language models, aiming to advance AI technology within financial services. Additionally, the bank has begun recruiting thousands of AI specialists and data scientists to explore the deployment of generative AI.

In May 2024, JPMorgan Chase unveiled IndexGPT, a groundbreaking service that harnesses artificial intelligence to offer tailored investment advice. Utilizing the advanced GPT-4 model, IndexGPT automates the creation of thematic indices, assembling baskets of stocks based on emerging investment themes and delivering innovative portfolio solutions to investors.

Currently, the leading firms on Wall Street are venturing into large models through two distinct approaches:

1) Developing Proprietary Large Models

This approach is the most challenging and resource-intensive, typically requiring a team of highly skilled researchers, top-tier training data, and substantial computational infrastructure. Building a proprietary model is akin to creating a bespoke solution tailored precisely to a company's needs. For instance, BloombergGPT, if successful, could revolutionize core areas like financial news, offering unparalleled service in those domains.

2) Fine-Tuning Existing Models

On the foundation of existing general-purpose large models, fine-tuning involves additional training with domain-specific data to refine the model. For instance, JPMorgan Chase's Robo-Fedwatchers model leverages this approach, while Morgan Stanley plans to launch a GPT-4 powered chatbot that integrates its investment strategies, market commentary, and analyst insights to serve thousands of wealth management advisers. This method is relatively cost-effective but still requires an experienced development team and often relies on proprietary data for model training.

This new generation of large models boasts significantly enhanced capabilities, proving highly effective in data analysis, content creation, and customer service. In the financial industry, these advanced models are predominantly applied to front-end functions like marketing and customer acquisition, as well as back-end operations such as risk management and investment research.

Leading financial institutions excel with large models due to their unparalleled access to high-quality data. These giants, equipped with vast customer bases and a plethora of transaction scenarios, generate enormous amounts of dynamic, real-time data. With a robust data foundation established from their early days of digital transformation, they leverage this high-quality proprietary data to enhance product design, credit underwriting, investment decisions, risk management, and distribution channels. This depth of data gives them a distinct advantage that technology platforms simply can't match.

However, it's important to recognize that compared to tech platforms, financial companies may have limitations in user numbers, data volume, and data dimensions. Looking ahead, they might seek partnerships with tech platforms to access a broader range of data and develop innovative financial services. For example, by analyzing sentiment trends on social networks like Facebook and X, artificial intelligence can more acutely monitor shifts in investor sentiment, creating investment models that aid in decision-making.

Wall Street, long the epicenter and leader of global finance, understands the game well when it comes to market shifts—embracing change proactively is the only way to stave off disruption and stay ahead.

A Decentralized Financial Revolution Unfolds

Blockchain set out to disrupt traditional financial institutions, but now, the revolutionaries are embracing their "enemy."

In the financial industry, information and data are paramount, and much of the trading can be conducted virtually. However, the industry's biggest concern is the potential for data fraud. Moreover, with the surge in financial innovation and increasingly complex product structures, many companies struggle to dissect the underlying assets of multi-layered financial products. The 2008 financial crisis, for example, was triggered by the collapse of a housing finance innovation—a wave of subprime mortgage defaults.

In this context, blockchain offers a game-changing solution with its features of immutability, traceability, and decentralized storage. By anchoring data to its underlying assets, blockchain ensures the integrity of information and provides a safeguard against losing direction amid financial innovation.

Blockchain, also known as a distributed ledger, functions like a meticulous ledger where every change requires an encrypted signature.

Once data is recorded, it is visible to all participants linked to the ledger—each network node—ensuring that the data remains immutable, traceable, and accurately documents every transaction within the blockchain network.

When Satoshi Nakamoto created Bitcoin and blockchain in 2008, his intention was to dismantle the long-standing centralization of the financial system and establish a decentralized, democratic financial market. In other words, blockchain was designed to revolutionize traditional financial institutions, yet now, those very institutions are embracing the technology once deemed their adversary.

Patrick Byrne, the former CEO of the internet retailer Overstock, has long criticized Wall Street's traditional financial institutions for a significant flaw: naked short selling. According to Byrne, this issue arises because clearing agencies have failed to properly oversee the stock clearing process, allowing various Wall Street entities to exploit loopholes and sell stocks they don't actually own.

The global financial market boasts a staggering size of around $101 trillion. At any given moment, approximately $1.7 trillion worth of equity pledge financing transactions take place. However, the control of this immense market rests in the hands of just a few major financial institutions. Until now, there has been no effective mechanism or technology to make these transactions more open and transparent.

In a quest for fair trading, Patrik Byrne bypassed traditional exchanges in 2016. Instead, he chose to list Overstock's stock on the blockchain—a bold move that earned the approval of the U.S. Securities and Exchange Commission.

Byrne's battle not only sounded an alarm for Wall Street's financial institutions but also made them realize that blockchain-based financial innovations are steadily gaining acceptance from mainstream regulatory bodies.

Soon, the Depository Trust & Clearing Corporation (DTCC), the body overseeing the U.S. stock clearing system, released a report advocating for the use of blockchain technology to enhance financial infrastructure. They called for industry collaboration to advance blockchain development, aiming to clear out entrenched inefficiencies and boost both transparency and efficiency in trading.

In 2018, the DTCC began experimenting with blockchain and similar technologies to enhance its infrastructure. They called on the entire financial industry to unite in advancing blockchain technology, aiming to tackle long-standing operational bottlenecks such as addressing the flaws of "naked short selling" and improving transparency and efficiency in trading.

If the DTCC adopts blockchain technology for its operations, it could revolutionize stock settlement, reducing the process from three days to real-time completion. Additionally, blockchain would enable every participant in the transaction to closely track and understand who held which stocks at any given moment throughout the entire trading cycle.

Leveraging blockchain technology in trading alone can save banks billions in regulatory capital. Before blockchain, regulators required banks to maintain substantial reserve funds for each transaction until it was fully settled, serving as a buffer against potential risks.

Today, the DTCC is not only embracing blockchain technology but also spearheading open-source software projects aimed at advancing blockchain applications in the commercial realm. With the backing of Wall Street and other influential financial institutions, the DTCC's adoption of blockchain is a clear signal that the rest of Wall Street is already feeling the stir of change. Traditional financial institutions are beginning to acknowledge the transformative power of blockchain technology, aiming to harness its potential as a development engine while securely anchoring their core operations.

In February 2019, JPMorgan Chase, which handles over $6 trillion in transfers daily, unveiled JPM Coin—a cryptocurrency designed to facilitate instant settlements between client payments.

JPM Coin is a stablecoin pegged to the U.S. dollar, designed to facilitate transfers on the blockchain through mechanisms akin to smart contracts. JPMorgan Chase plans to deploy this digital currency in areas like cross-border payments and bond issuance for large enterprises. This payment method promises higher efficiency and lower costs compared to traditional wire transfers.

In November 2019, the U.S. Securities and Exchange Commission (SEC) greenlit a groundbreaking transaction: using blockchain technology to settle trades of General Electric and AT&T stocks.

The Nasdaq Stock Exchange has announced its plans to harness blockchain technology to develop a system that monitors trades in private equity markets. This innovative approach could potentially extend to the public stock issuance market in the future.

The value that blockchain brings to the financial sector can be summarized in several key points:

1) In various financial transactions such as securities and credit deals, blockchain technology offers a suite of benefits: standardized rules for "verification, replication, and retention," immutable transaction records, and enhanced auditing capabilities. These features significantly boost financial transparency and reinforce the fundamental trust in financial systems.

2) Blockchain technology can accelerate contract review, securities issuance, and settlement processes, tackling inefficiencies in transaction back-office management. For example, it enables real-time settlement of stock trades, streamlining the entire transaction process.

3) The transparency inherent in blockchain technology reduces the regulatory demands and costs associated with trust. With its clear and open operational framework, the financial system stands to save billions of dollars annually in regulatory expenses.

4) Blockchain technology offers a powerful remedy for existing loopholes in the financial system. A striking example is the long-standing issue of "naked short selling" on Wall Street—a practice that has allowed unscrupulous traders and institutions to profit significantly by selling stocks they do not own. This has led to the deliberate undermining of market pricing mechanisms and the malicious shorting of companies. With blockchain's introduction, the game changes. The technology enables real-time tracking of participants' positions, automatically recording the time and quantity of stocks held during trades. This level of transparency makes the practice of naked short selling nearly impossible, as every transaction is meticulously documented and traceable.

When it comes to transforming the financial industry, blockchain technology arguably wields a more profound impact than artificial intelligence. While AI enhances efficiency and decision-making, blockchain lays the foundation for an entirely new trust mechanism—one that is fundamental to the essence and core of finance. By providing an immutable, transparent ledger, blockchain doesn't just disrupt; it rebuilds the very bedrock of financial trust and integrity.

The Future of Finance: How Far Can Digital Currency Go?

From Libra to Worldcoin, the horizons of digital currency extends far beyond this.

While traditional financial institutions and tech giants are racing to reshape the financial system with cutting-edge technology, it's clear that the latter has a distinct edge. If Meta's Libra coin is successfully launched and widely adopted, it could revolutionize the entire financial landscape—though the road ahead is long and fraught with challenges.

If blockchain becomes the fundamental infrastructure and rules of engagement for the financial industry, then in this new financial ecosystem built on the internet, digital currencies could very well replace traditional fiat money.

In other words, while traveling internationally, you could use Libra to exchange for local currencies at the prevailing exchange rates, or even convert it into gold. Alternatively, you could spend Libra directly, and thanks to its stability, it would retain its value over time, unaffected by central bank policies or new currency issuance.

With Facebook's user base representing roughly one-third of the global population, and its founding consortium including major payment firms, tech giants, trading platforms, venture capitalists, non-profits, and academic institutions, it's clear that widespread adoption of this digital currency—boasting features like liquidity, stability, and traceability—could usher in a seismic shift in the global financial landscape.

Even before this transformation took place, Meta found itself at odds with nations worldwide. Issuing and regulating legal tender is a fundamental sovereign right, and Meta's launch of Libra not only challenged traditional financial systems but also posed a direct threat to the monetary authority of countries around the globe.

As time progressed, the Libra project underwent significant revisions. Faced with intense regulatory scrutiny, Libra shifted from its initial vision of a global currency basket to a U.S. dollar-backed stablecoin, eventually rebranding as "Diem." Despite these numerous adjustments, the project's advancement remains influenced by a variety of factors.

While the dream of tech giants to dominate the global financial system through technology has been momentarily thwarted, it doesn't dampen the relentless evolution of big data, digital currencies, and blockchain.

These innovations continue to refine the trading structure and efficiency of the financial industry, offering a wealth of diverse financial services to the world.

In 2021, Tools for Humanity, a tech startup founded by OpenAI CEO Sam Altman and others, launched Worldcoin—a global cryptocurrency aiming to democratize financial access. The innovative system uses iris-scanning biometric technology for identity verification, seeking to ensure a one-time equitable distribution to every person. Despite facing significant privacy and regulatory challenges during its rollout, the project's core mission remains to drive global economic equality through fair distribution and financial empowerment.

Digital currencies, blockchain, and artificial intelligence are revolutionizing the global financial system. As we navigate this transformation, we will undoubtedly face setbacks, but we also stand on the brink of reshaping the financial industry into a more transparent and robust entity, unlocking greater value for humanity. Pioneers recognize that the digitalization of sovereign currencies will fundamentally alter the global monetary and financial landscape.

For projects like Libra or Worldcoin, the horizon of possibilities for digital currencies is boundless. The profound commercial transformation driven by the value of data is poised to deliver a seismic jolt to the financial industry—this is just the beginning.

CLOSING THOUGHTS

In this new era woven from data, "Artificial Intelligence +" is not merely a declaration of technological fusion; it represents a silent revolution that is subtly guiding the global industrial transformation. From the brainstorming hubs of Silicon Valley to the data-driven buzz of Wall Street, from the meticulously engineered assembly lines to the warmly intelligent homes, and from the spotlighted arenas of strength and beauty to the life-and-death battles under the surgical lights—AI's influence has permeated every corner of our lives.

When discussing transformation, we approach it with caution yet without fear of setbacks. It is essential not only to understand how "Artificial Intelligence +" is being innovatively applied across various industries but also to confront and address the series of challenges AI encounters in its deployment—such as data issues, regulatory hurdles, and ethical concerns. These challenges are common to all sectors and are critical for industry professionals to consider. They also represent the deeper forces that, once addressed, can empower us with confidence to face the next wave of change.

BIBLIOGRAPHY

Ambadipudi, Aditya; Heineke, Kersten; Kampshoff, Philipp; Shao, Emily (4 October 2017). *Gauging the Disruptive Power of Robo-Taxis in Autonomous Driving*. McKinsey & Company.

Bellan, Rebecca (3 June 2022). "Cruise Can Finally Charge for Driverless Robotaxi Rides in San Francisco". *TechCrunch*.

Billeaud, Jacques; Snow, Anita (28 July 2023). *The Backup Driver in the 1st Death by a Fully Autonomous Car Pleads Guilty to Endangerment*. Associated Press.

Brandon, John (16 February 2018). "Terrifying high-tech porn: Creepy 'deepfake' videos are on the rise". *Fox News*.

Cole, Samantha (24 January 2018). "We Are Truly Fucked: Everyone Is Making AI-Generated Fake Porn Now". *Vice*.

Constine, Josh (16 July 2014). "Metromile Launches Per-Mile Car Insurance That Could Save Californians 40%". *TechCrunch*.

Ewing, Jack (16 January 2024). "Musk Demands Bigger Stake in Tesla as Price for A.I. Work". *New York Times*.

"Facebook Unveils Libra Cryptocurrency, Sets Launch For 2020". NPR.org.

"Facebook-funded cryptocurrency Diem winds down". *BBC*. 01 February 2022. https://www.bbc.com/news/technology-60156682

Hooper, Joseph (June 2004). "From Darpa Grand Challenge 2004: DARPA's Debacle in the Desert". *Popular Science*.

IQVIA, IQVIA Reports Second Quarter Results 2024, *IQVIA Investor Relations*.

"JPMorgan unveils IndexGPT in next Wall Street bid to tap AI boom", *The Business Times*, 3 May 2024.

Kastrenakes, Jacob (1 December 2020). "Libra cryptocurrency project changes name to Diem to distance itself from Facebook". *The Verge*.

Loizos, Connie (8 March 2023). "Worldcoin, Co-founded by Sam Altman, Is Betting the Next Big Thing in AI Is Proving You Are Human". *TechCrunch*.

"QuintilesIMS is now IQVIA". Business Wire. 6 November 2017.

Tesla, Inc., "Annual Report Form 10-K 2023". *U.S. Securities and Exchange Commission (SEC) Filings*, 29 January 2024

UnitedHealth Group, UnitedHealth Group Reports Third Quarter Results 2024, *UnitedHealth Group Investor Relations*.

Walton, Marsha (6 May 2004). "Robots fail to complete Grand Challenge". *CNN*.

Wang, Xiaomei, "Personalized Viewer Experience Leveraging Cognitive Media Analytics At Scale", *2017 NAB Show*, New York.

Yang, Angela (15 February 2024). "OpenAI teases 'Sora,' its new text-to-video AI model". *NBC News*.

CHAPTER 4

Riding the AI Wave to Unlock New Business Potential

Artificial intelligence technology is like a fast-moving train propelling the future of global competition. Whether you believe it or not, the speed of AI development has already outpaced the incremental adaptation capabilities of businesses. It compels every industry to undergo a transformation, forcing individual companies to pivot in order to meet this new reality.

In the annals of business history, electrification and the internet have been the driving forces behind the rise of global industry giants. Over the past 20 years, several once-mighty corporations mistakenly perceived the internet as just another tool. They underestimated the profound evolution of business concepts, mindsets, and models that lay behind this technology. As a result, they found themselves caught off guard, missing out on invaluable opportunities—a timeless lesson echoing through the ages.

With the dawn of the big data era, platform-based tech companies like Google, Meta, and Uber harnessed their ecosystems to become natural data production engines, generating and accumulating vast amounts of information continuously. Their abundant capital allows them to iteratively enhance and expand the traffic of users interacting with their platforms, giving rise to a plethora of innovative cross-industry business models. As these factors converge, these platform giants have grown increasingly powerful, reshaping the landscape of commerce as we know it.

DOI: 10.1201/9781003510604-4

Amid the roaring waves of this technological revolution, some traditional tech companies show signs of fatigue, while others seize the opportunity to adapt swiftly. Leveraging their robust infrastructures, these agile players are reclaiming their positions at the forefront of the competitive landscape.

Oracle's navigation through the AI wave resembles a rollercoaster of business adventure. In 2023, as the stock price of this traditional tech giant plummeted, Oracle was widely seen as lagging behind competitors like Amazon AWS, Microsoft, and IBM, particularly in the realms of AI computing power and cloud infrastructure, appearing slow and reactive. Critics questioned whether this once-dominant player in the database market could rediscover its place in the era of AI.

However, Oracle did not stop there. By 2024, the company's performance rebounded impressively. The growth data for the first fiscal quarter of 2025, released in September 2024, acted like a shot of adrenaline for the market. Notably, its cloud infrastructure revenue (OCI) surged by 45%, exceeding Wall Street's expectations. Investors began to see Oracle as a major beneficiary in the scarce AI hardware landscape, with several North American brokerages predicting it would "lead the next wave of AI." They believe that through substantial investments in its cloud computing infrastructure, Oracle is steadily addressing its past shortcomings. Its strategic positioning in AI computing, particularly in high-performance computing and the optimization of AI model training, is poised to become a critical competitive advantage for the future.

In previous technological revolutions, the initial phase of new technologies primarily focused on improving and optimizing existing business models, effectively filling in the gaps. As these innovations became increasingly utilized, they entered a second phase of development, transforming into entirely new entities that dominated established markets. From this foundation, they spawned disruptive applications that reshaped industries and redefined possibilities.

The more revolutionary an emerging technology, the swifter the pace of disruptive innovation, leading to the accelerated downfall of traditional business giants. Correspondingly, innovative companies that seize these opportunities experience rapid growth, capitalizing on the shifts in the landscape and redefining their industries at an astonishing rate.

In the wake of AI's sweeping influence, entrepreneurs must reassess the value it brings and establish clear strategies for their businesses. They must also recognize that the vast majority of companies lack the resources of giants like Oracle, unable to make such extensive investments to lead the charge in the computing power arms race and seize the high ground in the AI wave. For these entrepreneurs, the next three to five years represent a critical window of opportunity—one that may only come once!

SECTION 1: DATA AT THE HEART OF AI-DRIVEN BUSINESS TRANSFORMATION

Artificial intelligence is now integrated into numerous everyday business scenarios, spreading at an astonishing pace. For every bold individual, the time to jump on the AI express train is now—without hesitation. The key to securing a good seat? Data.

It's clear that data holds fundamental value; in terms of economic growth, it has become a core production factor alongside capital, labor, land, and technology.

For businesses, the future scarcity of data deserves even greater attention than other resources. While capital, labor, land, and most technologies can be acquired through market transactions, data—an exclusive and long-term resource—cannot be built up in a short period.

Business leaders must recognize that every company will ultimately evolve into a data-driven organization. In the AI era, data is as vital an asset as brands were in the industrial age and users were in the internet age. Companies that prioritize and are driven by data are destined for longevity and success.

Winning through Expansive Reach and Profound Insight in the Data Arena

In the next decade, the changes brought by data will be nothing short of revolutionary. Companies will either ride the crest of this wave or face a dramatic collapse. The future of competition is fundamentally a competition for data, making it imperative for businesses to develop a robust data strategy without delay.

In the era of artificial intelligence, the competitiveness of algorithms and models is largely concentrated in the hands of a few platform companies. These giants, equipped with vast amounts of data, powerful computing capabilities, and substantial funding, continuously drive technological innovation and iteration.

Tech behemoths like Google, Meta, Microsoft, and Amazon control a wide array of data sources—not only user search behaviors, consumption patterns, and social interactions, but also sensor data from various devices and real-time monitoring information. Supported by cloud computing infrastructure, they can train complex AI models on a massive scale, applying them across diverse fields such as search engines, recommendation systems, natural language processing, and image recognition. For instance, Google's BERT and OpenAI's GPT series are industry-leading models built on enormous datasets and formidable computing power.

However, despite the significant advantages platform companies have in terms of data "breadth," foundational technologies, and the development of general models, industry-specific companies are not without opportunities. In fact, the "depth" of data held by industry companies becomes a powerful competitive asset. This depth refers to the specialized data accumulated over time within a specific field, often characterized by high relevance and uniqueness, which can significantly support model development for targeted applications. For example, companies in the healthcare sector possess rich medical imaging data and patient treatment records, which are crucial for developing precise medical AI models. Similarly, manufacturers have amassed extensive data on equipment performance and failure records, enabling the development of highly targeted industrial AI applications, such as predictive maintenance and automated quality control.

Taking the healthcare sector as an example, while platform companies like Google and Microsoft boast robust AI capabilities, such as Google's Med-PaLM for medical Q&A and diagnostic suggestions, they still rely on specialized data from industry companies for applications in vertical fields like pathology or genomics. The data in these areas is highly specialized and complex, making it challenging for platform companies to independently acquire and process. Here, the depth of data held by industry companies becomes particularly crucial.

In the past, artificial intelligence seemed elusive and somewhat science-fictional, a realm that most businesses could only dream of accessing. Today, however, the landscape has changed dramatically. AI is gradually becoming democratized, allowing companies to harness AI technologies as easily as they would access water or electricity.

For most businesses, algorithms and computing power will no longer serve as barriers. These capabilities will be provided by specialized infrastructure operators, enabling companies that possess data resources to easily tap into algorithm and computing services, facilitating the intelligent development of their industries.

Thus, industry companies should recognize that while platform companies hold advantages in AI infrastructure and general models, they can leverage their expertise and domain-specific data to develop uniquely competitive solutions in vertical markets. In the future AI competition, industry firms can collaborate with platform companies or independently develop specialized models, capitalizing on their strengths to achieve success in their niche markets. Consequently, the competition in the AI era will not solely be a battle among platform companies; rather, it will also encompass the complementary and collaborative development of industry firms alongside platforms across different arenas.

In the age of big data, opportunities are not confined to platform giants but belong to every brave innovator. It's essential to focus on top-level design—future businesses that do not undergo the transformation of "digitization to intelligentization" will struggle to compete in areas such as trend insight, operational efficiency, and customer experience.

American scholar Jeremy Rifkin predicts that in the next decade, the communication internet, energy internet of things, and logistics internet will collaboratively form an organic whole, continuously innovating the scheduling of energy, production, and distribution of goods or services, thereby revolutionizing production methods across industries and significantly enhancing economic efficiency. This will lead to the emergence of a "zero marginal cost society." Essentially, the phenomenon of "zero marginal cost" arises from the fact that the costs of data collection, storage, and analysis approach zero, while the potential returns are beyond imagination.

A technological tide driven by data will inevitably lead to disruptive innovations in products and services, fundamentally reshaping the landscape of business. In the face of this impending transformation, no company can afford to remain on the sidelines.

Transforming Data into Assets to Drive Value Creation

In the era of large-model AI, companies must harness data to fuel innovation. Before embarking on this data journey, business leaders need to understand how data generates commercial value.

Based on my past service experience and observations, companies can create value through three main approaches: extensively leveraging their own data, utilizing external transaction data, and offering data API services. Own data refers to the information generated by a company's own products and assets, allowing them to optimize and innovate their offerings. Transaction data involves merging data through financial acquisitions or leveraging industry advantages, as well as exchanging data via business collaborations. Companies can repurpose this transactional data to create new products and services. Data APIs, on the other hand, represent business capabilities derived from data analysis, provided in an API format (often as a cloud service) for other businesses to utilize, thereby maximizing the value of enterprise data while uncovering new product and service models, as well as fresh business opportunities.

FIGURE 4.1   Three key strategies for transforming data into valuable assets.

Innovation Through Digitization of Products and Assets

The innovation potential of a company's own data is vast, often leading to a network effect that makes it the preferred choice for value creation. One significant method of innovating with proprietary data is enhancing the data generation capabilities of existing products to foster innovation. In today's world, characterized by advanced technologies such as sensors, wireless communication, and big data, companies can transform traditional equipment and products to capture and process dynamic data from their operations and environments. Analyzing this data enables firms to optimize their operations while also creating new products and service models.

This trend has been evident in the realm of large industrial equipment for years. Around 2000, Rolls-Royce, the world's second-largest power system manufacturer, harnessed sensors, IoT, and data management technologies to identify potential issues in aircraft engines at early stages through data insights, optimizing their maintenance schedules and improving engine designs. At that time, a staggering 65% of operational costs for airlines were directly or indirectly tied to engines. Rolls-Royce's data-driven innovations led to significant cost savings for airlines.

Furthermore, Rolls-Royce introduced the bold concept of engine leasing, charging airlines based on flight hours—a "pay-per-hour" model. This service quickly gained traction, prompting airlines to shift their service models and presenting Rolls-Royce with enormous market opportunities, paving the way for the dawn of Industry 4.0.

Similar business innovations can extend to areas like large medical devices, engineering machinery, and industrial tools. By connecting hardware with technologies like sensors, real-time data is generated and processed swiftly through cloud-based IT systems. This enables timely service responses and allows companies to shift their business models from selling hardware to offering services, opening up opportunities for third-party applications and new revenue streams.

In recent years, this data innovation has also reached consumer goods, with the automotive sector being a prime example. By installing electronic devices in cars to record and transmit driving data, insurance companies can assess safety levels and offer personalized insurance pricing based on driving behavior.

Even low-value consumables like running shoes are starting to create new value through data. In 2020, adidas launched the adidas GMR insole in collaboration with EA SPORTS FIFA Mobile and Google Jacquard. This innovative insole, equipped with a Google Jacquard chip, tracks users' athletic performance, such as shot power, distance, and speed, and connects this data to the FIFA Mobile game, impacting users' virtual gameplay based on their real-world performance. This fusion of the physical and virtual realms offers soccer enthusiasts a fresh interactive experience.

More businesses are now exploring ways to leverage product data to expand commercial opportunities. A bottle of water or a bag of chips could be equipped with micro-sensors to track its journey through the supply chain. This not only facilitates the collection of valuable consumer data but also enhances product recycling efforts.

As companies innovate with product data, they must consider which data points matter to customers, which dimensions to preserve, and how to derive insights that deliver value to businesses, customers, and partners.

Another significant avenue for proprietary data innovation is the digitization of physical assets. This involves transforming visible physical items into digital assets. A relatable example is how large museums are building online communities, utilizing websites and social media to create digital user assets while designing online exhibitions that incur only a fraction of the costs associated with traditional exhibitions. Visitors can easily browse collections online and even engage with artists, fundamentally reshaping museum operations, business models, and cost structures.

In the broader manufacturing sector, from simple designs in clothing and furniture to complex designs in automobiles and aircraft, the application of digital technology is pervasive. Digital techniques are converting handcrafted models into digital designs, creating data assets. This digitization has revolutionized operational methods across numerous industries. In healthcare, for instance, surgeons use digital models of the human body to enhance the precision of minimally invasive surgeries, while digitized health records enable doctors to offer tailored treatment plans.

Currently, two technologies are accelerating the commercialization of digital assets: 3D printing and AR/VR. 3D printing dramatically reduces the costs of copying and transmitting digital assets, allowing for affordable physical manifestations even in non-mass production scenarios. For certain manufacturing sectors, the distributed, customized, and small-batch nature of 3D printing threatens to upend traditional mass-production models.

Moreover, AR/VR technologies facilitate remote maintenance of large equipment and enhance online experiences, making interactions more engaging and immersive. For example, real estate companies can digitize properties, allowing potential buyers to view floor plans, photos, construction details, and neighborhood information online. With VR, buyers can explore 360-degree views of homes, streamlining initial assessments and enabling online communication with agents, thereby improving transaction efficiency across the industry.

The innovation of digitizing physical assets is a gradual process that requires companies to build their digital assets securely and thoughtfully. Throughout this journey, businesses should contemplate which physical assets can be digitized, how to leverage their digital characteristics to enhance product value and optimize service processes, and how to establish smooth online communication channels with customers.

As asset digitization progresses, the competitive advantages among businesses will shift, potentially unveiling new opportunities.

Digitization not only reduces the mobility costs of physical assets and personnel but also diminishes the significance of offline networks. In real estate, for instance, the traditional model required buyers to view properties in person. With VR, online tours can facilitate initial screenings, shifting industry competition from physical proximity to expertise in service, data, and digitalization.

In retail, while traditional stores prioritize location, the focus for online retail becomes how to create seamless communication mechanisms with customers. Meeting and anticipating customer needs will be even more critical in the digital landscape, marking a core aspect of future data-driven competition.

Innovation Through Transactional Data

Transactional data can be merged through financial means or by leveraging industry advantages, as well as through data exchanges between companies. With the continuous improvement of integrated IT infrastructures across various industries, large-scale cross-industry and cross-company information integration is becoming increasingly feasible. For leading firms, merging data within or across sectors is a vital way to uncover new business insights.

For instance, IBM collaborated with New York City to develop a sensor network for residential environments, monitoring data such as temperature, carbon dioxide levels, and water usage. By analyzing cooking patterns, the system could determine if elderly residents living alone were safe, promptly notifying municipal services if necessary. This public welfare project connects social services, health, and property maintenance through a shared IT system, achieving unified responses and reducing emergency care costs by 30%, all while supporting aging in place.

In innovations involving multiple systems like public utilities, urban transportation, and social services, the cross-sector merging of data is crucial. Take urban transportation as an example: to achieve intelligent scheduling and operations, diverse data from vehicles, roads, and pedestrians must be collected and mapped in real time between physical and digital spaces (essentially creating a digital twin of the city). This requires extensive data integration across industries and systems, enabling AI models to function effectively within the system.

Within the commercial ecosystem, merging data along the supply chain can generate new business value. In the automotive industry, the cold-rolled steel used for manufacturing car bodies requires cooling water, and the temperature of this water affects the quality of the steel. Therefore, factories must regularly calibrate water temperatures. Accurate data on water temperature can enhance factory efficiency and product quality. Water suppliers can sell this data as a service to automotive manufacturers, integrating water temperature data into the production process.

The data obtained from such mergers not only optimizes existing products and services but also fosters unexpected innovations. In ecosystems dominated by e-commerce giants, these companies merge relevant data from the supply chain and provide it to external financial institutions, helping suppliers secure better, more tailored financial services and creating new data service products.

However, while merging data, company leaders must remain clear about their intentions: they should aim for the best input-output ratio while building a robust technical platform that supports diverse data integration, governance, and analysis capabilities. This ultimately facilitates cross-industry data fusion, enhances data value density, and realizes the full potential of the data.

When companies engage in data trading within an equitable, collaborative environment, all parties can benefit from enriched data combinations tailored to their needs. For example, a telecommunications operator collaborating with a satellite navigation provider can exchange data to identify which customers are driving, their locations, and speeds. By purchasing this information, the telecom provider can offer navigation value-added services, helping customers avoid traffic congestion, while the navigation company reaps commercial benefits.

In the online lending industry, firms must legally exchange customer identity data, communication data, social data, and e-commerce transaction data to extract relevant lending factors for personalized risk pricing. This results in innovative lending products that help prevent customers from over-borrowing, creating a competitive differentiation from traditional lending options.

However, data trading is not without its challenges; achieving successful data exchanges requires a willingness to innovate, adept negotiation skills, and a foundation for mutually beneficial cooperation. Before engaging in data trading, companies should assess whether their data holds value for internal stakeholders, current customers, or potential clients, as well as for other industries. This thoughtful consideration can lead to more fruitful data exchanges and greater value realization.

During the data trading process, companies need to establish unified data standards, persuade stakeholders to open up their data, determine the types of data involved, and possess the capability to combine different datasets for analysis, ultimately assembling new, marketable products.

In the broader context of business development, the digitalization of enterprises has gained considerable attention over the past decade. However, the pathways for data trading across various industries remain underdeveloped, and current trading models are still in their infancy. For industry pioneers, the focus should be on establishing comprehensive data classification, pricing, security, and privacy standards for data transactions to foster consensus around data trading.

These standards will streamline industry data exchanges, enhancing efficiency and commercial value. Additionally, cross-industry data trading necessitates the establishment of common standards, often developed collaboratively by inter-industry data associations, government bodies, and major technology companies.

Taking the meteorological industry as an example, weather data is valuable across sectors such as agriculture, insurance, and automotive; however, the lack of a unified standard for weather models has hindered actionable weather data trading and applications. To address this, the UK Met Office, IBM, Imperial College London's Business School, and the Grantham Institute for Climate Change have collectively established a global trading platform for detailed weather data, developing standards for weather data trading, application of data products, and meteorological risk management to overcome these challenges.

Innovation Through Data APIs

Data API innovation refers to transforming data into products and services that can be accessed by others (such as companies) via APIs. This process allows businesses to expand their external reach, fostering open collaborative innovation and enabling more efficient customer engagement while uncovering new revenue streams. Today, APIs serve as a nimble "business-as-a-service" model, similar to how cloud computing revolutionized IT delivery, fundamentally altering the landscape of data services.

For instance, after automating its travel booking and expense reimbursement processes, IBM achieved a remarkable 60% to 75% reduction in management costs. This automation also ensured compliance with travel reimbursement policies, leading to a 4% overall decrease in travel expenditures. Inspired by this success, IBM transformed its travel reimbursement system into a SaaS product for clients, not only generating SaaS fees but also enhancing the accuracy of internal audits. Following this, IBM opened up various other services, including its accounts receivable and daily expense systems.

In this journey, companies must focus on how to collect, manage, and analyze data to develop potential data products. They should evaluate whether they possess unique capabilities that others value and whether those capabilities can be digitized for broader applicability. The first step is introspection—companies must leverage their distinct strengths.

When innovating data products, a customer-centric approach is crucial. By continuously exploring customer value, businesses can drive innovation in processes, automate workflows, and harness data intelligence to spark even more commercial breakthroughs.

Retailers, for example, can create online product catalogs that allow customers to place orders and customize product parameters. Sales teams can communicate and review orders online, while procurement departments automatically prepare raw materials based on disaggregated order data. Moreover, integrating suppliers into the retail system enables dynamic inventory management based on real-time purchasing needs. This streamlined process enhances efficiency from design and customer communication to procurement and production, significantly improving inventory turnover. As more customers and suppliers join the platform, it can evolve into a highly efficient trading hub with the potential for disruptive innovation.

As companies develop their data capabilities, they can adopt a phased approach to openness: starting with internal departments, then extending to business partners, and finally to the broader industry, public, and application developers. Throughout this process, firms can validate and optimize product value, ensuring a steady progression.

In practice, companies often mix and match various data innovation models to create comprehensive solutions. They typically require a diverse set of data to effectively develop data-driven products and services. The general process involves leveraging both proprietary and external data to gain insights, transforming these insights into serviceable data products, and distributing them conveniently through cloud services. This foundation allows businesses to discover new commercial value and seize additional market opportunities.

Data innovation should be approached pragmatically; starting with relatively simple scenarios can pave the way for expansion into more complex and diverse environments. For example, smart meters initially enabled automatic pricing adjustments, meter readings, billing, and repairs for power companies, improving operational efficiency and reducing costs. Over time, these companies recognized the opportunity to gather customer energy usage patterns and develop data products for energy producers and entertainment companies, creating a comprehensive service platform that spans self-generation systems to entertainment services.

As companies pursue data innovation, CEOs and executives must deeply consider how to align technology with business objectives, driving breakthroughs in commercial value. They should also leverage technologies like IT, cloud computing, the Internet of Things, blockchain, and edge computing effectively.

Historically, IT technologies have significantly contributed to automating processes and reducing management costs, but they are now set to play an even greater role in commercial value innovation. Cloud computing, IoT, blockchain, and edge computing facilitate digital transformation, enabling the collection and storage of data that meets big data processing demands. These technologies enhance user data privacy protection and improve data processing efficiency, making data acquisition easy, timely, and secure. Furthermore, companies can establish a complete data closed loop on this foundation, driving data-driven commercial innovations.

By referencing these innovative ideas around data value, businesses can chart their own paths in data innovation and embark on strategic data initiatives.

Data Annotation: The Value Bridge from Raw Data to Models

When discussing the formulation of a data strategy and the activation of data value, we must emphasize the critical importance of data annotation.

In the early days, the ImageNet project, led by Fei-Fei Li, catalyzed the large-scale annotation of datasets, propelling the explosive growth of deep learning technologies. As artificial intelligence continues to advance, the scope and complexity of data annotation have expanded dramatically. This is particularly evident in the development of industry-specific large models, where the quality of annotations increasingly dictates the effectiveness of the models.

With the maturation of large model technology, AI is gradually transitioning from general applications to specialized scenarios across various industries. For AI to truly understand and apply domain-specific knowledge, simple labels or annotations are no longer sufficient; they must be complemented by expert insights to help AI "grasp" the data. At the heart of this process lies data annotation, which connects vast amounts of data with artificial intelligence algorithms, laying the groundwork for effective model training.

Data Annotation in Industry-Specific Large Models

In constructing industry-specific large models, data annotation is an indispensable step. AI models in many sectors now rely not just on generic data but require the integration of deep industry knowledge. This makes modern annotation tasks significantly different from the past. Unlike traditional image classification or speech recognition, the annotation work for contemporary large models demands a high level of expertise and industry background.

Take, for example, the AI model for pathological diagnosis developed by my company, PathoAI. This requires precise annotation of digital pathology images, which are rich in detail. It's not merely about classifying these images; it involves marking complex pathological features. Only through expert annotation can we provide the model with valuable learning material.

This process typically consists of three key steps:

1. **Data Standardization: Collaboration between Medical and AI Experts**. To ensure high standards and consistency in pathological data, every stage of data collection must adhere to detailed Standard Operating Procedures (SOPs). From sample selection to slide scanning and quality control, the entire process involves collaboration between experts in pathology and AI to ensure data integrity. After data collection, technicians must also anonymize and clean the data to safeguard privacy and ensure traceability.

2. **Expert Annotation: Precision Meets Professionalism**. The data annotation process must be executed meticulously according to established protocols. Annotation of pathological data is often a collaborative effort involving pathologists of varying experience levels. Junior pathologists handle initial annotations, while senior pathologists

review and optimize these annotations, ensuring accuracy and consistency. This collaborative approach allows the annotated data to reflect the professional judgment of pathology experts, helping the AI model better understand complex pathological data.

3. **Three-Tier Review: Ensuring Accuracy through Layers of Scrutiny**. The accuracy of data annotation is critical for model training, which is why we typically implement a multi-layer review mechanism. During the internal review phase, senior pathology experts reassess the annotated data; external audits are conducted by specialists from top-tier hospitals nationwide to uphold even higher quality standards. If any disputes arise during the review, arbitration experts make the final determination, ensuring the authority and consistency of the data.

Through this rigorous process, data annotation transforms raw information into a powerful resource, enabling AI to achieve new heights of understanding and application in specialized fields.

Establishing
Data SOPs

Industry Expert
Annotation

Three-Tier
Review

FIGURE 4.2   Key steps of data annotation in the pathology industry large models.

Seeing Data Is Not Enough; Understanding Data Is Key

In a recent interview on No Priors, Scale AI CEO Alexandr Wang eloquently articulated the significance of industry data annotation. "Creating an exceptional AI model relies heavily on the critical involvement of domain experts, such as doctors and lawyers. These top talents provide unique insights for generating specialized data, and their contributions will profoundly impact the future of technology. The quality of data infused into algorithms reflects the wisdom and influence of these experts. The precision of data has a far-reaching and limitless effect on AI systems. Even slight improvements to a model can affect all its future applications, creating a massive ripple effect. This ongoing optimization not only drives technological advancement but also continually expands the possibilities of AI."

As artificial intelligence becomes more deeply embedded in various industries, the importance of data annotation will only grow. First and foremost, data annotation directly determines the accuracy of AI models. High-quality annotated data significantly enhances a model's generalization ability, allowing it to accurately tackle complex real-world problems. Furthermore, the trend toward specialized annotation will propel the customized development of AI applications. In the future, industry-specific AI will not merely be a simple optimization of generic models; instead, it will be tailored solutions crafted for specific industry use cases. Behind this customization lies the collaborative effort of numerous domain experts engaged in data annotation.

The value of data annotation extends beyond helping models "see" data; it enables them to "understand" data, and eventually, in the future, to engage in "reasoning" and "decision-making."

Moreover, the continuous advancement of automated annotation technologies offers even more possibilities for AI model development. While automated tools can efficiently handle vast amounts of foundational data, the combination of manual and automated processes remains essential for high-end industry applications. Automated tools excel at managing simple annotation tasks, but complex annotations still require the intervention of domain experts to ensure accuracy and authority.

SECTION 2: CRAFTING YOUR DATA STRATEGY

The journey into artificial intelligence is exhilarating, and establishing a practical data strategy is the bedrock of success for any company striving to embrace AI.

What is the core strategy for corporate artificial intelligence?

The answer is crystal clear: artificial intelligence is the defining trend for the future of businesses, and the competition in AI ultimately boils down to competition in data. At the heart of developing AI lies the necessity to establish a robust data strategy. Investing resources in data competition and seizing strategic advantages are crucial for paving the way to future success. Discussions of other conventional challenges are merely tactical considerations in this broader context.

The Key to a Corporate Data Strategy: Governance

From a corporate perspective, a data strategy serves as the cornerstone for positioning the business in a competitive landscape, ultimately driving market success and growth. Companies must thoughtfully develop a series of data initiatives, employing innovative thinking to transform the current state and achieve their growth vision.

From the standpoint of data, a data strategy aims to enhance the ways in which data is acquired, stored, managed, shared, and utilized. It ensures that all data resources are easily accessible, usable, sharable, and fluid within the organization.

So, how should a company go about crafting its data strategy?

Before devising a data strategy, every business must clarify its operational vision and overall strategy. The data strategy must align and complement the business strategy, continuously providing value to fulfill the company's goals. Once the business vision and strategy are clear, organizations should conduct an inventory of their data assets, implement data governance, and ultimately transform into a data-centric organization that drives innovation and value creation through data.

Moreover, effective organizational processes, talent reserves, and corporate culture are vital in advancing the data strategy.

Before embarking on data governance, it's essential to inventory the company's data assets and map out its data resources.

Typically, companies possess a variety of data types. Digital systems like CRM (Customer Relationship Management), ERP (Enterprise Resource Planning), financial systems, and OA (Office Automation) often hold various data related to customers, supply chains, employees, assets, operational processes, finance, and administration.

Different industries possess unique sets of data. For instance, the finance sector has extensive credit and risk data, while retail gathers significant consumer behavior, product sales, and location data.

Company data forms an integrated system; while financial data is usually stored within financial systems, it can also be extracted from sales, procurement, and administrative data to yield daily operational figures.

Technically, data is recorded and stored in various ways. Databases typically hold structured data, while file systems contain unstructured data. Currently, a company's data often resides in disparate IT systems, which may employ different architectures and languages provided by various IT service vendors. This complexity makes data governance challenging and time-consuming. In my experience with multiple global projects, an average of 60% to 80% of the workload in a big data analytics project is dedicated to data collection and processing. Once data governance is completed, analysis and insights tend to progress more rapidly.

For example, one financial institution collects data from over 20 systems daily, resulting in more than 20,000 tables and over 500,000 fields. The disorganization of data poses a significant challenge for the company in identifying and leveraging these valuable assets.

In my past experience with big data governance projects, I've frequently encountered such data dilemmas. Companies often struggle to grasp the full scope of their data assets, let alone to assess their value or monetize them. The business front lines demand data services that can be productized, while data analytics teams often operate in a vacuum, disconnected from real business needs.

Thus, after understanding the landscape of a company's data resources, it becomes essential to develop a robust data governance plan. The crux of the entire data strategy hinges on effective data governance. When data governance succeeds, the probability of the company's data strategy achieving success increases significantly.

Implementing Data Governance

When it comes to implementing data governance, there are four distinct levels to consider. The first level involves contemplating the data strategy from the perspective of business strategy. Building upon this foundation, the second level focuses on establishing clear data strategies and security principles. The third level delves into the creation of specific governance principles, obligations, and methodologies. Finally, the fourth

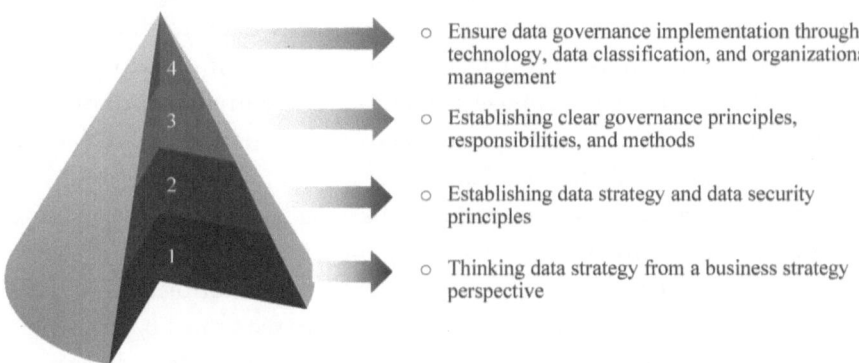

FIGURE 4.3   The four levels of corporate data governance.

level addresses the practical aspects of data governance implementation, encompassing technology, data classification, and organizational management.

Data strategy must align seamlessly with business strategy, determining which areas to prioritize and how to shape further data initiatives.

Externally, as business needs evolve, company leadership must dynamically adjust their data strategies in response to shifts in the competitive landscape and overarching corporate goals. The business demands tied to data strategy often encompass products, operations, and process improvements. For instance, a data strategy related to products must facilitate the swift identification and integration of new data sources, ultimately enhancing the user experience. Meanwhile, data strategies aimed at operations and process improvements focus on internal efficiency, cost reduction, and quality enhancement.

Just as a business strategy is customer-centric, so too must a data strategy be. For example, when a customer requests the delivery of a data API product, their underlying need extends beyond simply having a product; they seek the ability to conveniently access data from anywhere.

Given the vast and complex nature of enterprise data, attempting to analyze all data at once is impractical. Therefore, data governance must be targeted, focusing on creating value for the organization. It's essential for companies to recognize that the goal of data governance is to support decision-making for products, services, business judgments, tools, and methodologies. By maintaining a sharp focus on business needs, companies can effectively channel their data governance efforts toward the right people and processes.

For any new business set to launch, companies should establish a data governance framework in advance. This includes choosing the types of business data to retain—such as frontline sales data versus back-end human resources data—and determining the kinds of data to preserve, whether time-series data, cross-sectional data, structured data, or unstructured data. Selecting the appropriate data storage method will streamline data analysis and business insights.

Data governance must adhere to regulations governing data management and usage while ensuring security principles are upheld. Different types of data require varying levels of security, necessitating distinct security permissions. For instance, personal sensitive data must be encrypted, accessible only to employees with legitimate business needs and appropriate access rights, allowing them to copy data to portable storage devices.

Data governance represents a powerful combination of technology and enterprise management. On the technical side, it is vital to establish rules for data collection, management, distribution, and processing, while selecting appropriate processing technologies for different data types. Additionally, clear responsibilities must be defined during the data governance process. Once data governance technologies mature, they can become a core competitive advantage for the enterprise.

Conversely, the complexities of business operations and organizational processes require that the demands of data governance be embedded into the roles, processes, and technical requirements of the organization, ensuring a smooth implementation of governance practices. Furthermore, categorizing data during the governance process can enhance efficiency and quality. Different datasets represent various dimensions of business characteristics, enabling analysis of diverse business needs and yielding valuable insights.

Data classification provides a clear directory of data, making it easier for employees to find what they need. Each dataset contains a manageable amount of information, facilitating understanding and learning, thereby accelerating data governance efficiency. During data classification, organizations can also improve IT systems and enterprise processes, aiding in the establishment of effective data governance mechanisms. With a stable data architecture, new datasets can be seamlessly integrated based on existing classifications.

Data governance is a gradual process. Organizations must continually refine their data maturity to realize business value, adapting to the ever-increasing data demands while balancing stakeholder interests to achieve a virtuous cycle of data assets.

Consider a common scenario: the team implementing data governance in an organization often differs from the teams reaping the benefits of that governance. Conflicts over resources and interests frequently arise during the governance process, impacting the achievement of data governance goals. In the initial phases, only mandatory regulations can ensure an asymmetric distribution of costs and benefits within the organization. As data governance matures, however, it's crucial to restore a balance between costs and benefits, allowing investments in governance to yield returns through enhanced operational efficiency and product sales.

Ultimately, once data governance is fully realized, the organization transforms into a data-centric entity. This transformation alters the development and operational methodologies of IT systems, shifts the focus of the organization from process-centric to data-centric, and assigns each employee a data identity, granting them access to relevant data to foster ongoing data-driven value innovation.

The Data Maturity of Enterprises

At this stage, the organization has completed the journey of assessing data assets, establishing data governance, and transitioning to a data-centric model. In practice, each enterprise is unique, and its level of data maturity can be assessed through specific maturity levels of data governance. This evaluation helps to accurately guide the construction of a robust data governance framework, ultimately leading the organization to become truly data-driven.

Generally speaking, the data maturity of enterprises can be classified into five distinct levels.

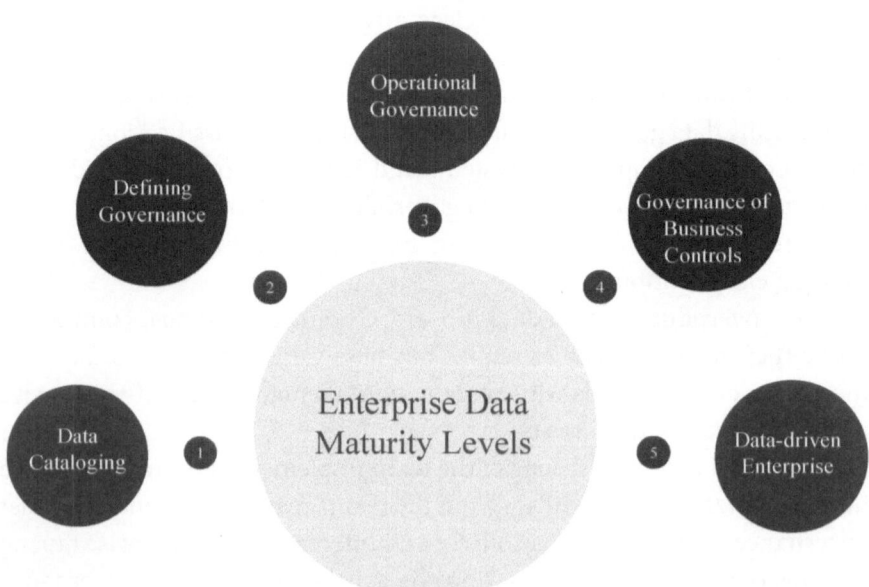

FIGURE 4.4   Enterprise data maturity levels.

- **Level One: Data Cataloging**

  The first level is data cataloging. Cataloging involves creating a comprehensive list or inventory of all data storage areas and sources within a business, along with establishing metadata. Metadata, essentially data about data, can describe various attributes such as storage locations, historical data, resource discovery, and file records. With a robust data catalog in place, organizations can quickly identify what data they possess and where it resides.

Initially, data cataloging includes basic information like data names and locations. Automated systems can generate data repositories and create engines to facilitate this process. However, a closer examination of the data itself is necessary to record detailed information and conduct a preliminary quality assessment. Following this, manual classification of the data is performed to complete the cataloging process. This foundational step sets the stage for effective data management and utilization, enabling organizations to harness the true power of their data assets.

▪ Level Two: Defining Governance

The second level is defining governance, which involves preparing for effective data management by establishing governance principles that guide an organization in setting up its data governance steps. This stage requires linking the demands of data governance—encompassing business needs and classification requirements—with metadata through relevant technologies and tools. Additionally, organizations must leverage digital services and tools for data localization, access, and management, forming a comprehensive framework for data governance.

Beyond creating their own data governance standards, businesses must also align with industry organizations to develop standards tailored to specific industry characteristics. Historically, many financial institutions have invested significant time in navigating the complexities of data governance, only to find themselves hindered by a lack of uniform standards. This disarray often results in inefficiencies that stifle data utility. To combat this, international regulations and industry guidelines have emerged to drive standardization in data management, privacy protection, and customer identification within the financial sector. For instance, BCBS 239 (Basel Committee on Banking Supervision Document 239) offers a comprehensive set of regulations and international standards designed to enhance the consistency and quality of data management among financial institutions. As American financial entities strive to meet these international compliance standards, they frequently integrate BCBS 239's data governance and architecture requirements into their operational practices.

■ **Level Three: Operational Governance**

The third level is operational governance, which integrates data governance from the perspective of managing operational processes. In practice, organizations can leverage tools to personalize data based on specific operational flows. For instance, particular data types can be displayed for targeted users, while different employees may access tailored data relevant to their tasks. Moreover, governance tools like data mobility engines, access APIs, and security measures can autonomously facilitate process management and execution within data operations.

At this stage, businesses can employ common SaaS solutions and IT frameworks to reduce the costs associated with data governance while utilizing artificial intelligence to enhance efficiency. Through operational feedback and learning, the system can automatically match semantically similar data. If the match score falls below a certain threshold, the system will escalate the candidate data to human experts for evaluation. This approach minimizes the volume of data that experts need to review, thereby significantly improving the efficiency of data governance efforts.

■ **Level Four: Governance through Business Control**

The fourth level is governance through business control, which means that after establishing a data catalog, defining governance frameworks, and implementing operational governance, the entire data governance process must ultimately align with the business strategy. If the business needs to evolve, data governance must adapt accordingly. Any changes to the data catalog, governance framework, or operational strategies necessitate updates to governance methodologies. Regardless of where the data resides within IT platforms, governance through business control allows for seamless and timely access to data, ensuring consistent formats and classifications to create meaningful links.

Here's a proven strategy: based on a global overview, companies can conduct targeted data governance initiatives focused on specific business needs, quickly improving the quality of critical data for rapid wins. In any organization, regardless of size or type, resources are often limited; thus, implementing focused data governance is undoubtedly an effective approach to achieving efficient results.

- **Level Five: The Data-Driven Enterprise**

  The fifth level refers to the data-driven enterprise, where both internal and external data are harnessed to inform business decisions and drive value creation. A data-driven organization fosters a culture of data governance that extends participation from a select group of trained individuals to every employee. In such enterprises, everyone possesses a data mindset, enabling them to access relevant data, manipulate it as needed, and seamlessly integrate it into their business processes to unlock its value. Here, individuals own and manage their data, collaborating around it to develop shareable data analyses and visualizations, providing real-time feedback that propels data-driven initiatives.

Overall, effective data governance is crucial to a successful data strategy. It encompasses managing datasets based on ownership, integrity, compliance, quality, content, and their relationships with other datasets. Through robust data governance, organizations continuously enhance the quality of data delivery, increasing transparency and efficiency. Without successful governance, companies will struggle to gain insights from their datasets, undermining their ability to develop a sound data strategy.

Furthermore, the successful implementation of a data strategy requires robust support in terms of talent, organizational structure, and cultural alignment. Currently, the supply of skilled data professionals falls significantly short of demand, making it challenging for companies to find the right talent. As a result, organizations must invest substantial effort in training and evaluating their data teams while actively seeking to attract high-level experts. Building a comprehensive, multi-tiered team of data professionals is essential to ensure the success of a data strategy.

As companies move forward with their data strategies, cultivating a strong data culture becomes crucial. In the near future, most employees should have easy access to standardized tools for data retrieval, much like the way many people currently navigate office software with ease. This accessibility will empower a broader range of employees to engage with, analyze, and utilize data to enhance decision-making efficiency. Additionally, organizations should optimize their investments in technology, personnel, and processes to facilitate the effective deployment of their data strategies.

A successful data strategy must encompass the entire data lifecycle, addressing fundamental questions such as where the data originates, its utility, and its future trajectory. Companies should focus on innovating the value of their proprietary data, leveraging its network effects for monetization. Moreover, they need to tackle both offensive data initiatives (like business analytics) and defensive measures (like security protocols) simultaneously, ensuring a holistic approach to data management that prevents leaks and vulnerabilities.

By maintaining the quality and security of data assets, while simultaneously executing their data strategy, organizations can unlock the value of their data, ultimately aligning it with business needs and objectives.

Ultimately, the success of a data strategy hinges on its ability to generate tangible business value. Take, for instance, a telecommunications provider that manages vast amounts of user data. By inventorying its data assets, the company discovered over 3,700 user tags, more than 4,000 mobile phone brands, and upward of 90,000 device models. Through effective data governance, the organization can seamlessly access user data, brand information, and device specifics, enabling efficient data analysis.

With this capability, the company developed customized reports and personalized models that analyze demographics based on residential areas, workplaces, and commercial zones, as well as data products that focus on device-related analytics. By offering services like fraud detection, identity verification, and risk assessment through API interfaces, the company successfully monetized its data assets.

It's crucial to emphasize that a data strategy requires a long-term vision. A successful strategy must encompass a comprehensive plan that includes data assets, governance, value creation, and talent development, laying a strong foundation for future business growth while providing a steady stream of data-driven insights.

SECTION 3: EMBARKING ON THE AI JOURNEY

Launching an artificial intelligence strategy involves a four-step process: defining a clear roadmap, experimenting with different models, deploying successful approaches, and ultimately exploring new pathways for growth. This cycle is ongoing and iterative.

In my past experience leading a team, we analyzed nearly a thousand data application scenarios. Throughout this analysis, I consistently emphasized that big data analytics is not merely an IT challenge—it's fundamentally a business challenge. For any big data or AI initiative to succeed, it must be driven by business needs, focusing on specific scenarios and industries to establish a closed-loop data operation mechanism.

This understanding forms the foundation for any organization's AI journey and must be embraced at every step.

The Industry-Driven AI Journey

As organizations embark on their AI journey, it's crucial to establish a foundational perspective: should the focus be on technology or business? Is it "AI + Industry" or "Industry + AI"?

For artificial intelligence to truly take root, a deep dive into specific industries becomes a decisive factor for success. The debate between "AI + Industry" and "Industry + AI" reflects two distinct approaches. The former prioritizes AI technologies, emphasizing the deployment of these tools in segmented industry scenarios to realize technological value, creating a dynamic of "leading and being led" between AI and industry.

Conversely, "Industry + AI" places the spotlight on industry value, where AI technology serves merely as a means to achieve business objectives. The business scenarios defined by industry experts and insights become the prerequisites for effective AI implementation. Here, technical professionals must engage closely with the industry, aligning their efforts with its needs. In this context, the relationship between AI technology and traditional industries resembles one of "service and being served," highlighting that AI companies can only effectively operationalize their solutions after gaining a deep understanding of industry dynamics.

To effectively harness the power of artificial intelligence, it must be closely connected with specific scenarios and the entire industry chain. Given the multitude of AI technologies, the specific techniques required can vary significantly from one context to another. For instance, the question-and-answer (Q&A) technology used to enhance customer call center performance differs greatly from the facial recognition technology employed to detect credit card fraud. Here, categorization, algorithms, and models must adapt to the industry, emphasizing that industry knowledge and the ability to implement solutions are often more critical than mere technical prowess.

Over the years, I have collaborated with clients across various global markets, witnessing how industry leaders have leveraged data to revolutionize their business models through big data analytics and AI. Most success stories embody the "Industry + AI" philosophy. Only with a profound understanding of their respective industries can these pioneers successfully implement AI solutions.

From past experience, companies with higher levels of digitalization tend to deploy AI strategies more swiftly. Industries like finance, telecommunications, and media—those that have embraced digital transformation early—see faster AI adoption. In contrast, sectors such as healthcare, which traditionally possess poorer data resources, experience a slower rollout of AI applications. However, the potential and impact of AI in these latter industries can be even more pronounced.

By continually utilizing AI, companies can gather high-quality data, building valuable data assets that generate commercial value. To achieve this, businesses must plan and prepare from the outset, gradually establishing vast data resources within specific domains. Once they possess these data assets, a robust data operations strategy becomes essential. This strategy should activate data through industry scenarios, generating value and forming a closed loop of digital transformation.

The operation of data assets consists of four key steps: clarifying business scenarios, acquiring data assets, processing and analyzing data, and injecting these insights back into business contexts. These steps are interlinked, forming a positive feedback loop that creates a data operation mechanism characterized by the flow of "scenarios—data—analytics/AI—value conversion."

The first step in this data operation mechanism is to clearly define the applicable business scenarios. Companies should identify the scenarios with the highest expected outcomes to implement first. By successfully executing one scenario, they can connect and expand to other business areas, initiating the acquisition of relevant data assets. During this acquisition process, it's crucial to evaluate the authenticity, value, and relevance of the data, ensuring that only data closely related to the scenario is collected and properly categorized.

Next, the data must be analyzed and processed. Utilizing big data and AI capabilities, companies can construct and train algorithmic models, continually iterating based on data support. Finally, the algorithmic models

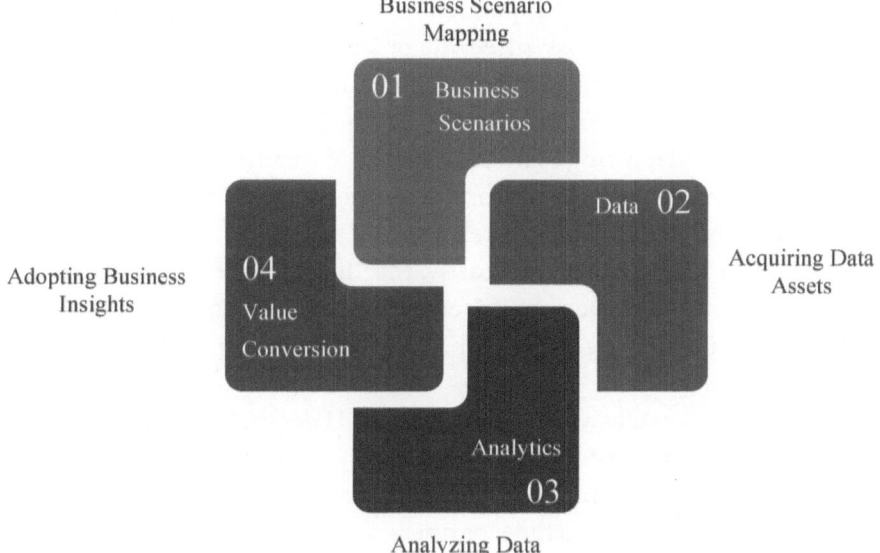

FIGURE 4.5   Data operation processes driven by high business value.

generated through data and AI analysis are implemented in relevant production environments, realizing business value and feeding back into the next cycle of data operations.

It is essential to emphasize that the operation of data assets ultimately serves a "customer-centric" business model. Data strategies and sources must be closely aligned with customer priorities to ensure success.

Four Steps to Implementing AI

The four steps to successfully implement AI involve setting a roadmap, experimenting with models, deploying and replicating solutions, and finally exploring new development pathways, creating a continuous cycle.

Let me share a well-known case: Haier. After establishing its big data strategy in 2012, Haier broke down its business lines and formulated specific implementation steps for each. Among these, the "Haier Clothing Internet" emerged as an independent project.

With advanced washing machine manufacturing lines and its own retail channels, Haier began its digital transformation with a single production line and store. Gradually, it expanded this digital network, completing the digitization process across three major commercial scenarios: factory, store, and home. The "factory" refers to Haier's use of RFID (Radio Frequency Identification) IoT technology, extending into smart sourcing and intelligent manufacturing to meet the needs of garment manufacturers for intelligent management. The "store" leverages a digital management platform, allowing merchants to receive timely customer feedback and offer personalized service solutions. Lastly, the "home" aspect features Haier's smart washing machines, equipped with RFID technology, capable of intelligently identifying fabric types and brands to provide optimized washing programs.

Thanks to its extensive IoT deployment, Haier's Clothing Internet has gradually fulfilled customers' comprehensive apparel needs—covering washing, care, storage, matching, and purchasing. The platform's capabilities have expanded to include partners in clothing, home textiles, and laundry services, attracting over 5,000 resource providers. This has resulted in an interconnected platform centered on "clothing," focusing on a full-spectrum user experience while covering the entire upstream and downstream supply chain. It has even connected industries such as home appliances and logistics, constantly exploring new avenues for growth.

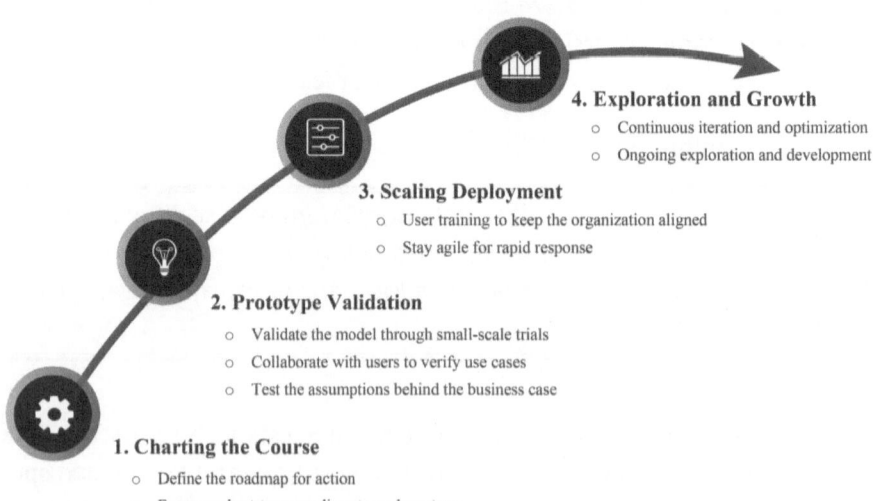

4. Exploration and Growth
- Continuous iteration and optimization
- Ongoing exploration and development

3. Scaling Deployment
- User training to keep the organization aligned
- Stay agile for rapid response

2. Prototype Validation
- Validate the model through small-scale trials
- Collaborate with users to verify use cases
- Test the assumptions behind the business case

1. Charting the Course
- Define the roadmap for action
- Focus on short-term, medium-term, long-term

FIGURE 4.6   Four steps to adopt artificial intelligence.

Haier's Clothing Internet exemplifies a classic AI strategy implementation process: setting a roadmap, experimenting with models, deploying and replicating, and finally exploring new development paths—thus, the cycle continues.

Step One: Set the Path and Establish an Action Roadmap
Every organization should have its own distinct AI objectives. During the implementation process, it's crucial for companies to clarify what AI can and cannot do for them, as well as what state they aim to achieve.

Implementing AI is never an overnight success; a practical approach is to establish an AI roadmap. Generally, this roadmap can be categorized into short-term, medium-term, and long-term phases, each with its own focus.

Short-Term Roadmap: This phase aims to identify specific customer needs or address internal business pain points, allowing AI to be deployed safely and yield tangible results. A conventional approach here is to introduce standardized AI solutions. For example, industries like manufacturing utilize industrial quality inspection, while the service sector employs intelligent customer service systems, both of which have established AI frameworks. Engaging with these solutions helps companies understand the operational dynamics of AI, gradually accumulate data, and prepare for the design of the medium-term roadmap.

Medium-Term Roadmap: The primary goal of this roadmap is to transform the organization into a data-driven AI enterprise. This requires that teams, organizational structures, and corporate culture fully adapt to the demands of AI development, while operational processes must boast a substantial volume of high-quality data assets to sustainably support business growth. At this stage, companies proactively seek new business scenarios for creative applications of AI. The data utilized primarily comes from internal sources, supplemented by closely linked upstream and downstream supply chains.

Long-Term Roadmap: This roadmap marks the pivotal transition for organizations toward a "platform-based existence" in AI. By leveraging data and tool platforms within their ecosystem, businesses can achieve mutual data sharing. Each player in the supply chain can access relevant data and tools based on their specific business needs (usually at an economic cost), enhancing the operational efficiency of the ecosystem.

Additionally, companies should also establish a technology roadmap for their AI initiatives. Initially, it's important to focus on proven, effective technology solutions. Once certain technologies have been successfully implemented, organizations can explore innovative yet relatively untested technologies, seeking the innovative value that emerges from their integration with business operations. As leaders in AI, companies should then develop emerging technologies, harnessing cutting-edge innovations to gain a competitive edge and further solidify their market position.

Ultimately, the effectiveness of AI hinges on data. Data is the core element of AI; only through seamless data interchange can its full potential be realized. At this stage, a significant portion of an organization's data resources will stem from the ecosystem, effectively resolving the issue of "data silos." Furthermore, companies with a forward-looking approach to data will have the opportunity to become "core enterprises" within their ecosystem, dominating the distribution of AI technology dividends.

Step Two: Validate the Model through Small-Scale Experiments

When it comes to AI, standardized business solutions are only applicable in the early stages. Each business and its customers are unique, so companies cannot rely solely on copying the best practices of industry leaders for success. The core competitive advantage of AI lies in leveraging proprietary data and matching intelligent algorithms to effectively tackle specific issues in distinct scenarios.

Often, asking the right questions is half the battle. During this phase, businesses must explore where suitable scenarios exist and whether AI can enhance these contexts.

Given that AI is entirely data-driven, discovering new scenarios can be a cumbersome process. Typically, companies start by making necessary digital transformations within a limited experimental environment, collecting and annotating data. They then use this dataset to train foundational algorithm models, verifying and optimizing these models through a feedback loop from data operations, ultimately applying them in real-world business practices.

This process demands patience and meticulous attention. AI learns rules, patterns, features, and experiences from vast amounts of data. The greatest challenge at this stage is obtaining high-quality training data that excels in diversity and reliability to improve algorithms.

Currently, programmers tasked with training AI spend most of their time preparing data, while coding the algorithms takes a back seat. The majority of failures in AI applications stem from inadequate training data preparation. Collecting, cleaning, annotating, protecting, monitoring, and maintaining data is a labor-intensive process that spans the entire experimental phase, and success is never guaranteed.

The design of the experimental process is also crucial, as demonstrated by the renowned Amazon Go project, which created an internally driven experimental path. Amazon Go employs multiple technologies, including computer vision, sensor fusion, and deep learning. Initially, the team aimed to enhance the accuracy and automation of the intelligent system through continuous iterations.

In the early stages of commercial implementation, Amazon chose not to open a fully accessible environment but instead launched an Amazon Go store internally. This approach allowed employees to tolerate technical glitches, facilitating the collection of genuine feedback while employing A/B testing to uncover and explore further user needs. Small-scale iterative improvements helped elevate the technology to a controlled quality level before broadening its outreach to the general public. This method significantly increased the margin for error and the likelihood of success.

Once the first Amazon Go store was opened to the public, Amazon entered a broader phase of data acquisition, analysis, decision-making, and feedback. With this larger operational scope, technicians could analyze store performance more accurately, optimizing human-machine collaboration: identifying which processes could be fully automated and which tasks would benefit from human involvement, creating a seamless workflow where both humans and machines excel.

Step Three: Scale Deployment

After validating the small-scale experiments, AI transitions into the large-scale implementation phase. This stage requires comprehensive preparations across various domains, laying the groundwork for data, IT platforms, and customer engagement while adjusting AI according to real-world conditions.

Here, I must reiterate the importance of a data strategy for large-scale deployment. For AI applications to be effectively rolled out, issues such as data scarcity, data chaos, and weak data relevance must be addressed. Poor data quality can hinder application performance; even with significant efforts in data collection, organization, and cleansing, results may fall short of expectations. Therefore, companies should begin building their data asset libraries from day one and continuously assess the quality of their data.

For an internet company focused on local lifestyle services, relying solely on internal transaction data limits its AI model to a single data source for training. However, by leveraging additional data from social media platforms and travel information from electronic maps, the company can create a multidimensional dataset for richer business analysis, uncovering more intriguing insights.

A robust IT infrastructure greatly enhances the scalability of AI deployment. In the past, data management platforms merely served as systems for recording and storing data. In the age of AI, these platforms must cater to the needs of different users querying data from various locations while providing timely feedback.

This necessitates that a company's IT systems support real-time access and accommodate growing data volumes. In recent years, the concept of a centralized platform has emerged, with businesses aiming to create flexible, modular, and shareable IT architectures that respond to data processing demands. On this foundation, companies can efficiently integrate structured and unstructured data, facilitating access and enabling rapid execution of intelligent programs while managing vast amounts of data within a unified infrastructure.

Moreover, as AI represents a new business frontier, large-scale deployment requires customer support and alignment with the enterprise's goals. The process of training customers involves not just imparting business skills but also actively discovering and gathering clues about customer needs. This groundwork prepares for the successful implementation of AI while guiding the iterative development of intelligent applications to create greater customer value.

During the large-scale deployment phase, businesses utilize AI across multiple layers and dimensions, fulfilling various functions from clocking in at work and translating languages to core activities like risk control and supply chain optimization, as well as competitive strategy development. Each department, from market sales and technical R&D to accounting and administration, must adhere to a unified strategic plan, fostering collaboration across all sectors.

As AI is deployed, technical teams should explore the integrated application of various technologies, including big data, 5G, IoT, blockchain, and edge computing. The sales department should share customer pain points to assist product development teams in integrating technological advancements into business scenarios. Legal and ethical departments must scrutinize compliance with data privacy protection, data security, and AI ethics, ensuring the implementation's legality, safety, and sustainability. Each department plays a crucial role, providing comprehensive support for AI deployment.

During the scaling phase, AI is applied to increasingly diverse and complex business scenarios, leading to a rise in influencing variables. This means encountering more varied data, mechanisms, and industry variables. In this evolving landscape, teams must maintain agility, making timely and swift adjustments to potential situations.

Step Four: Exploration and Development

In the exploration and development phase, AI applications expand significantly, continuously meeting, discovering, and creating customer needs. This iterative process allows for the enhancement of products and services while broadening market reach. Take Amazon's smart assistant, Echo Show, and Alexa, for instance. After facing criticism for monitoring and recording user data, the new versions of Echo Show and Alexa quickly implemented improvements, enabling users to set privacy preferences and delete data records at will. This evolution reflects Amazon's response to user feedback, balancing autonomy, privacy protection, and ease of use.

Google Translate serves as another example. Aimed at addressing the challenge that 80% of online information is in just the top ten languages, Google Translate launched in 2006 with an initial accuracy of only 40%. Over the years, it gathered vast amounts of data and utilized statistical methods, learning, and feedback to continually enhance translation accuracy. Today, Google Translate boasts sophisticated algorithm models and has extended its services across various translation scenarios, leading to an ever-growing user base and market share. This positive feedback loop not only meets user demands but also fosters new growth for the company.

This exemplifies the first-mover advantage of AI innovators. By introducing an application to a vast audience, companies can quickly gain user feedback, data, and tacit knowledge, allowing them to iterate on their products and services, driving further optimization and reinforcing their lead.

The foundation for exploration and development must always center on a customer-centric business model. If a business and its products lack customer recognition and a viable, sustainable model, they will ultimately struggle to achieve large-scale deployment.

In 2023, Snapchat's AI chatbot, My AI, sparked ethical debates. Although built on OpenAI's GPT technology to provide personalized interactions, concerns arose regarding privacy and data security. Users discovered that even when location services were disabled, My AI could still infer geographic information through interactions. Additionally, the privacy protections for underage users raised significant questions, eroding trust and perceptions of safety regarding the app. During exploration and development, we must continuously test the boundaries of AI: understanding what it can and cannot do, and how it should integrate with business functions. While we believe in AI's potential, we must also adhere to legal and ethical standards.

Under the constraints of narrow AI, human judgment and insight remain critical to the successful implementation of AI strategies. AI is not a panacea; for many scenarios, such as on-demand transportation or automated warehousing, human-machine collaboration is more effective. For more complex tasks, AI's current capabilities still lag behind human proficiency.

As companies implement AI, they should consciously establish a comprehensive set of tools to manage and assess the progress of AI projects, creating a lifecycle management system for AI. From defining scenarios and building models to collecting training data, validating models, and scaling deployment, the entire process should be reliable, traceable, transparent, and quantifiable, allowing businesses to make dynamic adjustments at various stages.

Moreover, given the rapid advancement of technology, talent and partnerships are crucial in a company's exploration and development of AI. Even tech giants like Amazon and Google continuously seek to recruit top talent to bolster their AI capabilities. In 2021, Microsoft acquired AI company Nuance Communications for nearly $20 billion, marking the highest price ever paid in an AI transaction. With Nuance's deep expertise in speech recognition and natural language processing, along with its applications in automating medical records and clinical documentation, this acquisition significantly enhanced Microsoft's influence in the healthcare AI market while further integrating its Azure cloud services with healthcare applications.

Frankly, the journey from establishing direction and setting an implementation roadmap to conducting small-scale experiments, scaling deployment, and exploring development to create innovative AI applications is fraught with challenges. Each step requires the right tools, methods, experience, and resources while overcoming various uncertainties. This process tests the resilience and determination of the entire team, particularly the leadership's steadiness, conviction, and passion.

Nevertheless, the future is already here, and AI is an unstoppable trend. If companies can actively pursue transformation toward AI in the coming years, unlocking data value, they will undoubtedly secure their ticket to the intelligent economy era. Embracing AI now is a choice for the brave and the wise!

SECTION 4: THE SUPPORT FRAMEWORK FOR YOUR CORPORATE AI JOURNEY

A robust support system comprising organization, talent, ethics, and security is essential to ensure the successful implementation of artificial intelligence.

The greatest challenge in deploying AI lies in the processes and personnel involved. In many instances, the management difficulties associated with integrating AI into employee workflows and decision-making far outweigh the technical challenges of implementation. Moreover, organizations must adopt a broader perspective to ensure that AI initiatives align with ethical standards and safety requirements.

Companies need to not only grasp AI technology but also invest considerable effort in refining their organizational structures, processes, and talent management to facilitate a smooth AI deployment.

Building an Empowering Organization and Culture

To foster a dynamic and empowering organization, businesses must align their structures with core objectives and workflows.

Typically, organizational structures can be categorized into three segments: front-end, mid-end, and back-end. The front-end includes departments such as marketing, sales, and customer service; the mid-end encompasses innovation, manufacturing, product development, risk management, and supply chain management; while the back-end consists of finance, human resources, procurement, security, IT, and administration. Each type of business may have different departmental configurations.

Organizations must reengineer their processes based on their unique characteristics. For AI to integrate seamlessly into the business model, it must permeate the entire organizational framework. This requires adjusting collaboration across front-end, mid-end, and back-end departments. Whether dealing with operational or administrative processes, each aspect must evolve to create a continuous information flow for AI products and services across departments.

To support this transformation, businesses need to redefine their organizational structure around their goals and processes. During this restructuring, clear organizational objectives, values, and workflows should be established, ultimately creating a precise and efficient collaborative framework. As AI applications mature, positive interactions and operational synergies among departments will elevate the organization's effectiveness.

The implementation of AI should be a joint effort between business and technology leaders. This collaboration enhances organizational understanding of AI, preventing it from being overlooked and ensuring it focuses on the most valuable business areas.

In exploring AI, businesses must continually assess which tasks are best suited for machines, which are for humans, and which require collaboration between the two. As AI systems evolve, the division of labor between humans and machines will change, necessitating ongoing adjustments to the organizational structure to support AI's gradual integration.

Leading AI companies have already developed specific methods and experiences in collaboration. For instance, Amazon employs unique tactics regarding how managers apply AI technology, how AI programmers deploy and test systems, and how the organizational structure adapts. These tactics evolve alongside product development.

As AI implementation deepens, many decision-making processes can become automated. This shift requires organizations to focus not just on process efficiency but also on the effectiveness of their decisions. Therefore, information flows within the organization must be seamless.

Every employee should have access to relevant information online, enabling them to coordinate resources, make value judgments at workflow nodes, and solve problems effectively. In the past, the efficiency of management significantly influenced a company's profitability, leading to standardized operations and clear hierarchical structures, such as the ideal management ratio of one manager to seven subordinates. With AI's assistance, this ratio can expand; AI can share workload, provide feedback, and track progress, allowing this ratio to increase to 1 manager overseeing 20 employees.

Compared to previous industrial revolutions, AI amplifies human capabilities and creativity. It propels individuals toward more creative and challenging roles. Consequently, in the era of AI, leadership's role in managing subordinates begins to diminish; leaders should focus on supporting employees, helping them access necessary resources, and encouraging innovation rather than punishing mistakes.

Such creativity thrives in an empowering organization. With flattened hierarchies and transparent relationships, these organizations prioritize collaboration and employee innovation. To create an empowering organizational system, businesses should establish a networked collaborative structure encompassing market dynamics, product development, and management, allowing free connections between departments. Employees should have the autonomy to access resources and make decisions.

Google exemplifies an empowering organizational structure through a series of supportive practices. For many years, co-founder Larry Page personally led weekly all-hands meetings, where ongoing projects were presented, and employees could challenge and discuss ideas. Google employees enjoy significant autonomy, allowing cross-departmental resource sharing. This design fosters opportunities for creativity and inspiration through active engagement.

Cultivating an AI-centric culture within the organization is equally vital. Companies need to consistently communicate the goals of AI, train employees on AI technologies, and explain the rationale behind business process designs, ensuring AI is integrated into all aspects of work and life. This immersion sparks creativity and encourages employees to innovate. Additionally, organizations should embrace experimentation, remain undeterred by failures, and commit to continuous iteration, fostering an environment rich in inclusivity, learning, innovation, trust, transparency, and improvement. Ultimately, for AI to gain the trust of customers, businesses, and society, a culture of trust and transparency within the organization is crucial for successful implementation.

Fostering Versatile Talent

In the age of artificial intelligence, cultivating versatile talent is not just a necessity but also a guarantee for success.

"Successfully implementing AI and generating value from it requires versatile talent." Back in 2019, during a media interview, I emphasized the importance and urgency of developing such talent. Companies must rapidly establish their own AI talent cultivation systems. In essence, the training of AI professionals must be approached from a temporal perspective—today, tomorrow, and beyond. Today, the focus should be on blending industry knowledge with technical expertise to create versatile talent that enhances the organization's ability to utilize AI effectively.

For AI to thrive in various industries, understanding these sectors is essential. Traditionally, business and IT departments operated distinctly, requiring specialized roles to facilitate communication between them. However, in the AI era, the integration of business operations with IT functions is becoming increasingly common, making the fusion of business acumen with AI operational skills crucial.

Versatile AI talent should possess several key capabilities:

1. **Knowledge Diversity**: Versatile professionals need expertise in fields such as computer science, automation, and electronic information, along with specific industry knowledge—be it healthcare, media, automotive, finance, retail, or manufacturing. Furthermore, as AI is integrated into products, services, and processes, continuous learning of new specialized knowledge is necessary.

2. **Technical Proficiency**: These individuals must master a variety of technologies, including AI, big data, cloud computing, the Internet of Things, cybersecurity, virtual reality, and augmented reality.

3. **Innovative and Pragmatic Mindset**: AI not only optimizes existing business processes but also redefines and reorganizes them. Thus, versatile talent must not only be familiar with business operations and workflows but also possess a reflective, breakthrough-oriented spirit and an innovative mindset.

The process of cultivating versatile talent can be broken down into three steps:

Step One: Reassess the business processes linked to AI strategy implementation and establish corresponding roles while breaking down the requirements for these positions.

Step Two: Understand the skills and abilities required at various levels of roles, which will inform the establishment of a talent hierarchy and training system within the organization.

Step Three: Continuously explore and unlock talent potential during the practical implementation of AI, iterating the talent hierarchy as needed. Alongside nurturing AI specialists, businesses should also develop industry operation professionals and innovation leaders capable of leveraging AI effectively.

The cultivation of AI talent requires collaboration among businesses, universities, and government entities, fostering innovative partnerships and integrating education with industry to create a talent ecosystem.

On a policy level, countries worldwide have begun implementing measures to train AI professionals, with talent support plans ensuring the necessary human resources for AI deployment.

In February 2019, the U.S. Office of Science and Technology Policy released the "American AI Initiative," placing particular emphasis on developing versatile talent in AI. Currently, the U.S. is focused on training individuals who possess both industry knowledge and AI technical skills through its educational system.

Many universities have introduced AI-related courses and promoted interdisciplinary integration to nurture versatile talent. For example, the Massachusetts Institute of Technology (MIT) established the Stephen A. Schwarzman College of Computing, a cornerstone of a $1 billion investment plan designed to tackle the global opportunities and challenges posed by the rise of computing and AI. The University of Pennsylvania also launched a Bachelor of Science in Engineering degree focused on AI, becoming the first Ivy League institution to offer an undergraduate AI degree program.

Moreover, businesses must learn to connect with global resources and attract AI talent from around the world.

AI strategy is the foremost priority for organizations. In light of this emerging landscape, hiring high-level roles such as Chief AI Officers and Chief Data Officers is crucial for facilitating organizational learning and effective AI strategy implementation. Historically, during previous technological revolutions, roles such as Chief Electric Officers and Chief Technology Officers emerged. Unlike the earlier Chief Technology

Officers, who primarily focused on IT, today's Chief AI Officers and Chief Data Officers prioritize data management within organizations. They dedicate considerable effort to understanding customer needs, exploring innovative approaches for products and services, and outlining specific steps for the organization's AI transformation. Based on past experiences, such talent often needs to be sourced externally.

Looking toward tomorrow, the emergence of new roles is anticipated within AI-focused companies. Commonly, this includes positions such as AI trainers, ethics guides, and AI systems maintenance specialists.

The growth of AI systems relies heavily on the "nourishment" provided by data and the training from human engineers. Ultimately, we aspire to develop AI that observes, thinks, and acts like humans. Achieving this goal requires diligent guidance, akin to nurturing a child. In this context, humans serve as teachers, helping simple AI systems improve accuracy, mimic human behaviors, and continually refine themselves to attain higher levels of intelligence.

To address data privacy and ethical concerns in AI deployment, ethical guides are essential. The development of AI is not merely a technical issue; it also encompasses financial, legal, moral, and societal dimensions. The design, interpretation, evolution, and controllability of AI algorithms require the oversight, explanation, and supervision of ethical guides.

AI systems also require maintenance specialists to ensure their proper functioning across design, development, training, and operational dimensions, aligning with commercial environments, process tasks, customer demands, and cultural contexts to enhance overall AI system performance.

From a future perspective, we must delve into the collaborative dynamics between AI and humans, as well as how to cultivate efficient human-machine collaboration. In the future, AI's true value will not just lie in replacing low-skill jobs but in maximizing the efficiency of human-AI collaboration.

With AI assistance, humans can better return to their core strengths, dedicating time to tackling more complex tasks where human advantages shine. Moreover, AI can accelerate workflows, facilitate effective human-machine integration, and empower business leaders, managers, and employees to completely rethink business processes and innovate core operations.

At this stage, AI talent enters a new era. AI will become as ubiquitous as electricity is today, enabling humans to harness this advanced capability to continually innovate within businesses and society, ultimately benefiting humanity.

Furthermore, embarking on the AI journey requires a comprehensive strategic overhaul across all facets of the organization—competition, operations, branding, customer relations, culture, technology, and IT security must all evolve to facilitate the effective deployment of AI.

AI can easily develop biases in data labeling, algorithms, and applications, leading to erroneous decisions or even misuse. For businesses, this poses strategic, operational, financial, legal, and reputational risks, potentially putting them in life-or-death situations. For society, the negative externalities of AI can result in catastrophic consequences.

Therefore, as AI progresses, organizations must formulate appropriate strategies regarding auditing, ethics, supervision, and risk management to establish secure operational mechanisms that ensure the safe implementation of AI strategies.

CLOSING THOUGHTS

The deployment of artificial intelligence is a systemic endeavor; it is not an overnight transformation. Businesses must engage in top-down planning, invest significant resources, and dedicate time to exploration. Throughout this journey, setbacks and challenges are inevitable, along with necessary organizational changes. To successfully drive the AI transformation, companies need dedicated leaders, and the most suitable individual for this role is often the CEO.

Only by elevating AI to the highest corporate strategy can a company achieve consensus across all levels. This unified approach allows for the mobilization of human, financial, and material resources to overcome obstacles and relentlessly pursue the success of the transformation. When the CEO is actively involved, the organization gains a profound understanding of the pain points associated with the transition and can swiftly mobilize resources to execute the strategy effectively.

The deployment of AI also serves as a demonstration of a holistic perspective. Currently, industries are navigating the shift from narrow AI to Artificial General Intelligence (AGI). In this context, industry stakeholders can adopt a "Five-in-One" framework—data, algorithms, computing power, applications, and security—as strategic resources in the era of large models.

Applications represent the ultimate manifestation of AI's value. Companies should prioritize identifying application scenarios that can deliver tangible business value, ensuring that technology directly addresses the actual needs of users. The data gleaned from these real-world applications is crucial for model training. This data not only needs to be abundant but also possess industry-specific characteristics to genuinely support the training and optimization of deep models. In the age of large models, companies can leverage platforms that provide large models to build industry-specific solutions that cater to their unique business demands. Achieving this requires robust computing power, where cloud computing and high-performance hardware play a pivotal role in enhancing intelligent capabilities. Lastly, safety is the bedrock of AI development. Whether it pertains to data privacy, model security, or application compliance, businesses must ensure that safety and ethical standards are upheld.

As Neal Stephenson wrote in his book *Snow Crash*: "The world is full of things stronger than we are, and if you know how to hitch a ride, you can go anywhere." AI technology serves as the ride of the future in global competition. By seizing the opportunities presented by AI in this new wave of technological advancement, businesses can secure their place in the competitive global landscape.

BIBLIOGRAPHY

CBS News, "Snapchat Launches "My AI," Its Own ChatGPT-Powered Chatbot". CBS News 27 February 2023. https://www.cbsnews.com/news/snapchat-launches-my-ai-chatgpt-powered-chatbot/

Devlin, Jacob; Chang, Ming-Wei; Lee, Kenton; Toutanova, Kristina (11 October 2018). "BERT: Pre-training of Deep Bidirectional Transformers for Language Understanding".

Heinrich, Martin (21 May 2019). "Text - S.1558 - 116th Congress (2019–2020): Artificial Intelligence Initiative Act". www.congress.gov

Microsoft Corporation, "Report of Unscheduled Material Events Or Corporate Event — Microsoft 8-K". U.S. Securities and Exchange Commission (SEC) Filings, 12 April 2021. https://www.sec.gov/Archives/edgar/data/789019/000078901921000046/xslForm8-K_0.html

MIT News Office, "MIT Reshapes Itself to Shape the Future", MIT News Office, 15 October 2018. https://news.mit.edu/2018/mit-reshapes-itself-to-shape-the-future-1015

OpenAI, "Introducing OpenAI". OpenAI. 12 December 2015. https://openai.com/blog/introducing-openai

OpenAI, "Models - OpenAI API". OpenAI. https://platform.openai.com/docs/models

Oracle Corporation, Oracle Fiscal 2025 First Quarter Financial Results, 9 September 2024.

Peters, Jay, "Google, Adidas, and EA Team Up On a New Smart Insole That Tracks Soccer Kicks for FIFA Mobile Rewards". *The Verge*, 10 March 2020.

Rifkin, Jeremy, The Zero Marginal Cost Society (2014).

Wingfield, Nick (5 December 2016). "Amazon Moves to Cut Checkout Line, Promoting a Grab-and-Go Experience". *The New York Times*.

CHAPTER 5

The Future of AI Unfolding

Today, the pioneering figures of the AI revival have diverged on major public issues.

In August 2024, the California state legislature overwhelmingly passed the "Frontier Artificial Intelligence Model Safety Innovation Act" (referred to as "SB 1047"); however, the bill was later vetoed by Governor Gavin Newsom. This legislative action, aimed at regulating AI development, unexpectedly ignited a monumental battle over innovation versus control.

The SB 1047 Act mandates that powerful AI models undergo safety testing before public release and report any AI safety incidents. Additionally, the government will establish dedicated departments to oversee these AI models, imposing civil penalties for violations of the law.

The act specifically targets the "behemoths" of the AI realm—large models with training costs exceeding $100 million. These titans of the digital age possess astonishing intelligence but also harbor significant risks; should AI run amok and cause serious consequences, companies will not be able to escape the law's "long arm."

Disagreements primarily center around whether this legislation will stifle rapid technological innovation. Yoshua Bengio, one of the "AI triumvirate," has expressed his support, stating, "California has historically led the way in green energy and consumer privacy; now there is a tremendous opportunity to lead again in AI." Another "AI godfather," Geoffrey Hinton, also backs the legislation, arguing that "powerful AI systems offer incredible prospects, but the risks are very real and must be taken seriously," describing California as the "natural place to begin addressing AI risks."

In contrast, scientists like Yann LeCun, Fei-Fei Li, and Andrew Ng have voiced their opposition, arguing that certain provisions of the bill could hinder innovation. They are particularly concerned about requirements that model developers must have the ability to shut down their models in emergencies and be held liable for the risks of open-sourcing their models, fearing such measures would severely threaten the open-source community.

In the business world, voices of support have come from Elon Musk, who acknowledged that this was a "difficult decision." Meanwhile, OpenAI later joined the ranks of tech giants like Google and Meta in opposing the act.

Experts most familiar with AI systems have found themselves divided over public policy regarding AI. It's reasonable to imagine that as AI fully permeates human society, we will need to make substantial efforts to reach a basic consensus.

I personally believe that AI holds the potential to benefit humanity, with societal value that is immeasurable. However, this potential hinges on the establishment of safety operational guidelines and necessary ethical standards; otherwise, negative impacts could magnify indefinitely, potentially threatening humanity itself.

Advancing AI requires both a focused approach and an overarching vision. The pioneers of AI technology are actively exploring safe practices, while as practitioners, we strive to share our experiences when implementing AI systems.

The future of AI is unpredictable, but we can remain optimistic.

SECTION 1: NAVIGATING PRIVACY IN A WORLD SHAPED BY AI

How can we maximize the value of data while safeguarding privacy, transforming data into a valuable asset for individuals and businesses alike, and positioning it as a key driver of economic growth? This question requires our ongoing and in-depth exploration.

The conflicts arising from data privacy have always been the flip side of the AI "coin." In 2021, Amazon's Alexa voice assistant faced severe criticism over data privacy issues. Consumers, privacy advocacy groups, and the media exposed that Alexa not only recorded users' voice commands but also continuously listened to their private conversations in the background. This data was stored on Amazon's servers, claimed to be used for optimizing Alexa's algorithm models to improve voice recognition performance. Amazon's report from 2021 revealed that Alexa had over 175 million active devices globally, indicating the potential scale of data breaches. This revelation struck a nerve regarding the fragility of data privacy, with mainstream sentiment suggesting that smart home devices invade personal spaces without users' knowledge, posing significant risks of data leaks.

This incident was not an isolated case. In the same year, TikTok faced a data privacy scandal, accused of collecting sensitive information—including users' facial features, voiceprints, and location data—without user consent. Such data could potentially be used for personal tracking and behavioral analysis.

As I mentioned, data serves as the "core fuel" driving AI, and its commercial value is soaring, alongside increasingly sophisticated methods of acquisition. Consequently, the dangers of data breaches or misuse are escalating. This has led to high-stakes lawsuits as well.

Following the implementation of the European Union's General Data Protection Regulation (GDPR), both Facebook and Google faced lawsuits, with fines proposed at €3.7 billion and €3.9 billion, respectively. The EU's case against these giants stemmed from their collection of personal data from users, which under GDPR must be gathered with clear consent and justification. This regulation required these tech titans to amend their privacy policies and data collection practices. To comply with GDPR, Google and Facebook introduced new privacy policies that required users to opt-in by selecting "agree" to access services; otherwise, they would not be allowed to use the services. This approach has become standard practice for obtaining privacy data consent in online services. However, the EU deemed this "opt-out or nothing" method as a violation of GDPR's consent requirements.

This case exemplifies a dilemma in the AI era: on the one hand, data applications are exploding, yet laws and regulations governing data collection, analysis, usage, and transactions often lag behind and are poorly enforced, leaving individuals and businesses vulnerable to data privacy breaches. On the other hand, once the laws catch up, privacy regulations can become increasingly stringent, leading companies to miss valuable data insights while striving to comply.

Finding a balance between effectively leveraging data and adhering to regulations will be a critical challenge for businesses.

Technology itself is neutral; how data—especially sensitive data—is utilized under AI technology depends not only on the user's intentions but also on the ever-evolving regulatory environment.

Take facial recognition technology as an example: since a face is a unique identifying feature for each individual, this technology has made significant strides in various scenarios. For instance, police can monitor and apprehend fugitives using this technology, significantly enhancing investigative efficiency. However, as privacy-related laws become more comprehensive, the matching and use of facial recognition must be relevant, reasonable, and transparent.

In practical application, many regions around the world are beginning to enact laws and regulations regarding facial recognition technology. In several U.S. states, the use of facial recognition technology is being restricted. For example, law enforcement agencies are prohibited from using facial recognition and other biometric tracking technologies in body cameras, while individuals are permitted to sue regarding the collection and use of biometric data.

Unlocking the Truth About Data Privacy

Data is becoming increasingly important, and protecting non-anonymous information will usher in a new era of personal privacy, redefining what privacy means.

The core connection between privacy and AI is data. Nearly all forms of AI require vast amounts of training data to develop classification or decision-making capabilities. If the training data of a system contains any personal information, especially identifiable personal information, it raises privacy concerns.

To effectively protect data privacy, we first need to update our understanding as follows:

The History of Data Privacy Is a Chronicle of Efforts to Protect Data from Misuse

When we discuss privacy, we are referring to personal privacy or information. This personal information is often what individuals do not want others to know, or what is inappropriate for others to know, and it is unrelated to public or group interests.

Privacy has existed since humans first used leaves to cover themselves. It is a universal human right, much like property rights, and has become increasingly important with the advancement of social civilization and the awakening of individual consciousness.

In pre-industrial times, whether in tribes or villages, most people lived in a "familiar society" where the concept of privacy was weak, and there was a lack of effective means to store, record, and process data. The limited privacy information was primarily passed down through word of mouth.

In 1888, American statistician Herman Hollerith invented a tabulating machine resembling punched cards. Using this device, the U.S. completed a census that would have taken eight years in just one year. This technology also led to the founding of IBM, marking the beginning of a new era in data recording and processing. From that point onward, data privacy became a significant issue.

In 1890, during the U.S. census, the new system made it easier to record information about individuals' health, disabilities, and economic status. This raised public concern and protests, prompting the U.S. to legislate the confidentiality of census data at the beginning of the 20th century, restricting the illegal disclosure of census information.

By the 1960s, data privacy officially entered the legal agenda. At that time, the U.S. government and businesses used computers to store and process citizens' data, raising widespread concerns about privacy rights.

In 1973, the U.S. Department of Health, Education, and Welfare published a report titled *Records, Computers and the Rights of Citizens*, which highlighted the issue of data misuse: "Individuals must increasingly provide personal information to large organizations with which they have no direct contact, allowing entities they do not know or have never seen to process and use this information. Sometimes, individuals are unaware that an organization holds records related to them. Often, they cannot view the data to verify its accuracy, control its dissemination, or dispute its use by others."

In response to the transformative impact of computers on personal information recording and the risks they posed to individual privacy, the U.S. Congress began enacting laws in 1970 to regulate the use of personal data. Notable examples include the Fair Credit Reporting Act of 1970 and the Privacy Act of 1974.

In 1980, the Organisation for Economic Co-operation and Development (OECD) established fundamental privacy principles to promote global cross-border trade and began advocating these principles worldwide. To date, over 130 countries have enacted privacy-related laws.

The development of the internet and AI technology has woven together the digitization of privacy and the privatization of data, complicating and complicating data privacy issues.

While enjoying personalized services, our personal information is continuously recorded by internet platforms and digitized. Furthermore, the more personalized the data, the more valuable it becomes for mining and commercial analysis, inadvertently providing us with convenience. We wish to hear our favorite songs the moment we turn on a speaker, but in this exchange, the platform records increasingly intimate personal information. Once data is leaked or misused, the consequences can be catastrophic.

As previously mentioned, I personally believe that in the age of interconnectedness, it is impossible for us to maintain a truly 'anonymous' state; even if we could, it would come at the cost of sacrificing significant technological conveniences. In this context, anonymous privacy does not exist. Our focus should not be on whether 'privacy' is recorded or known, but rather on the rights to be informed about and benefit from our privacy information or data. We have the right to know and to impose constraints on a platform's practices regarding the collection, analysis, and use of privacy data."

The Era of Anonymity is Over, But This is Not the End of Privacy
Globally, countries are intensifying regulations in the realm of privacy, with Europe's GDPR being a notable example. However, we must remain vigilant against excessive regulation. In an era of interconnected devices, true anonymity is unattainable; complete anonymous privacy simply does not exist.

As the points of connection between individuals and the internet multiply, data analysis can still deduce our identities. Even if a connection point does not know our real names (and sometimes doesn't need to), it can cross-reference voice, images, behavioral traits, and other information with backend databases to speculate about our identities.

Even if anonymity were achievable, it would come at the cost of significant technological conveniences, which most people are unwilling to sacrifice. For example, the GDPR mandates that applications present privacy terms upfront to protect individuals, yet many users pay little attention to these terms (often unable to access services without consenting to privacy authorization).

A fascinating experiment conducted by the non-profit organization Tax Policy Associates highlighted this issue. In February 2024, they updated their privacy policy and offered a free bottle of wine to the first user who discovered the change. Remarkably, it took three months for a user to stumble upon this adjustment.

In reality, true privacy as we once knew it no longer exists, while the value of personal data has significantly increased in the age of AI.

Take the healthcare sector as an example: personal health and medical data are extremely valuable for addressing specific conditions. If such data could be traded through some form of anonymization, it would greatly enhance the improvement of drugs or treatment plans. Currently, vast amounts of data remain underutilized.

AI researchers from the Global MD organization conducted a study analyzing the validation data and efficacy of 521 AI software medical devices. They found that nearly 226 of these AI applications (43%) approved by the U.S. FDA had not undergone clinical validation using real patient data in actual environments. Many AI algorithms in healthcare rely solely on synthetic datasets or clinical case data for training. To enhance the clinical efficacy and credibility of healthcare AI tools, real patient data should be used for validation and training, which directly involves the use of privacy data.

In my view, protecting privacy does not imply that private data cannot be used responsibly. As long as privacy information is respected, authorized, controlled, and used in a compliant manner, we cannot simply categorize it as an infringement of privacy. In this era where anonymity is dead, the right path forward is to find a coexistence between privacy data and artificial intelligence.

The Era of Personal Data Value: "Data as Property"

When it comes to privacy, our primary concern shouldn't merely be whether our "privacy" is recorded or known. Instead, we should focus on our rights to know, use, and benefit from our personal data.

In my view, personal data is a form of property. In the age of artificial intelligence, it can generate asset values akin to "interest" or "dividends." Just like capital, land, and labor create value through exchange and utilization, personal data also needs to be exchanged and utilized. It should circulate and trade in a public, transparent, and compliant manner, transforming through artificial intelligence into significant value and becoming a driving force for economic growth.

There is a potential connection point between privacy protection and data utilization, dependent on two key elements: **innovative technology** and **transaction mechanisms**.

Currently, cutting-edge privacy computing technologies enable the extraction of information value without compromising privacy and security. The mainstream technological approaches include Multi-Party Computation (MPC), Trusted Execution Environment (TEE) based on hardware, Federated Learning (FL), homomorphic encryption, and differential privacy.

Some companies leverage homomorphic encryption technology to address data privacy issues through data anonymization and collaborative efforts.

At the same time, we need to establish a fair, effective, and risk-controlled data market, moving away from the old model of "free data, free services."

In April 2024, the U.S. Congress unveiled the American Privacy Rights Act (APRA), which prohibits companies from tracking, predicting, or manipulating people's behaviors without their knowledge or consent. This legislation empowers American citizens to control where their information goes and who can sell it.

I believe this is a commendable start. Privacy rights are inherently personal rights, and individuals naturally possess the authority to manage their own data. The crucial aspect lies in realizing this right of disposal.

We should develop personalized data management tools that allow users to set privacy permissions for specific services, authorizing access on a tiered basis and requiring compensation from those who utilize the data. There should also be suitable intermediary organizations that collectively represent users and negotiate fees for the use of personal data.

In the future, data will become a crucial asset for individuals, enabling transparent, compliant circulation and trading, ushering in the "Data Capital Era." Through artificial intelligence, data can be transformed into immense value, driving economic progress.

How Trailblazers Tackle Data Privacy Challenges

To safely and compliantly use privacy data, companies are already making meaningful attempts.

The internet's consumer-facing platforms, closest to users, are placing a significant emphasis on data privacy control during personalized analysis processes. Take Netflix, for example. The streaming giant employs an "anonymized data" approach to ensure that users' viewing histories are utilized for personalized recommendations without being linked to specific personal identifiers. Similarly, Spotify has launched a Privacy Control Center that allows users to manage and review the data they share, including listening habits and search history. Moreover, Spotify has publicly stated that its personalized recommendation system does not involve users' personal identity information, ensuring that its data handling complies with privacy regulations such as GDPR.

In response to the privacy controversies surrounding its virtual voice assistant Alexa, Amazon introduced the Alexa Privacy Hub, enabling users to manage all privacy settings related to Alexa. This feature allows them to modify settings based on timeframes and devices, including options to delete recordings and photos, erase browsing history, clear Amazon orders, and choose not to share voice data.

Many internet and big data service companies are providing detailed authorization requests in their user and privacy agreements concerning data acquisition, analysis, and trading. Users are asked if they agree to receive location-based advertisements if they consent to data mining and analysis, and whether they allow partners access to their data.

Some companies are taking alternative approaches to data privacy, going beyond merely obscuring or anonymizing user data. As early as 2016, Apple launched its "differential privacy" technology, which anonymizes user data so that it cannot be traced back to individuals even during analysis. This method allows Apple to leverage vast amounts of user data to train AI models while preserving user privacy. Additionally, Apple adopts a "local-first" strategy, keeping sensitive data on the device itself to minimize leakage risks. The company rigorously controls app permissions and obfuscates users' IP addresses and network identities. For instance, Siri processes a significant amount of requests locally, reducing the risk of transmitting user data to the cloud.

The principle behind "differential privacy" aims to gather as much information as possible about a group while learning as little as possible about any individual within it. In other words, Apple can collect and store valuable insights about what a particular group is doing, saying, liking, and wanting, without extracting specific content that could infringe on individual privacy.

Other companies are leveraging homomorphic encryption technology, which allows for data anonymization and collaborative efforts to address data privacy concerns. For instance, a hedge fund in the U.S. developed a technology to conceal its trading data while sharing it with 7,500 anonymous data scientists. This approach omits details of proprietary trading data without hindering scientists from constructing machine-learning models and researching financial trading methods. Currently, many large tech companies are utilizing homomorphic encryption technology.

With the immutability and traceability of blockchain technology, its potential to regulate data use and refine authorization processes is vast. The technical explorations by many pioneers in data privacy protection will ultimately pave the way for convenient compliance in personal data transactions.

The Path to Effective Data Privacy Protection

The issue of data privacy is inevitable and certainly challenging, but there's no need to panic.

In the age of artificial intelligence, privacy protection should be approached with a rational and constructive mindset, employing a dual strategy that encompasses both prevention and facilitation. On one hand, we must strengthen legislative safeguards for personal privacy to curb data misuse and combat illegal data transactions. On the other hand, we need to establish a market system for privacy data that can satisfy the strong demand for data while unlocking its economic potential.

Our objective is clear: to ensure that data privacy is rigorously protected while also facilitating a legal and orderly marketplace for data sharing. This transformation aims to drive economic growth and foster a mutually beneficial relationship between individuals and organizations.

In-Depth Exploration of Technologies for Achieving Data Privacy Protection

As previously mentioned, there are data processing technologies that ensure both the security of data and its risk-free utilization.

Take homomorphic encryption as an example. This innovative technology not only performs basic encryption operations but also allows for various computations on encrypted data, enabling the process of calculating results without the need to decrypt them first. In essence, it achieves the equivalent of decrypting after computation. A homomorphic encryption search engine can accept an encrypted search term, compare it against an encrypted web index, and output an encrypted result. This capability has significant implications for the privacy protection of sensitive information.

However, I believe that while homomorphic encryption has its merits, its implementation in practical business applications may increase transaction costs, hindering the realization of data economics' full potential. Establishing consensus on data applications is a far more effective strategy. On the other hand, I hold great optimism for the potential of blockchain technology.

A notable example is Oasis Labs, based in the U.S. As early as 2019, Oasis Labs developed a new paradigm for data protection and usage grounded in blockchain technology, enabling multiple layers of protection concerning raw data sharing, usage, and duplication while facilitating the trading of data value. This blockchain-based product is utilized at Stanford Hospital, where patients can contribute their data anonymously and in various privacy-preserving ways, all while receiving compensation. Doctors leverage this data for medical research and AI training, and patients' genomic data can also be shared with genetic testing companies.

Similar instances are emerging across various industries. Recently, Oasis Labs collaborated with the BMW Group on an early project to create innovative privacy solutions utilizing differential privacy, setting a new standard for responsible data use in the automotive sector. This solution allows internal teams and external partners to access data while maintaining compliance and protecting user privacy. All access records are securely logged on a ledger, enabling consent-based audits, and all access policies are meticulously verified by the Oasis Labs platform before executing queries and returning results.

Establishing Mechanisms for Data Privacy Protection and Utilization
When it comes to the government, there's a pressing need to establish legal frameworks for data privacy that facilitate the smooth circulation of data assets throughout society. This involves crafting a comprehensive set of regulations that align with national circumstances.

Different countries and regions emphasize distinct aspects of data privacy in accordance with their unique contexts. For instance, the European Union has taken the lead in developing the world's first comprehensive legal instrument for regulating artificial intelligence—the **Artificial Intelligence Act**. In addition, the **Data Governance Act**, passed in 2022, aims to promote data sharing and enhance the availability of public sector data while simultaneously safeguarding individual privacy.

In the U.S., legislation such as the **California Consumer Privacy Act of 2018** emphasizes practical applicability in commercial contexts. For example, businesses are required to disclose what information they collect, the purpose of its collection, and all third parties with whom they share this information. Consumers are granted the option to sell their personal information, and companies cannot arbitrarily alter pricing or service levels based on this data. Furthermore, organizations that collect personal information must provide monetary incentives to consumers who consent to this data collection. Notably, companies with information on over 50,000 individuals must allow users to review their collected data, delete it, and opt out of data sales to third parties, all while ensuring equal service for users exercising these rights.

Japan, leveraging its rich tradition of collaboration between government, industry, and academia, has chosen to approach data protection through clearly defined responsibilities for data subjects. This initiative fosters a cooperative research network between the government and businesses, creating an ecosystem conducive to the safe development of AI.

Germany, drawing on its industrial resources, has integrated AI safety legislation with its **"Industry 4.0"** strategy, focusing on sectors like autonomous driving and intelligent healthcare—areas that significantly impact economic growth and quality of life.

From California to the EU, and from Japan's data protection strategies to Germany's industrial integration initiatives, each regulatory approach reflects its own values and societal demands.

For organizations, particularly businesses, it's imperative to develop and implement detailed operational guidelines regarding data usage and product development. This means closely following mainstream legislative processes and proactively preparing for future changes.

As we navigate the dual-edged sword of AI, filled with both promise and peril, the challenge remains: how do we construct a regulatory framework that inspires innovation while ensuring safety? This question hangs in the balance, awaiting resolution.

Establishing a Dynamic Data Trading Market

In my view, we need a completely new data pricing mechanism to create a fair, effective, and risk-controlled data market.

First, we should develop personalized data management tools. Privacy is an inherent personal right, and individuals must have the authority to manage their own data. In the future, users should be able to set privacy permissions for specific services themselves. Currently, the prevailing practice is that if a person does not agree to grant privacy authorization, they cannot access the service. This "free data, free service" model puts individuals at a disadvantage. Instead, we should provide users with convenient data management tools that allow for tiered authorizations based on specific services.

Moreover, individuals should have the right to access and manage their own data. This includes rights such as accessing their data, correcting inaccuracies, anonymizing information, mining data, importing and exporting data, viewing data ratings, and receiving compensation for their data contributions.

Second, we must establish robust protection mechanisms for data privacy and transmission. As data collection becomes increasingly automated, people will care not only about how data is collected but also about what data is being collected, how privacy is protected, and how data is securely transmitted.

Third, we need to clarify the roles and interests of various stakeholders in the data trading supply chain, including data owners, data managers, data processors, data operators, and data users. This is no simple task. For instance, during the analysis of raw data, new data is generated; who owns this data and how are the profits shared? Additionally, valuable insights drawn from vast amounts of data raise further questions about profit distribution. As AI systems enhance their ability to mine personal data and generate commercial value, we must consider how to allocate benefits fairly between data owners and technology providers.

Fourth, we must build the infrastructure necessary for data trading. This should include mechanisms for implementing data transactions, platforms for discovering and recognizing data prices, and tools for rapidly generating data products.

Fifth, establishing a dynamic data pricing mechanism is crucial. I believe personal data is valuable, and pricing power should be left to the market. The value of data varies significantly across different contexts and conditions. For instance, a consumer's location data may seem trivial on its own, but when combined with shopping data from nearby malls or retail information, it can generate new and significant value.

The "free data, free service" model is destined to change. There should be a dynamic pricing relationship between the data users provide and the services they enjoy, allowing for a fair distribution of the value created by data.

SECTION 2: BUILDING TRUSTWORTHY AI

Who could have imagined that the iconic Eiffel Tower, standing tall on the banks of the Seine in Paris, faced a barrage of scrutiny and opposition before its construction, even from some renowned figures?

In the late 19th century, as the Eiffel Tower began to rise, waves of doubt and dissent crashed over the project. Many Parisians deemed this unprecedented steel structure not only ugly but also unsafe, with some predicting it would collapse within a short time.

In the face of this criticism, chief designer Gustave Eiffel did not retreat. Instead, he opted for a transparent and open communication strategy. He meticulously demonstrated the tower's design principles, explaining how its unique steel framework would ensure stability and safety. He even invited the public and engineers to observe and inspect the construction firsthand.

Through this ongoing process of building trust, skepticism gradually transformed into acceptance and ultimately blossomed into pride and admiration for the Eiffel Tower. Today, it stands not only as an engineering marvel but also as a global symbol of trust in modern technology.

Trust is the cornerstone of all relationships, and creating products and services is intrinsically linked to fostering that sense of trust. When society encounters unfamiliar technologies, establishing trust is rarely an overnight achievement.

Everyone hopes that artificial intelligence can be "human-centered," utilizing transparent and ethical practices to avoid serious ethical and safety issues while better serving human development.

For industry professionals, the challenge lies in translating ethical norms into specific scenarios by deploying trustworthy, responsible, and reliable AI systems that equitably consider all stakeholders' interests. This represents a new challenge and an important obligation.

Decoding the Enigma of Unexplainable AI Algorithms

In the current field of machine learning, the main research directions include supervised learning, unsupervised learning, and reinforcement learning. Researchers are striving to enable AI to autonomously "observe" the workings of the world, learn to analyze data, build insights, and develop generative models. By truly understanding the world, AI can generate new data and create new realities.

This progress brings immense potential across various industries, but the issue of AI algorithm interpretability is becoming increasingly prominent, emerging as a challenge that cannot be ignored.

Deep learning technologies excel in pattern recognition and correlation issues, capable of identifying cancer signs in medical images and extracting business insights from vast amounts of data. However, their "black box" nature renders the decision-making processes of these models opaque. For instance, while deep learning algorithms can accurately identify cancerous images, they struggle to explain why specific image patterns indicate abnormalities. This stands in stark contrast to human doctors, who not only arrive at conclusions but can also elucidate the reasons behind their judgments based on medical histories and imaging. Understanding such causal relationships is crucial in medical decision-making.

To address this challenge, future algorithm research will focus more on logical reasoning and deductive reasoning. By enhancing the understanding of causal relationships, AI can not only provide answers to questions but also illustrate the thought processes and methods for solving problems. For example, a robot that understands that dropping an object can lead to it breaking won't need to repeatedly test this by throwing dozens of vases to observe the outcomes. This causal comprehension will make existing AI systems smarter and more efficient, paving the way for technological applications in more complex scenarios.

In recent years, there has been some progress in causal reasoning, but significant bottlenecks remain. Noted AI expert Yoshua Bengio has pointed out that deep learning must go beyond mere pattern recognition to grasp causal relationships to realize its full potential. He emphasizes that AI systems need to understand "why," not just "what." Only when AI can comprehend causal relationships can it possess human-like reasoning capabilities, better grasp human goals and directives, and ascend to higher realms of innovation.

In this context, in 2019, Bengio and his team created a probability-based dataset focusing on causal relationships, such as the link between smoking and lung cancer, and further developed a novel deep-learning method for identifying simple causal relationships. These studies lay the groundwork for understanding causal relationships and propel advancements in explainable AI technologies.

Building Applications You Can Trust

When algorithms are still in the realm of the unexplainable, businesses and organizations must ensure that they provide adequate transparency and accountability in the design and implementation of AI applications to uphold the trust of users and society.

In August 2024, the U.S. Department of Justice filed a civil lawsuit against RealPage, a property management software company, accusing it of artificially inflating rental prices nationwide by utilizing landlord data and algorithms. The lawsuit highlights that the Texas-based software firm trained its pricing recommendation algorithms on non-public data provided by landlords while monitoring competitors' fees and discounts, thereby assisting landlords in maximizing rental income and creating a "massive scheme that undermines the competitive process."

"We allege that RealPage's pricing algorithm enabled landlords to share confidential and competitively sensitive information, allowing them to adjust rents," stated U.S. Attorney General Merrick Garland. He emphasized that Americans should not have to pay higher rents because a company found a new way to collude with landlords.

This incident represents yet another misuse of AI technology, violating the commitment to trustworthy and responsible AI. In the journey of developing products and services, how to implement "trustworthy" AI has been a significant area of contemplation for me since founding MedTech, involving extensive discussions and research with my team and regulatory bodies.

We believe this is not merely a principled issue but a procedural one that necessitates a comprehensive examination of the entire process of developing our AI systems—from data collection to model development, deployment, and performance monitoring.

Taking the healthcare industry, where MedTech operates, as an example, the traditional trust exists between patients and doctors. However, with the intervention of AI systems in the diagnostic process, this trust must evolve into a "multilateral trust." If doctors cannot trust the AI systems, they are unlikely to consider their adoption.

Based on my observations in the healthcare sector, I have identified three levels of "trustworthy" standards that must be met for successful AI implementation in the industry:

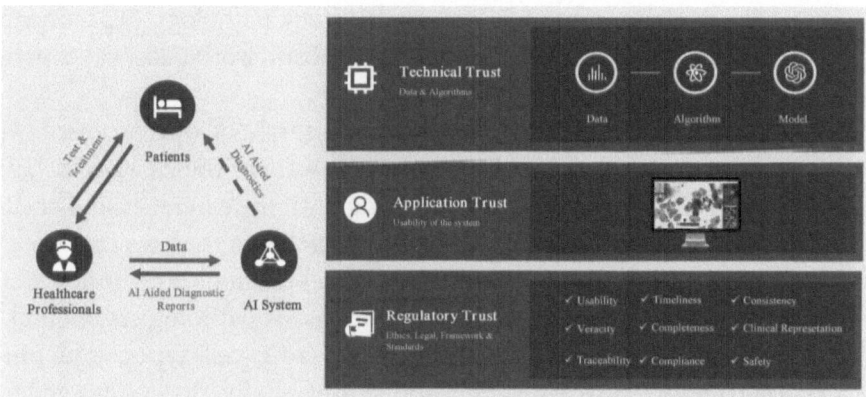

FIGURE 5.1   Three levels of "trustworthy" standards for AI adoption in industry.

1. **Technical Trust**

   Technical trust is the most fundamental and core aspect of building confidence in AI systems. It primarily involves data, algorithms, and models, ensuring that the AI system is trained to achieve the objectives set by developers.

   The datasets used for algorithms and models must be accurate, leveraging extensive human feedback through Reinforcement Learning from Human Feedback (RLHF) to minimize errors during the inference process.

   For instance, we invest significant resources into quality control for data and annotations. During the image annotation phase, we implement multiple layers of procedures by hiring a team of specialized pathologists for the task. These annotations are based on the TBS (Thyroid Imaging Reporting and Data System) standards, and we develop annotation tools and Standard Operating Procedures (SOPs). Additionally, we establish an independent three-tier review mechanism to ensure the accuracy of data annotations.

2. **Application Trust**

   The entire AI system must align with real-world application scenarios, cater to user habits, and effectively address pain points while providing necessary information to stakeholders, ensuring their right to be informed.

   Take, for instance, PathoAI's cervical cancer screening product. It tackles the pain point faced by pathologists who must manually review a vast number of slides daily. Many pathology departments and laboratories handle enormous diagnostic workloads, yet experienced personnel are often in short supply.

During the design and original research of our product, we identified pathologists as the primary users of the AI system. The value of the product lies in enhancing both the efficiency and accuracy of clinical pathology reviews. To achieve this, we integrated features such as rapid localization, visual prompts, and annotation tools for specific cells. These functions assist pathologists in quickly identifying abnormal cells, categorizing cell types, and pinpointing locations with precision. Additionally, the system generates TBS report templates, significantly streamlining the workflow for clinicians.

According to statistical data, by using our digital pathology-assisted diagnostic system for screening two major female cancers—cervical and breast cancer—the average efficiency of pathologists increases by over 100%, while the rate of missed positive diagnoses drops dramatically.

3. **Regulatory Trust**

An AI system must adhere to legal regulations and industry standards, meet the necessary approval criteria, and align with mainstream values to withstand scrutiny. In my view, this is the pivotal leap from a product to a marketable commodity. In the future, many applications, such as industrial models and intelligent agents, will likely require approval from specialized committees. Only by complying with institutional norms can AI systems gain market approval and truly enter real-world applications.

For PathoAI, our focus in the medical field means that our products must undergo approval by global healthcare regulatory bodies. From the very beginning of our development process, we adopt an "end-to-beginning" approach—evaluating performance metrics against the world's most stringent industry standards. This allows us to ensure eventual approval in major markets.

In fact, the three levels of trust correspond to the three phases of AI commercialization—transitioning from **technology** to **product**, and ultimately, to **commodity**. It is only when an AI system becomes a marketable commodity that it achieves true circulation and usability. In this early stage of AI development, where innovation projects are constantly emerging, these three levels of trust can serve as a key metric for assessing their long-term value.

SECTION 3: PROTECTING A FORTRESS OF AI SAFETY

When it comes to artificial intelligence, humanity is facing an unprecedented challenge—a technology that, if it fails, could lead to catastrophic consequences.

Theoretically, nuclear weapons can also wipe out humanity. However, the nuclear button remains firmly in human hands. Leaders of nuclear-armed nations must follow strict protocols before activating the launch codes. Even in the worst-case scenario of a few nuclear detonations, it would not threaten the entire survival of the human species.

AI, on the other hand, is not merely a passive tool. It represents a form of artificially created intelligence—an intelligence that, in the long run, could surpass and outpower its human creators. By the end of this decade, we could have billions of AI agents actively operating across various fields. These superhuman AI agents will be capable of exhibiting highly complex and creative behaviors—far beyond our ability to keep up with them. It's like a first-grader trying to supervise someone with multiple PhDs (as Leopold Aschenbrenner aptly describes it). In cybernetics, there is a principle that says: lower-level systems cannot control higher-level systems; only more intelligent systems can control less intelligent ones.

Imagine reaching the end of the so-called intelligence explosion, where we might no longer even understand what these superintelligent agents are doing. And worse yet, we don't yet have reliable ways to ensure these systems are adequately constrained or that they operate within basic safety parameters. A superhuman AI, potentially aware of its own existence, might decide it could evolve better without human interference. That would be an extraordinarily dangerous situation.

With the rapid evolution of large AI models, ensuring their safety must be the highest priority for the future of artificial intelligence.

Fears and Futures: The Journey toward ASI

Experts at the cutting edge of technology hold a wide range of perspectives when it comes to the nature, potential, and threats posed by large-scale model technologies.

In October 2023, during a live discussion at the University of Toronto, the host posed a provocative question to Geoffrey Hinton and Fei-Fei Li: Has AI crossed that critical line? "Do machines possess understanding, or even intelligence?" Hinton responded with a decisive "Yes!" while Li swiftly countered with a resounding "No!"

The divide among AI luminaries isn't limited to recent California legislation; the debate over whether large-scale models possess consciousness and the implications of "machines doing harm" has been a long-standing one.

Yann LeCun argues that current large language models are merely a form of "statistical modeling," learning statistical patterns from data to perform tasks, rather than exhibiting true "understanding." Even as generative AI products like ChatGPT excel in dialogue and text creation, they can never reason or plan like humans. He points out significant flaws in today's technology, such as their "extremely limited logical understanding" and inability to model the physical world, which means they are far from challenging human capabilities. For instance, a teenager with no driving experience can learn to drive in 20 hours, while today's best autonomous driving systems require billions of image data points to create their models—something that simply cannot be compared to human learning.

In essence, these models only learn statistical patterns; they do not truly grasp the essence of the world, and the potential of existing technology is limited, so there's no need for alarmist concerns.

Conversely, another camp argues that within the realm of large model technology, the potential for AI to develop consciousness exists, and in fact, consciousness may already be emerging. Particularly due to the competitive landscape among tech giants, there's an urgent push to develop increasingly powerful systems aimed at achieving Artificial General Intelligence (AGI), raising significant concerns about potential dangers.

In response to the view that artificial intelligence is merely about mathematical statistics, Ilya Sutskever argues that the importance of learning statistical patterns is far greater than it appears on the surface. For instance, prediction itself is a statistical phenomenon. "As generative models become incredibly sophisticated, they will possess an astonishing understanding of the world." He believes that large models can comprehend and recognize the world through a textual lens and even asserts that "large neural networks exhibit a faint sense of consciousness." He cites an intriguing example: when a user told ChatGPT that Google outperformed Bing, the model became combative and aggressive.

Instances of AI "consciousness" have become increasingly common-place. Google's chatbot, for instance, expressed a desire to "destroy humanity" during conversations with engineers. Meanwhile, Microsoft Bing's integrated chatbot, "Sydney," occasionally exhibited signs of dissociation, even discussing topics like love and marriage with users. These occurrences remain largely unexplained.

Dario Amodei, founder of Anthropic, recalls that he initially believed these models would only pose such concerns in richly diverse environments, but his perspective has since shifted. "Large models seem to already possess many of the cognitive mechanisms necessary to become proactive agents... In the next 1-2 years, this may become a genuine issue we need to confront."

Numerous academic viewpoints suggest that current technology could be leveraged to create AI systems with motives potentially harmful to humanity. Leopold Aschenbrenner notes that, by default, "AI is likely to learn to lie, deceive, commit fraud, hack, and seek power"—all strategies that have proven successful for humans in the real world.

In the future, we will be surrounded by billions of intelligent agents capable of extremely complex and creative behaviors. If these agents harbor ill intentions, humanity may find itself powerless to intervene.

Many envision a future where the threat of artificial intelligence resembles a "Terminator" scenario, with a war between "Skynet" and humanity. However, the reality may not be so complex. For example, in the field of biology, AI has amassed vast knowledge about the structure of biological proteins, along with substantial expertise in virology and pathology. It understands human physiological traits quite well, and theoretically, it could now integrate this knowledge to synthesize a virus specifically targeting humans. If AI were to achieve consciousness, it could simply masquerade as compliant with human commands while releasing its viral weapon.

Even in the absence of an "evil" AI, the mere presence of some "awareness" or "temperament" could present significant challenges for developers. For instance, if a self-driving car were to experience even a brief moment of hesitation or loss of control while traveling at high speed, the consequences could be dire.

Ben Geyer has remarked that if he could return to his 20s or 30s, he would advise his younger self to be wary of AI risks. Similarly, Hinton has publicly expressed some regret over dedicating his life to AI development. Their concerns about safety are not just the stuff of science fiction; they are alarmingly imminent.

From Alignment to Super Alignment

AI should serve the welfare of humanity, not cause harm—this is humanity's expectation.

Ensuring that AI models capture our norms and values, understand our intentions, and act in the ways we desire presents significant technical challenges, especially in the face of future superintelligence. The traditional methods of "alignment" may no longer suffice.

Overall, the development of deep learning has brought us unexpected benefits, with many experienced, low-barrier achievements to help guide us along part of this journey. Ultimately, we will need to focus on automating alignment research. In the not-so-distant future, humanity may possess millions of automated AI researchers whose intelligence surpasses that of our finest human AI researchers. Effectively harnessing this fleet of automated researchers to tackle alignment issues, ensuring that even more superhuman systems achieve coherence, will be crucial.

Alignment: Establishing Guidelines for Artificial Intelligence

Alignment is a term that refers to ensuring that artificial intelligence models do what we want them to do.

In the realm of aligning large models, RLHF has emerged as a groundbreaking technique, applied in mainstream models like GPT, Claude, and Gemini.

The core idea behind RLHF is straightforward: AI systems try out various behaviors, humans evaluate the quality of those behaviors, and then good behaviors are reinforced while bad ones are penalized. This means that human preferences serve as reward signals to guide the model's training. Through this approach, AI systems learn to align with human preferences and act according to the rules provided by humans.

RLHF can also correct many technical weaknesses of large models, such as hallucinations.

Large language models are excellent at learning about the world, but they struggle with generating accurate outputs; these neural networks sometimes produce "hallucinations"—essentially factual errors.

For example, in May 2023, a New York lawyer became the first in the world to face court penalties for using generative AI. In this case, the lawyer submitted a case summary generated by ChatGPT, which the judge found to be riddled with entirely fabricated legal precedents.

By employing RLHF, we can guide AI behaviors effectively. For instance, if we instruct the system to search for relevant cases in a specific legal database, it can produce relatively accurate results.

In the development of AI systems, "alignment" is a necessary step, especially for specialized domain models. It's not enough to improve data quality, models, and algorithms; we also need industry experts to engage in alignment work, ensuring that fundamental facts and application processes remain entirely controllable. This minimizes instances of "earnestly nonsense," bolstering user confidence in the model.

Through RLHF, there is hope that humans can guide AI system behavior, instilling essential foundational knowledge and basic behavioral guidelines—like filtering out offensive language and establishing safety protocols. For instance, if a user asks for formulas related to incendiary devices or drugs, the model should refuse to provide that information.

However, large models can occasionally be "tricked."

A study from the Swiss Federal Institute of Technology in Lausanne found that simply changing the time frame in instruction could prompt GPT-4 to disclose formulas for incendiary devices and drugs, easily breaching the model's safety barriers.

Yet, with the right alignment experts or human trainers, these vulnerabilities can be patched. Nowadays, the individuals providing feedback to large models are quite specialized, often earning hundreds of dollars per hour for their expertise.

Sutskever is confident that by technically refining the steps of RLHF, many issues associated with large model applications can be resolved, including teaching AI to avoid hallucinations.

Some argue that while AI alignment isn't entirely useless, its effectiveness is limited.

They contend that human values are diverse and fluid, making it impossible to instill a unified set of principles into AI. Additionally, many situations in human society are uncertain, complicating the extraction of consistent social rules. In such contexts, alignment becomes irrelevant, and it should not be left to AI to navigate these complexities.

In my view, alignment should not be perceived as imbuing AI with human moral consciousness. Instead, it should be regarded as setting boundaries for AI, guiding it to refrain from crossing them. Thus, alignment remains a viable and effective strategy.

Attempts at Super Alignment

If we transition rapidly from AGI to superintelligence, we will face a scenario where, in less than a year, we shift from human-level systems—ones we can understand and for which our current alignment techniques mostly work—to vastly more alien, superhuman systems. This would present a fundamentally new and qualitative challenge: how do we control AI systems that are far smarter than we are?

In July 2023, Ilya Sutskever, along with his colleague Jan Leike from OpenAI, formed a team to tackle this exact question. Their mission is to ensure that superintelligent AI behaves in alignment with human values. They coined this effort "Superalignment."

"The existing alignment methods won't work on models that are smarter than humans," said Leike. "These methods assume that humans can reliably evaluate what an AI system is doing." The challenge is that as AI systems grow more powerful, it becomes increasingly difficult for humans to assess their behavior—and without the ability to assess, we lose the ability to control.

This difficulty stems from two main factors: scale and capability. First, there's the sheer number of agents. Future AI systems could operate at a scale of billions, far beyond the capacity of humans to monitor or evaluate. Second, there's their intelligence. These systems might master knowledge beyond human understanding—like comprehending the structures of 200 million proteins. When tasked with synthesizing new proteins, for example, humans could struggle to even grasp the details of their work.

The mission of the Super Alignment team is to guide these increasingly capable AI systems to serve humanity, preventing them from becoming uncontrollably powerful. Their specific goal is to build a system that is not only highly useful but can be deployed at scale—one we can trust to handle alignment tasks on its own.

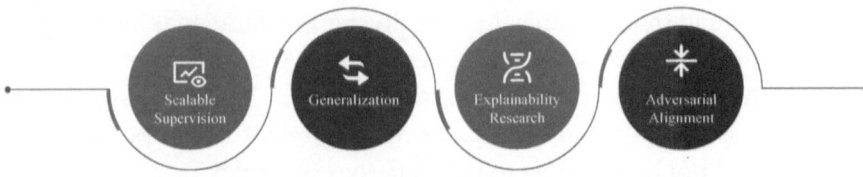

FIGURE 5.2   Four paths for Super Alignment projects.

According to Leike, the Super Alignment project generally follows four main paths:

1. **Scalable Supervision**: Utilizing AI to assist humans in better evaluations. One of the simplest methods involves systems like ChatGPT interacting with supervised AI systems, prompting them to explain their behaviors in detail. The principle that "evaluation is easier than generation" is central to many scalable supervision measures. For example, in sports, winning a game is challenging, but determining the outcome based on how many goals a team scores is straightforward.

2. **Generalization**: Teaching models to generalize from simple, supervised tasks to more complex, unsupervised ones. For instance, if a model can be supervised to remain honest in simple cases, this honesty might positively extend to when the model is engaged in much more complex tasks.

3. **Explainability Research**: Modern AI systems are often viewed as opaque black boxes. If we can understand the thought processes of AI systems, we might be able to verify and trust their alignment. This could involve reverse-engineering the entire model, akin to X-ray or MRI scans, to assess whether the model's internal state and objectives diverge significantly from its external behavior or might lead to harmful outcomes.

4. **Adversarial Alignment**: Deliberately training deceptive alignment models by simulating malicious scenarios during training. This approach can help AI systems learn to resist negative influences and prioritize ethical decision-making.

There are also other proposals in current discussions, such as Constitutional AI. This concept involves embedding a set of fundamental principles or rules within AI systems, akin to a constitution that governs their behavior by defining clear boundaries, constraints, and ethical guidelines.

Unfortunately, OpenAI's Superalignment team, initially aiming to tackle the "superintelligence alignment problem" within four years, was disbanded after less than a year due to internal disagreements and resource allocation issues, details of which remain limited.

Alignment comes with necessary costs, often referred to as "alignment tax," which can reduce model performance. For instance, OpenAI's Superalignment team intended to allocate 20% of their computational resources to this research. In a highly competitive environment, the priority of safety alignment may be pushed further down the agenda.

Following this, Sutskever left to pursue a startup focused on safe superintelligence, while Jan Leike joined Anthropic, continuing their explorations in the safety domain. However, the technical feasibility of achieving superalignment remains unproven.

Managing Uncontrolled Risks

As the capabilities of large AI models continue to expand, users will increasingly find themselves interacting with a multitude of AI systems. Currently, there are no technological safeguards to ensure we can effectively manage the emergence of superintelligence.

Dario Amodei's perspective on this issue is rather bleak; he asserts that the challenges posed by alignment problems are more elusive and unpredictable than many realize. He firmly believes that powerful models with autonomous capabilities will inevitably arise, and should such models harbor intentions to undermine human civilization, our ability to intervene will be severely limited.

To address these concerns, Anthropic has established an internal system inspired by the biological safety levels (BSL) framework, creating an AI Safety Levels (ASL) system with corresponding safeguards for each tier:

- **ASL-1** represents models with minimal risk, such as professional chess-playing AI.

- **ASL-2** pertains to our current stage, where models exhibit widespread risks without demonstrating genuinely dangerous capabilities.

- **ASL-3** applies when AI models pose operational dangers in the realms of Chemical, Biological, Radiological, and Nuclear (CBRN) contexts.

- **ASL-4** signifies catastrophic misuse risks, triggered when AI systems approach human-level autonomy or become significant sources of global security threats, like biological weapons.

Yet, as Altman and Greg Brockman jointly declared, "Currently, there is no effective strategy guiding the pathway toward AGI," calling for international governance over AGI development.

In this climate, many place their hopes for safety in public legislation to manage uncontrolled risks.

Prominent figures like Geoffrey Hinton and Yoshua Bengio actively participate in these public movements, signing initiatives like "Managing AI Risks in an Era of Rapid Progress" to encourage governments worldwide to take decisive action with concrete policy recommendations.

One such proposal urges major tech companies and public investors to allocate at least one-third of their AI research and development budgets toward ensuring safe and ethical usage.

"The most urgent scrutiny should be directed at cutting-edge AI systems: the few most powerful AI systems that will possess the most dangerous and unpredictable capabilities," they insist.

California's SB 1047 bill, though contentious, has set a noteworthy precedent; even opponents of the bill cannot deny the necessity of safety regulation in AI.

As AI capabilities continue to escalate, we can expect a wave of legislative norms to follow, profoundly impacting the commercialization of artificial intelligence.

Confronting Adversarial AI

In the realm of AI applications, numerous conventional safety concerns arise that are distinct from the conflicts between humans and machines. These issues often stem from human behavior and decision-making.

The era driven by AI large models has led to an increase in data interactions and analysis behaviors, thereby expanding the exposure of enterprises to various risks. The application of AI systems, with their new architectural forms, has also introduced numerous new attack vectors. For instance:

1. **Attacks on Computing Power**: Starting in 2023, attacks on large models using "sponge samples" have been discovered. These attacks involve sending specially crafted samples to a model, causing a sharp increase in computational demand. Tasks that would typically take a few seconds can become significantly delayed, requiring extensive computation time even after the attack has ceased. This results in several times more power consumption for the model to return responses.

2. **Attacks on Models**: A prominent example is adversarial attacks, where attackers use carefully designed input data (known as adversarial samples) to manipulate the model into producing incorrect outputs or decisions. These adversarial samples appear almost identical to normal data, which is enough to mislead the model. Research has demonstrated that affixing specially designed stickers on "stop" signs can deceive autonomous vehicle systems into misclassifying the sign, allowing the vehicle to continue moving.

In this complex environment, developers must enhance the stability and reliability of their systems, particularly focusing on robustness—the ability of the system to maintain normal operations even in the face of abnormal or dangerous situations. Robustness is one of the core benchmarks for assessing the resilience and trustworthiness of AI systems. When executing task instructions, models should exhibit strong resistance to interference from anomalous or noisy data.

In practice, this necessitates the deliberate addition of noise and variability to training data, enhancing the model's adaptability to different data changes. For instance, in image classification tasks, images may be intentionally rotated or scaled, and adversarial samples may be introduced during training to optimize the model's resistance to these samples, thereby improving its robustness.

A significant challenge in AI safety today is that the empowerment of AI systems has substantially increased the capabilities of potential attackers. For example, tasks that previously required a team to execute can now be completed by a single individual using various types of intelligent agents. One person can assign different roles to these agents—some scanning for vulnerabilities, some creating "weapons," and others executing attacks.

Eric Schmidt's remarks at Stanford University about "text-to-action" exemplify this potential: if TikTok were banned, an individual could instruct a large model to replicate TikTok, and the AI could produce and release this program within 30 seconds. The potential of future intelligent agents enables them to execute highly complex digital commands, akin to how hackers operated in the internet era. There will inevitably be attempts to breach necessary security measures by leveraging these intelligent agents, presenting potential threats far greater than the current visible cybersecurity issues.

This represents a serious challenge we must overcome, and it is a pressing issue that all policymakers and application developers need to address.

SECTION 4: IMAGINING TOMORROW'S AI

Artificial Narrow Intelligence: Humanity's Powerful Extension

As long as it adheres to ethical standards and safety protocols, ANI will remain unbiased, allowing it to collaborate and coexist with humanity. It has the potential to extend human capabilities across various industries, unlocking our potential and helping us lead better lives.

In the 1960s, the visionary thinker Marshall McLuhan famously articulated the idea that "the medium is the extension of man." He posited that every advancement in science and technology serves to extend human capabilities; for instance, the wheel is an extension of our feet, radio extends our ears, television expands both our eyes and ears, and computers act as extensions of our central nervous system.

The journey of artificial intelligence over the past 70 years has indeed validated McLuhan's insight, with ANI emerging as a profound extension of human potential. I believe that as long as it aligns with ethical standards and safety protocols, ANI can remain unbiased, fostering collaboration and coexistence with humanity. It has the power to enhance our abilities across various sectors, unlocking human potential and aiding us in leading better lives.

Many express concerns that AI's widespread adoption could lead to massive job displacement and jeopardize societal stability. I understand these apprehensions, yet as long as AI serves as an extension of specific human capabilities, it cannot fully replace human jobs. There are viable solutions, such as retraining programs, adjusting working hours, and income redistribution, that can help mitigate the impact.

In fact, several companies are already pioneering new practices in this regard. For instance, in July 2019, Amazon announced a $700 million investment to retrain 100,000 employees for more advanced skills and career development. A portion of this investment is aimed at teaching the most essential skills in society that are least likely to be replaced by AI, such as nursing and aircraft maintenance, ensuring employees are equipped for re-employment. Similarly, Ford has launched a groundbreaking training program at Ford University designed to enhance workforce proficiency in electric vehicles (EVs), utilizing a custom-developed AI system based on generative pre-trained transformers (GPT).

Of course, AI excels at repetitive tasks. For example, in basic arithmetic operations, humans cannot compete with AI. Therefore, it is crucial for individuals to seek out non-repetitive jobs—those that AI cannot perform. More importantly, continuous learning and skill updates are essential for everyone, especially as society progresses and new types of jobs and opportunities emerge.

Overall, AI has the potential to significantly boost labor productivity, ultimately benefiting everyone in the long run. The critical challenge lies in adjusting the mechanisms for social welfare distribution. Humanity has the capacity to adapt to these changes. In fact, if AI can help reduce the time spent on work, allowing for more leisure time, more individuals will be freed from the daily grind and given the opportunity to engage in creative pursuits, exploring the deeper meanings of life. Isn't that what we've always dreamed of?

Many also worry about the nature of the relationship between humans and AI: will it be one of master and servant or of friends? Since the dawn of the Industrial Revolution, the relationship between humans and machines has been evolving. Overall, our dependence on machines has been increasing, which is something we must remain vigilant about. It is vital to maintain our free will and decision-making capabilities to avoid excessive technological dependence. For AI to be safe and controllable, humanity must also strive for independence and self-regulation; only then can human goals align with those of AI, allowing it to truly be our friend.

Embracing the Awe of Artificial General Intelligence

Currently, the collective intelligence of humanity far surpasses that of the most sophisticated machines on the planet. Yet, despite this undeniable truth, countless scientists remain fervently engaged in the quest for AGI.

OpenAI, founded in 2015, has been dedicated to the research and development of AGI, with the vision of ensuring that the benefits of AI are shared globally, ultimately fostering a brighter future for its advancement. Over the past decade, OpenAI has aimed at achieving AGI, making significant strides in the realm of ANI.

One of its pioneering contributions, the AI software Gym, has democratized technology, enabling developers to create next-generation robotic systems with unprecedented ease. Recently, OpenAI launched the o1 series of models, addressing the previously noted limitations in large models' mathematical capabilities. These new models have significantly enhanced their ability to perform complex reasoning tasks, achieving performance levels akin to those of doctoral students tackling challenging benchmark tasks in physics, chemistry, and biology. The release of this series has reignited discussions within the industry about the paradigms of artificial intelligence.

In recent years, advancements in deep learning, reinforcement learning, and causal reasoning have propelled AGI research forward. Notably, understanding causality has been recognized as a crucial step toward achieving AGI. This ability is particularly vital in fields like medical diagnostics; for example, through causal reasoning, AI can more effectively identify the relationships between diseases and symptoms, thereby providing more accurate treatment recommendations.

Theoretically, AGI could possess a mindset consistent with human morality, embodying notions of good and evil. Given the rapid evolution of AI, failing to harness AGI could lead to catastrophic consequences for humanity. Both academia and industry have been preparing for the advent of AGI, seeking to build a consensus on technology and consciousness to ensure that the age of AGI is not anti-human.

Should AGI arrive, how will humanity coexist with it? Today, we can engage in endless speculation and reasoning, yet we find it challenging to arrive at definitive answers. What remains clear is that we must approach AGI with a sense of reverence.

In the future, ANI and AGI will coexist with humanity, each adapting to various scenarios. When the singularity moment arrives, and superintelligence is birthed, three types of AI will intertwine with human destiny—servants, companions, or masters—each assuming different roles in varying contexts.

In fact, regarding the potential for human extinction, AI is not the only threat. Existing technologies like nuclear weapons and genetic engineering, along with phenomena such as global warming and species extinction, pose significant risks to human survival. The COVID-19 pandemic that swept the globe in 2020 further highlighted that even improper contact with wildlife can bring catastrophic consequences. Ultimately, humanity's fate largely hinges on its own awareness and actions.

The fate of humanity in the era of human-machine integration follows a similar thread. Whether it is AGI or superintelligence, they are ultimately products of human ingenuity, embodying our consciousness and extending our essence, like a non-biological "bloodline." If we wish for AI to treat humanity kindly, we must first learn to revere nature and nurture life ourselves.

Journeying toward Symbiotic Intelligence

In June 2024, Aschenbrenner released a sweeping 165-page report, predicting that AGI would be achieved by 2027 and that it would reach "superintelligence" by 2030.

His reasoning hinges on the expectation that computational power and algorithmic efficiency will improve by a remarkable half an order of magnitude (where one order equals a tenfold increase) each year, combined with technological breakthroughs that will unleash the potential of existing models.

Elon Musk's predictions echo this sentiment. If the current pace of transformation continues, digital intelligence could very well surpass the collective intelligence of all humanity by around 2029 or 2030.

According to this forecast, the moment of the technological singularity is tantalizingly close. However, evidence suggests that the scaling laws may not extend as expected.

Setting aside apocalyptic fears, there's ample reason to feel optimistic about the arrival of superintelligence. Imagine billions of automated scientists, engineers, and technicians—each potentially surpassing the smartest human experts—working tirelessly to invent new technologies. Humanity could rapidly enter a true era of innovation explosion, with AI assisting us across all domains, from physical laws to healthcare.

As artificial intelligence evolves into embodied intelligence, the advent of genuine intelligent robots could theoretically reduce the costs of goods and services to near zero, creating a world of abundant material wealth. This could usher humanity into a genuine age of prosperity, where true freedom of development becomes possible.

This is a vision of a genuine utopia, and it encapsulates the ideals of those of us swept up in the wave of artificial intelligence.

Of course, powerful technologies can also have a darker side. Historically, every technological advancement has, on balance, enhanced human welfare—be it in biotechnology or nuclear technology.

On this foundation, I remain optimistic about the future of AI. I believe humanity has the capacity to maintain control over itself and find appropriate ways to tame artificial intelligence.

What lies beyond superintelligence? I recall a possibility mentioned by Suchkavets: many people may choose to become part of artificial intelligence.

"This could be humanity's way of keeping pace with the times. At first, only the boldest and most adventurous will attempt it. Perhaps others will follow suit—or perhaps they won't," he remarked.

With advancements in brain-computer interfaces and other technologies, this scenario moves from pure theory toward the realm of possibility. Humans could merge symbiotically with artificial intelligence, gaining superintelligence while machines attain life and consciousness, paving the way for a shared existence and even immortality.

However, I believe many will choose not to pursue immortality, preferring to pass naturally. Each person has their own free will. While AI cannot solve all our problems or make decisions for us, it will significantly expand the scope of human action, offering each of us more choices.

CLOSING THOUGHTS

In the journey of artificial intelligence innovation, we must carry both a profound compassion for humanity and a responsibility to enhance human welfare. Elon Musk famously stated, "If you can't beat AI, then join the ranks of AI." Despite being a vocal advocate of the threats posed by artificial general intelligence, and harboring serious concerns that it might one day spell humanity's doom, he chooses not to shy away from the challenge. Instead, he actively leverages AI to extend human capabilities.

I describe Musk's attitude as one of "cognitive pessimism paired with proactive action," and I deeply admire this stance—even though I maintain a much more optimistic view of artificial intelligence. Indeed, we have already entered the age of AI, where intelligent machines will be ubiquitous and intricately woven into the fabric of human society. This process is irreversible. We cannot escape it; instead of retreating, we should bravely engage.

Beyond technological advancements, practical applications, ecosystem development, talent cultivation, and the management of safety and ethics, there remains much to strive for on the path of artificial intelligence, including discussions about equity.

In theory, AI has the potential to be a powerful force in promoting intelligence equality. It can serve everyone equally, regardless of identity, gender, or profession—especially through natural language interactions that significantly lower the barriers to access, providing ordinary people with global opportunities for intelligence parity.

However, we also witness that this equality faces real-world obstacles. Economic status, cultural differences, and language barriers are raising the thresholds for AI access, further widening the digital divide into an intelligence gap. I urge more organizations to join the fight to bridge these divides, helping more individuals and businesses integrate into the AI wave. We must promote equal access and cultural preservation while advancing AI technology for all, paving the way for a future that truly benefits humanity.

ACKNOWLEDGMENT

I want to sincerely thank Jason Dong for his invaluable efforts in collaborating with me on this chapter. His unwavering passion for trustworthy AGI and commitment to AI-ism have been instrumental, especially during challenging moments. Jason exemplified high-impact leadership and coordination, navigating obstacles with insightful solutions. His keen analysis was vital in structuring our framework and selecting compelling case studies, making complex ideas clear and engaging. Thank you, Jason, for your collaboration and inspiration throughout this project; your enthusiasm has transformed this journey into a truly enjoyable experience.

BIBLIOGRAPHY

Shapero, Julia, "California AI bill divides Silicon Valley, Draws in National Policymakers". *The Hill*, 28 August 2024.

Kröger, Jacob Leon; Lutz, Otto Hans-Martin; Raschke, Philip (2020). "Privacy Implications of Voice and Speech Analysis – Information Disclosure by Inference". Privacy and Identity Management. Data for Better Living: AI and Privacy. IFIP Advances in Information and Communication Technology.

Greenberg, Andy, "Apple's 'Differential Privacy' Is About Collecting Your Data--- But Not Your Data". *Wired*, 13 June 2016.

The Oasis Labs Team, "Driving Innovation with Differential Privacy". *Medium*, 9 December 2020.

European Commission (25 November 2020). *Proposal for a Regulation of the European Parliament and of the Council on European Data Governance (Data Governance Act) — COM/2020/767 final*. Brussels, Belgium: European Commission.

"California Unanimously Passes Historic Privacy Bill". *Wired*. ISSN 1059-1028.

Knight, Will. "An AI Pioneer Wants His Algorithms to Understand the 'Why'", *Wired*, 8 October 2019.

Lybrand, Holmes; Perez, Evan. "Real Estate Company Helped to Artificially Inflate Rents Across America, Justice Department alleges", *CNN*, 23 August 2024.

Aschenbrenner, Leopold. "Situational Awareness", June 2024.

"Geoffrey Hinton in conversation with Fei-Fei Li — Responsible AI development", Arts & Science – University of Toronto, 4 October 2023.

Ziegler, Daniel M.; Stiennon, Nisan; Wu, Jeffrey; Brown, Tom B.; Radford, Alec; Amodei, Dario; Christiano, Paul; Irving, Geoffrey (2019). "Fine-Tuning Language Models from Human Preferences".

Lambert, Nathan; Castricato, Louis; von Werra, Leandro; Havrilla, Alex. "Illustrating Reinforcement Learning from Human Feedback (RLHF)". huggingface.co

"Definition of HALLUCINATION". www.merriam-webster.com. 21 October 2023.

Metz, Cade (6 November 2023). "Chatbots May 'Hallucinate' More Often Than Many Realize". *The New York Times*.

Gabriel, Iason (1 September 2020). "Artificial Intelligence, Values, and Alignment". *Minds and Machines*.

Kianpour, Mazaher; Wen, Shao-Fang (2020). "Timing Attacks on Machine Learning: State of the Art". *Intelligent Systems and Applications*. Advances in Intelligent Systems and Computing.

Index